3rd Workshop on Research in Computational Typology and Multilingual NLP (SIGTYP 2021)

Online
10 June 2021

ISBN: 978-1-7138-3028-3

Printed from e-media with permission by:

Curran Associates, Inc.
57 Morehouse Lane
Red Hook, NY 12571

Some format issues inherent in the e-media version may also appear in this print version.

Association for Computational Linguistics
209 N. Eighth Street
Stroudsburg, Pennsylvania 18360

Phone: 1-570-476-8006
Fax: 1-570-476-0860

acl@aclweb.org

Additional copies of this publication are available from:

Curran Associates, Inc.
57 Morehouse Lane
Red Hook, NY 12571 USA
Phone: 845-758-0400
Fax: 845-758-2633
Email: curran@proceedings.com
Web: www.proceedings.com

SIGTYP 2021

The 3rd Workshop on Research in Computational Typology and Multilingual NLP

Proceedings of the Workshop

June 10, 2021

SIGTYP 2021 is the third edition of the workshop for typology-related research and its integration into multilingual Natural Language Processing (NLP). The workshop is co-located with the 2021 Annual Conference of the North American Chapter of the Association for Computational Linguistics (NAACL 2021), which takes place virtually this year. Our workshop includes a shared task on robust language identification from speech.

The final program of SIGTYP contains 4 keynote talks, 3 shared task papers, 10 archival papers, and 14 extended abstracts. This workshop would not have been possible without the contribution of its program committee, to whom we would like to express our gratitude. We should also thank Claire Bowern, Miryam de Lhoneux, Johannes Bjerva, and David Yarowsky for kindly accepting our invitation as invited speakers. The workshop is generously sponsored by Google.

Please find more details on the SIGTYP 2021 website: `https://sigtyp.github.io/ws2021.html`

Organizing Committee:

Ekaterina Vylomova, University of Melbourne
Elizabeth Salesky, Johns Hopkins University
Sabrina Mielke, Johns Hopkins University
Gabriella Lapesa, University of Stuttgart
Ritesh Kumar, Bhim Rao Ambedkar University
Harald Hammarström, Uppsala University
Ivan Vulić, University of Cambridge
Anna Korhonen, University of Cambridge
Roi Reichart, Technion – Israel Institute of Technology
Edoardo M. Ponti, Mila Montreal and University of Cambridge
Ryan Cotterell, ETH Zurich

Program Committee:

Željko Agić, Corti
Emily Ahn, University of Washington
Isabelle Augenstein, University of Copenhagen
Emily Bender, University of Washington
Johannes Bjerva, University of Copenhagen
Claire Bowern, Yale University
Miriam Butt, University of Konstanz
Giuseppe Celano, Leipzig University
Agnieszka Falenska, University of Stuttgart
Richard Futrell, University of California, Irvine
Elisabetta Ježek, University of Pavia
Gerhard Jäger, University of Tubingen
John Mansfield, University of Melbourne
Paola Merlo, University of Geneva
Joakim Nivre, Uppsala University
Robert Östling, Stockholm University
Thomas Proisl, FAU Erlangen-Nurnberg
Michael Regan, University of New Mexico
Ella Rabinovich, University of Toronto
Tanja Samardžić, University of Zurich
Richard Sproat, Google Japan
Sabine Stoll, University of Zurich
Daan van Esch, Google AI
Giulia Venturi, ILC "Antonio Zampolli"
Nidhi Vyas, Apple
Ada Wan, University of Zurich
Eleanor Chodroff, University of York
Elizabeth Salesky, Johns Hopkins University
Sabrina Mielke, Johns Hopkins University
Edoardo M. Ponti, University of Cambridge
Damián Blasi, Harvard University
Adina Williams, Facebook
Ivan Vulić, University of Cambridge
Arturo Oncevay, University of Edinburgh
Koel Dutta Chowdhury, Saarland University

Elena Klyachko, National Research University Higher School of Economics
Alexey Sorokin, Moscow State University
Sylvain Kahane, Université Paris Nanterre
Taraka Rama, University of North Texas
Harald Hammarström, Max Planck Institute for the Science of Human History
Olga Lyashevskaya, National Research University Higher School of Economics
Kaushal Kumar Maurya, IIT Hyderabad
Johann-Mattis List, Max Planck Institute for the Science of Human History
Garrett Nicolai, University of British Columbia
Yevgeni Berzak, Technion – Israel Institute of Technology
Olga Zamaraeva, University of Washington
Zoey Liu, Boston College
Jeff Good, University at Buffalo
Priya Rani, National University of Ireland
Silvia Luraghi, University of Pavia
Beata Trawinski, University of Vienna
Miryam de Lhoneux, University of Copenhagen
Kemal Kurniawan, University of Melbourne
Andreas Shcerbakov, University of Melbourne
Ritesh Kumar, Bhim Rao Ambedkar University

Invited Speakers:

Claire Bowern, Yale University
Miryam de Lhoneux, Uppsala University / KU Leuven / University of Copenhagen
Johannes Bjerva, Aalborg University
David Yarowsky, Johns Hopkins University

Table of Contents

Non-archival Abstracts

Graph Convolutional Network for Swahili News Classification
Alexandros Kastanos and Tyler Martin
In this work, we demonstrate the ability of Text Graph Convolutional Network (Text GCN) to surpass the performance of traditional natural language processing benchmarks on the task of semi-supervised Swahili news categorisation. Our experiments highlight the more severely label-restricted context often facing low-resourced African languages. We build on this finding by presenting a memory-efficient variant of Text GCN which replaces the naive one-hot node representation with a bag of words representation.

Exploring Linguistic Typology Features in Multilingual Machine Translation
Oscar Moreno and Arturo Oncevay
We explore whether linguistic typology features can impact multilingual machine translation performance (many-to-English) by using initial pseudo-tokens and factored language-level embeddings. With 20 languages from different families or groups, we observed that the features of "Order of Subject (S), Object (O) and Verb (V)", "Position of Negative Word with respect to S-O-V" and "Prefixing vs. Suffixing in Inflectional Morphology" provided slight improvements in low-resource language-pairs despite not overcoming the average performance for all languages.

Multilingual Slot and Intent Detection (xSID) with Cross-lingual Auxiliary Tasks
Rob van der Goot, Ibrahim Sharaf, Aizhan Imankulova, Ahmet Üstün, Marija Stepanović, Alan Ramponi, Siti Oryza Khairunnisa, Mamoru Komachi and Barbara Plank
Digital assistants are becoming an integral part of everyday life. However, commercial digital assistants are only available for a limited set of languages (as of March 2020, between 8 to around 20 languages). Because of this, a vast amount of people can not use these devices in their native tongue. In this work, we focus on two core tasks within the digital assistant pipeline: intent classification and slot detection. Intent classification recovers the goal of the utterance, whereas slot detection identifies important properties regarding this goal. Besides introducing a novel cross-lingual dataset for these tasks, consisting of 13 languages, we evaluate a variety of models: 1) multilingually pretrained transformer-based models, 2) we supplement these models with auxiliary tasks to evaluate whether multi-task learning can be beneficial, and 3) annotation transfer with neural machine translation.

Plugins for Structurally Varied Languages in XMG Framework
Valeria Generalova
This paper aims to suggest an XMG-based design of metagrammatical classes storing language-specific information on a multilingual grammar engineering project. It also presents a method of reusing the information from WALS. The principal claim is the hierarchy of features and the modular architecture of feature structures.

Modeling Linguistic Typology - A Probabilistic Graphical Models Approach
Xia Lu
In this paper, we propose to use probabilistic graphical models as a new theoretical and computational framework to study linguistic typology. The graphical structure of such a model represents a meta-language that consists of linguistic variables and the relationships between them while the parameters associated with each variable can be used to infer the strength of the relationships between the variables. Such models can also be used to predict feature values of new languages. Besides providing better solutions to existing problems in linguistic typology such a framework opens up to many new research topics that can help us to gain further insights into linguistic typology.

Unsupervised Self-Training for Unsupervised Cross-Lingual Transfer
Akshat Gupta, Sai Krishna Rallabandi and Alan W Black
Labelled data is scarce, especially for low-resource languages. This beckons the need to come up with unsupervised methods for natural language processing tasks. In this paper, we introduce a general framework called Unsupervised Self-Training, capable of unsupervised cross-lingual transfer. We apply our proposed framework to a two-class sentiment analysis problem of code-switched data. We use the power of pre-trained BERT models for initialization and fine-tune them in an unsupervised manner, only using pseudo labels produced by zero-shot predictions. We test our algorithm on multiple code-switched languages. Our unsupervised models compete well with their supervised counterparts, with their performance reaching within 1-7% (weighted F1 scores) when compared to supervised models trained for a two-class problem.

Let-Mi: An Arabic Levantine Twitter Dataset for Misogynistic Language
Hala Mulki and Bilal Ghanem
Misogyny is one type of hate speech that disparages a person or a group having the female gender identity; it is typically defined as hatred of or contempt for women. Online misogyny has become an increasing worry for Arab women who experience gender-based online abuse on a daily basis. Such online abuse can be expressed through several misogynistic behaviors which reinforce and justify underestimation of women, male superiority, sexual abuse, mistreatment, and violence against women. Misogyny automatic detection systems can assist in the prohibition of anti-women Arabic toxic content. Developing these systems is hindered by the lack of the Arabic misogyny benchmark datasets. In this work, we introduce an Arabic Levantine Twitter dataset for Misogynistic language (LeT-Mi) to be the first benchmark dataset for Arabic misogyny. The proposed dataset consists of 6,550 tweets annotated either as neutral (misogynistic-free) or as one of seven misogyny categories: discredit, dominance, cursing/damning, sexual harassment, stereotyping and objectification, derailing, and the threat of violence. We further provide a detailed review of the dataset creation and annotation phases. The consistency of the annotations for the proposed dataset was emphasized through inter-rater agreement evaluation measures. Moreover, Let-Mi was used as an evaluation dataset through binary, multi-class, and target classification tasks which were conducted by several state-of-the-art machine learning systems along with Multi-Task Learning (MTL) configuration. The obtained results indicated that the performances achieved by the used systems are consistent with state-of-the-art results for languages other than Arabic, while employing MTL improved the performance of the misogyny/target classification tasks.

Our dataset is available at `https://github.com/bilalghanem/let-mi`

Towards Figurative Language Generation in Afrikaans
Imke van Heerden and Anil Bas
This paper presents an LSTM-based approach to figurative language generation, which is an important step towards creative text generation in Afrikaans. Due to the scarcity of resources (in comparison to resource-rich languages), we train the proposed network on a single literary novel. This follows the same approach as Van Heerden and Bas (2021), however, we explicitly focus and expand on fully automatic text generation, centring on figurative language in particular. The proposed model generates phrases that contain compellingly novel figures of speech such as metaphor, simile and personification.

Improving Access to Untranscribed Speech by Leveraging Spoken Term Detection and Self-supervised Learning of Speech Representations
Nay San, Martijn Bartelds and Dan Jurafsky
We summarise findings from our recent work showing that a large self-supervised model trained only on English speech provides a noise-robust and speaker-invariant feature extraction method that can be used for a speech information retrieval task with unrelated low resource target languages. A qualitative error analysis also revealed that the majority of the retrieval errors could be attributed to the differences in phonological inventories between English and the evaluation languages. With a longer-term aim of leveraging typological information to better adapt such models for the target languages, we also report on work in progress which examines the phonetic information encoded in these representations.

On the Universality of Lexical Concepts
Bradley Hauer and Grzegorz Kondrak
We posit that lexicalized concepts are universal, and thus can be annotated cross-linguistically in parallel corpora. This is one of the implications of a novel theory that formalizes the relationship between words and senses in both monolingual and multilingual settings. The theory is based on a unifying treatment of the notions of synonymy and translational equivalence as different aspects of the relation of sameness of meaning within and across languages.

Quantitative Detection of Cognacy in the Predictive Structure of Inflection Classes: Romance Verbal Conjugations against the Broader Typological Variation
Borja Herce and Balthasar Bickel
In recent years, Information Theory (with its core notion of entropy) has provided the theoretical background for a lot of empirical research on inflectional systems, and has inspired various metrics to capture (different aspects of) their complexity. So far, however, entropy-based metrics have chiefly been used to assess synchronic states. Here we explore their potential for capturing patterns in language change and phylogenetic relatedness. Specifically, we probe different aspects of an inflectional system for their stability within one language family, Romance, and for the degree to which they distinguish this family from unrelated and less closely related languages. Based on most metrics, Romance appears to be different from the control sample in the mean, variance, or both. The difference in variance is particularly interesting because it might suggest differences in relative diachronic stability and as phylogenetic signals of relatedness.

Subword Geometry: Picturing Word Shapes
Olga Sozinova and Tanja Samardzic
In this work in progress, we are investigating the structural properties of subwords in 20 languages by extracting word shapes, i.e. sequences of subword lengths.

A Look to Languages through the Glass of BPE Compression
Ximena Gutierrez-Vasques, Tanja Samardzic and Christian Bentz
One of the predominant methods for subword tokenization is Byte-pair encoding (BPE). Originally, this is a data compression technique based on replacing the most common pair of consecutive bytes with a new symbol When applied to text, each iteration merges two adjacent symbols; this can be seen as a process of going from characters to subwords through iterations.

Regardless of the language, the first merge operations tend to have a stronger impact on the compression of texts, i.e., they capture very frequent patterns that lead to a reduction of redundancy and to an increment of the text entropy. However, the natural language properties that allow this compression are rarely analyzed, i.e., do all languages get compressed in the same way through BPE merge operations? We hypothesize that the type of recurrent patterns captured in each merge depends on the typology and even orthography and other corpus-related phenomena. For instance, for some languages, this compression might be related to frequent affixes or regular inflectional morphs, while for some others, it might be related to more idiosyncratic, irregular patterns or even related to orthographic redundancies.

We propose a novel way to quantify this, inspired by the notion of morphological productivity.

Information-Theoretic Characterization of Morphological Fusion
Neil Rathi, Michael Hahn and Richard Futrell
Traditionally, morphological typology divides synthetic languages into two broad groups (e.g. von Schlegel, 1808; von Humboldt, 1843). Agglutinative languages, such as Turkish, segment morphemes into independent features which can be easily split. On the other hand, fusional languages, such as Latin, "fuse" morphemes together phonologically (Bickel and Nichols, 2013). At the same time, there has long been recognition that the categories "agglutinative" and "fusional" are best thought of as a matter of degree, with Greenberg (1954) developing an "index of agglutination" metric for languages. Here, we propose an information-theoretic definition of the fusion of any given form in a language, which naturally delivers a graded measure of the degree of fusion. We use a sequence-to-sequence model to empirically verify that our measure captures typical linguistic classifications.

OTEANN: Estimating the Transparency of Orthographies with an Artificial Neural Network

Xavier Marjou
Lannion, Brittany, France
xavier.marjou@gmail.com

Abstract

To transcribe spoken language to written medium, most alphabets enable an unambiguous sound-to-letter rule. However, some writing systems have distanced themselves from this simple concept and little work exists in Natural Language Processing (NLP) on measuring such distance. In this study, we use an Artificial Neural Network (ANN) model to evaluate the transparency between written words and their pronunciation, hence its name Orthographic Transparency Estimation with an ANN (OTEANN). Based on datasets derived from Wikimedia dictionaries, we trained and tested this model to score the percentage of correct predictions in phoneme-to-grapheme and grapheme-to-phoneme translation tasks. The scores obtained on 17 orthographies were in line with the estimations of other studies. Interestingly, the model also provided insight into typical mistakes made by learners who only consider the phonemic rule in reading and writing.

1 Introduction

An alphabet is a standard set of letters that represent the basic significant sounds of the spoken language it is used to write. When a spelling system (also referred as *orthography*) systematically uses a one-to-one correspondence between its sounds and its letters, the encoding of a sound (also referred as *phoneme*) into a letter (also referred as *grapheme*) leads to a single possibility; similarly the decoding of a letter into a sound leads to a single possibility as well. Such orthography is thus *transparent* with regards to phonemes with the advantage of offering no ambiguity when writing or reading the letters of a word, as illustrated in Figure 1.

In real life, no existing orthography is fully transparent phonemically. One reason is that a word spoken alone is sometimes different from a word spoken in a sentence. An even more consequential reason is that some orthographies like English[1] and French[2] have incorporated deeper depth rules that have moved them away from a transparent orthography (Seymour et al., 2003); this has created ambiguities when trying to write or read phonemically, as illustrated in Figure 2.

Many studies have discussed the degree of transparency of orthographies (Borleffs et al., 2017). These studies are mainly motivated by the estimation of the ease of reading and writing when learning a new language (Defior et al., 2002). Finnish, Korean, Serbo-Croatian and Turkish orthographies are often referred as highly *transparent* (Aro, 2004) (Wang and Tsai, 2009), (Turvey et al., 1984), (Öney and Durgunoğlu, 1997), whereas English and French orthographies are referred as *opaque* (van den Bosch et al., 1994). However, little work exists in NLP about measuring the level of transparency of an orthography. One noticeable exception is the work of van den Bosch et al. (1994) who have created grapheme-to-phoneme scores and tested them on three orthographies (Dutch, English and French).

This study extends such work with a method called OTEANN, which models a word-based *phoneme-to-grapheme* task and a word-based *grapheme-to-phoneme* task using an ANN. For the sake of simplicity, the former task is called a *writing* task while the latter task is called a *reading* task. The goal is not to build a perfect spelling translator or a spell checker. Instead the goal is to build a translator which can indicate a degree of phonemic transparency and thus make it possible to rank orthographies according to this criterion.

Interestingly, recent years have seen tremendous progress regarding NLP with ANNs (Otter et al., 2018). Sutskever et al. (2014) proposed an ANN

[1] https://en.wikipedia.org/wiki/English_orthography#Spelling_patterns
[2] https://fr.wiktionary.org/wiki/Annexe:Prononciation/français

Proceedings of the Third Workshop on Computational Typology and Multilingual NLP, pages 1–9
June 10, 2021.

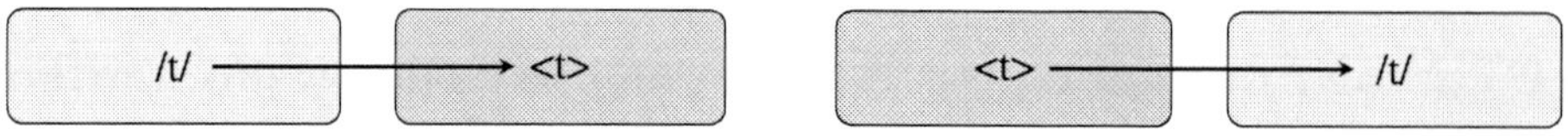

Figure 1: Example of unambiguous correspondence during writing and reading tasks in Esperanto.

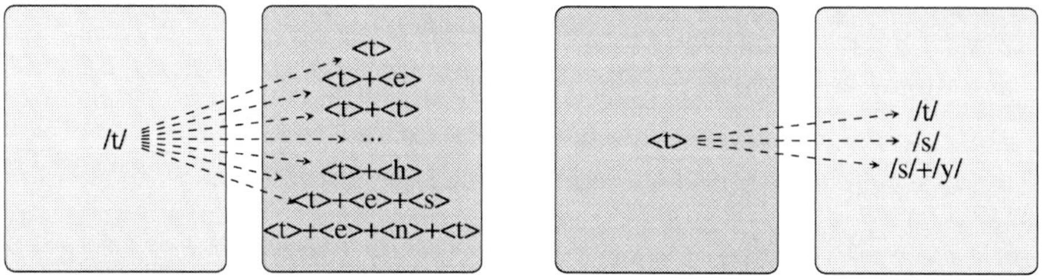

Figure 2: Example of ambiguous correspondence during writing and reading tasks in French. The /t/ phoneme can correspond to multiple graphemes, depending on the nature of the word and also depending on the nature of neighboring words in the sentence or even in a previous sentence. Similarly, the <t> grapheme can correspond to multiple phonemes.

called a Sequence-to-sequence (seq2seq) model that has proven to be very successful on language translation tasks. More recently, ANNs based on as *attention* (Bahdanau et al., 2014), (Vaswani et al., 2017) and *transformers* like Bidirectional Encoder Representations from Transformers (BERT), (Devlin et al., 2018) and Generative Pre-Training (GPT) (Radford, 2018) have again enhanced and outperformed seq2seqs. Considering writing a word and reading a word as two translations tasks allows re-using the transformers for our work. To this purpose, we used a minimalist GPT implementation (Karpathy, 2020) called *minGPT*. Notice that since we don't aim at building a perfect spelling translator, we do not have to translate a sequence of words into another sequence of words; our model only requires translating a spoken word into a spelled word (*writing task*) and a spelled word into a spoken word (*reading task*). In other words, our ANN operates at the character level within a sequence of characters of single words. The pronunciation and spelling of the word are both encoded as a sequence of UTF-8 characters; a pronounced word is encoded with the characters belonging to the set of phonemes of the target language, whereas a spelled word is encoded with the characters belonging to the alphabet of the target orthography. We directly re-used minGPT code with no modification. The only differences were the training data and the code for extracting the prediction at inference time.

We used OTEANN to test seventeen orthographies in order to evaluate their degree of phonemic transparency. Sixteen of them are the official orthographies of their respective language (Arabic, Breton, Chinese, Dutch, English, Esperanto, Finnish, French, German, Italian, Korean, Portuguese, Russian, Serbo-Croatian, Spanish, and Turkish) while the seventeenth is a phonemic orthography proposed for French.

A unique multi-orthography ANN model instance was trained to learn the writing and reading tasks on all languages at the same time. In other words, we used a single dataset containing samples of all studied orthographies. The multi-orthography ANN model was then tested for each orthography and each task with new samples, which allowed calculating an average percentage of correct translations. A score of 0% of correct translations represented a fully opaque orthography (no correlation between the input and the target), whereas a score close to 100% represented a fully transparent orthography (full correlation between the input and the target).

Our study first confirms that orthographies like Arabic, Finnish, Korean, Serbo-Croatian and Turkish are highly transparent whereas other ones like Chinese, French and English are highly opaque. For example, when solely based on a phoneme-grapheme correspondence, we estimated the chances of correctly writing a French word at 28%; similarly, when solely based on a grapheme-phoneme correspondence, we estimated the chances of correctly pronouncing an English word at 31%. For Dutch, English and French reading tasks, our obtained ranking is in line with the one of van den Bosch et al. (1994). One unexpected finding is that OTEANN also allows discovering

Orthography	Task	Input	Output
en	write	dʒɒb	job
en	read	job	dʒɒb

Table 1: Features of the multi-orthography dataset

certain mistakes performed by a new learner during writing and reading.

Remarkably, our method should apply to any orthography, provided a dataset is available.

2 Methodology

In order to evaluate a level of transparency of some orthographies two main steps were necessary: obtaining datasets and carrying out the training and testing experiments with the ANN.

2.1 Datasets

As displayed in Table 1, we needed a multi-orthography dataset with four features per sample: the orthography, the task (write or read), the input word (pronunciation or spelled word) and the output word (spelled word or pronunciation). A spelled word was represented by a sequence of graphemes whereas a pronunciation was represented by a sequence of phonemes. The characters representing phonemes are also called International Phonetic Alphabet (IPA) characters. Having a single dataset with multiple orthographies and tasks allows a single multi-orthography ANN model to learn to read and write all orthographies; otherwise, it would require one ANN model per orthography-task pair.

In order to build such dataset, we first generated one sub-dataset per orthography (e.g. one 'en' sub-dataset for English), each containing the pronunciation and the spelled word (e.g. 'dʒɒb' and 'job').

2.1.1 Baseline Orthographies

We first created baselines representing a fully transparent orthography and a fully opaque orthography.

Regarding a fully transparent orthography, we created a new artificial orthography called Entirely Transparent ('ent') orthography. We generated its samples by using the IPA pronunciation of real Esperanto words both as the pronunciation and as the spelled word, which resulted in a sub-dataset containing an 'ent' *bijective* orthography.

Regarding a fully opaque orthography, we also created a new artificial orthography called Entirely Opaque ('eno') orthography. We generated its samples by taking the IPA pronunciation of real Esperanto words mapping each of theirs phonemes to a random grapheme from a list of 25 graphemes, which resulted in a sub-dataset containing an 'eno' orthography with no correlation between the pronunciation and the spelled word.

2.1.2 Studied Orthographies

A sub-dataset was created for each of the following orthographies: Arabic ('ar'), Breton ('br'), German ('de'), English ('en'), Esperanto ('eo'), Spanish ('es'), Finnish ('fi'), French ('fr'), Italian ('it'), Korean ('ko'), Dutch ('nl'), Portuguese ('pt'), Russian ('ru'), Serbo-Croatian ('sh'), Turkish ('tr') and Chinese ('zh').

We incorporated the words from the corresponding Wiktionary[3] dump[4], with the exception of the following ones:

- Words containing space characters;
- Words containing more than 25 characters;
- Words containing capital letters (except for German words);
- Words containing non-standard characters with regard to the orthography's alphabet.

Two orthographies required additional processing:

- For German, proper nouns were discarded and the capital letter of common nouns was transformed into lower case;
- For Korean, the syllabic blocks words were converted in a series of two or three letters (one vowel and one or two consonants) pertaining to the Korean alphabet with *ko_pron*[5] Python library.

Regarding pronunciation, we directly extracted the IPA pronunciation when available in the associated Wiktionary dump, which was the case for 'br', 'de', 'en', 'es', 'fr', 'it', 'nl', 'pt' and 'sh'. The Esperanto ('eo') pronunciation came from the French Wiktionary. For the others ('ar', 'ko', 'ru', 'fi', 'tr'), we had to derive it from the spelled word with additional software. For Russian, the Russian Wiktionary dump did not contain the IPA. We thus used

[3]https://wiktionary.org
[4]https://dumps.wikimedia.org/
[5]https://pypi.org/project/ko-pron

wikt2pron ru_pron module[6] to obtain a pronunciation similar to the one displayed in the Russian Wiktionary web pages. For Chinese, we only selected Mandarin words in simplified Chinese and limited to one or two symbols (a.k.a. Hanzis); we then obtained their pronunciation from the *CEDICT*[7] dataset.

Extracting the phonemic pronunciation from Wiktionary may raise concerns given than IPA symbols can be used both for phonetic and phonemic notations and that there is no unified consistency between the different dictionaries. When processing the IPA strings, we nonetheless took care of preserving the highest surface pronunciation as possible: most pitches were removed since they represent no useful hint during the writing task (i.e. no consequence on the spelled word) and especially since they are generally impossible to predict when translating the spelled word into a pronunciation during the reading task. Nevertheless the /ː/ pitch was noticed as indispensable for some orthographies, for instance for predicting double vowels in the spelling of Finnish words or the *alif* letter in Arabic. Regarding the /ˈ/ pitch, it can slightly influence Spanish translation scores: it can lead to a better writing score as it can be a hint for predicting accented letters, but it can also lead to a lower reading score.

Another interesting orthography was a proposal of an alternative orthography for French called French Ortofasil ('fro')[8], which seeks to be phonemically transparent. Although not fully bijective (e.g. both /o/ and /ɔ/ map to <o> letter), it indeed seems highly transparent. We therefore used it to generate a sub-dataset for the 'fro' orthography.

It is debatable whether Chinese should be included in this study given the term *alphabet* is usually reserved for largely phonographic systems that have a small number of elements. We decided to include it because our ANN model allowed for *alphabets* with thousands of graphemes.

Table 2 summarizes the sub-datasets obtained.

2.1.3 Training and test datasets

$11,000$ samples were randomly selected in each of the 17 sub-datasets. Each sample from a sub-dataset produced two samples in the multi-orthography dataset: one sample for *write* task and one sample for the *read* task, as illustrated in Table 1. This multi-orthography dataset was subsequently divided into a training dataset ($10,000 * 17 * 2$ samples) and a test dataset ($1,000 * 17 * 2$ samples).

2.1.4 ANN architecture

We used minGTP (Karpathy, 2020) which runs on PyTorch[9]. Regarding the hyper-parameters, we configured a block size of 63 characters, 4 layers, 4 heads and 336 embedding tokens, which resulted in an ANN of $9,589,536$ trainable parameters and an episode training time of 2 hours and 10 minutes on a 4 GPU node. No effort was spent to shrink or prune the ANN, so its size could still be optimized. The data and code are available on Github [10].

2.1.5 Performance metric

We used a simple score in order to assess the performance of the ANN prediction during the testing step. When all the predicted characters were equal to those of the true target, a prediction was considered successful, hence allowing to score the percentage of successful predictions performed for each orthography-task pair.

2.1.6 Training and testing

We specified an episode as:

- **Generating the training and test datasets.** At the end of this step, each character present in these datasets was provisioned in the inventory of the ANN instance.
- **Training the ANN model**. The full training dataset was processed to be used as text blocks containing the concatenation of the four features (*orthography*, *task*, *input* and *output*) separated by a comma. Therefore, a single instance of the model was used to learn to write and read all 17 orthographies in one training.
- **Testing the ANN model for each orthography-task pair**. For each orthography-task pair, $1,000$ new samples were tested. Each sample was fed into the model with the concatenation of the three first features (*orthography*, *task* and *input*) separated by a comma. The model had to

[6] https://wikt2pron.readthedocs.io/en/latest/_modules/IPA/ru_pron.html

[7] https://github.com/msavva/transphoner/blob/master/data/

[8] https://fonétik.fr/v0/faq-en.html#mapping-table

[9] https://pytorch.org/

[10] https://github.com/marxav/oteann4

Orthography	Samples	Phonemes	Graphemes	Nb. of Phonemes	Nb of Graphemes
ar	12,057	32	47	8.0 ± 2.0	8.9 ± 2.3
br	17,343	45	29	6.6 ± 1.9	7.5 ± 2.2
de	529,740	41	30	10.2 ± 3.1	11.5 ± 3.4
en	42,206	42	29	7.3 ± 2.7	7.6 ± 2.6
eo	26,845	25	28	8.8 ± 2.6	8.6 ± 2.5
es	40,824	34	33	8.1 ± 2.7	8.7 ± 2.6
fi	105,352	28	27	10.4 ± 3.5	10.4 ± 3.5
fr	1,214,248	35	41	9.0 ± 2.7	11.2 ± 2.9
fro	1,214,262	35	32	9.0 ± 2.7	8.6 ± 2.6
it	26,798	34	32	9.1 ± 2.8	9.1 ± 2.6
ko	64,669	41	67	10.6 ± 4.0	8.3 ± 3.0
nl	13,340	45	28	7.8 ± 3.1	8.6 ± 3.4
pt	12,190	37	38	7.7 ± 2.3	7.9 ± 2.3
ru	304,514	30	33	10.5 ± 3.1	10.7 ± 3.1
sh	98,575	27	27	9.1 ± 2.8	8.9 ± 2.7
tr	117,841	36	31	10.3 ± 3.7	10.1 ± 3.6
zh	27,688	32	4813	9.9 ± 2.2	1.8 ± 0.3
eno	26,845	25	25	8.8 ± 2.6	8.8 ± 2.6
ent	26,845	25	25	8.8 ± 2.6	8.8 ± 2.6

Table 2: Summary of the sub-datasets. For each sub-dataset, a line indicates the number of samples available, the number of different phoneme UTF-8 characters, the number of different grapheme UTF-8 characters, the mean number of phonemes in words, and the mean number of graphemes in words.

predict a value equal to the *output* feature, which was the target to be found.

We performed 11 episodes to measure the mean and standard deviation of each orthography-task pair and thus assess the consistency of our results.

Future work may use more test samples to gain a statistical insight on the different types of errors depending on the orthography at hand.

3 Results

First, regarding the results of the two baseline orthographies, the 'eno' opaque orthography obtained a score of 0% in both writing and reading, which was in line with the expectations given that there was no correlation between its phonemes and its graphemes; on the other hand, the 'ent' transparent orthography scored above 99.6% on the writing and reading tasks, which indicated a high level of correlation between its phonemes and its graphemes. We thus considered our ANN model satisfactory for our objective of comparing the performance of different orthographies.

Figure 3 and Table 3 present our main results. They are significantly different between writing and reading since these tasks are generally not symmetrical. Two features are likely to influence the symmetry, and therefore the efficiency of each task. As recalled by Figure 2, the most important feature would undoubtedly be the number of possible phoneme-to-grapheme and grapheme-to-phoneme ambiguities per tested orthography. Unfortunately we did not possess such data. Another impacting feature may be the number of possible values (graphemes or phonemes) for a given target character. The higher the number of values, the harder the prediction should be for the ANN. Future work should investigate the relative importance of these features on the OTEANN performances.

Comparing OTEANN's reading results with those of van den Bosch et al. (1994), OTEANN first seems to naturally assimilate the grapheme complexity (e.g. for French, it successfully learnt that "cadeau" should be pronounced /kado/). Regarding grapheme-to-phoneme complexity (*G-P complexity*), they ranked English (*G-P complexity*=90%) more complex than Dutch (*G-P complexity*=25%) which, in turn, was more complex than French (*G-P complexity*=15%). OTEANN results preserved the same ranking with transparency scores of 31%, 57% and 79*s*% for English, Dutch and French. Admittedly, OTEANN's scores were different in terms of scale but OTEANN had to deal

Orthography	Write	Read
ent	99.6 ± 0.3	99.8 ± 0.1
eno	0.0 ± 0.0	0.0 ± 0.0
ar	84.3 ± 0.8	99.4 ± 0.3
br	80.6 ± 0.6	77.2 ± 1.6
de	69.1 ± 1.0	78.0 ± 1.5
en	36.1 ± 1.5	31.1 ± 1.3
eo	99.3 ± 0.2	99.7 ± 0.1
es	66.9 ± 2.0	85.3 ± 1.3
fi	97.7 ± 0.3	92.3 ± 0.8
fr	28.0 ± 1.4	79.6 ± 1.7
fro	99.0 ± 0.3	89.7 ± 1.1
it	94.5 ± 0.8	71.6 ± 0.9
ko	81.9 ± 1.0	97.5 ± 0.5
nl	72.9 ± 1.7	55.7 ± 2.2
pt	75.8 ± 1.0	82.4 ± 0.9
ru	41.3 ± 1.6	97.2 ± 0.5
sh	99.2 ± 0.3	99.3 ± 0.3
tr	95.4 ± 0.7	95.9 ± 0.6
zh	19.9 ± 1.4	78.7 ± 0.9

Table 3: Phonemic transparency scores. (OTEANN trained with 10,000 samples)

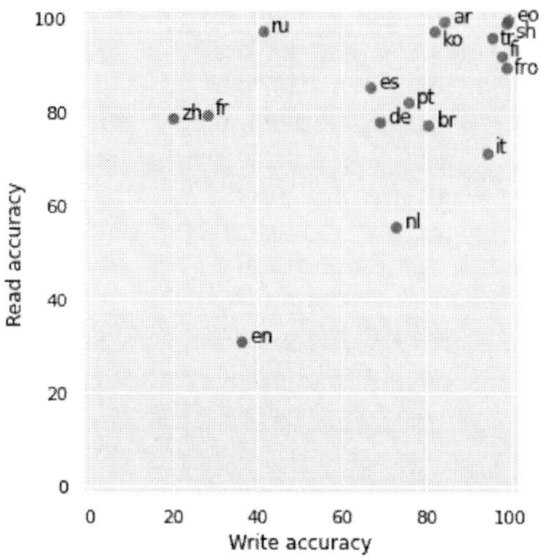

Figure 3: Scatterplot of the mean scores. (OTEANN trained with 10,000 samples)

with more orthographies as well as with the writing task.

Figure 3 also allows categorizing the studied orthographies with respect to their degree of transparency:

- **Esperanto**: With scores above 99.3%, Esperanto orthography is nearly as transparent as the 'ent' baseline. The most common error occurred on a doubled letter in the input, which was incorrectly translated to a single letter.

- **Arabic, Finnish, Korean, Serbo-Croatian and Turkish**: Their scores above 80% both in writing and reading confirmed that their orthography is highly transparent as indicated in (Aro, 2004), (Wang and Tsai, 2009) and (Öney and Durgunoğlu, 1997). The Arabic score is high on in the read direction, which is likely due to the use of diacritics in the dataset; without them, the score would undoubtedly be lower. Regarding Korean, its orthography became a little less transparent during the twentieth century; its high scores suggest that further work should check the dataset and evaluate new scores.

- **Breton, German, Italian, Portuguese and Spanish**: With all their scores above 65% their orthography was also measured as fairly transparent. For Spanish, the detailed results showed that the most common failure during writing occurs with accents: the ANN had great difficulty predicting whether a vowel should contain an accent or not. For Italian, typical errors observed in the results were the prediction of /ɛ/ instead of a /e/ and /ɔ/ instead of a /o/, which were harder to discriminate. Future work may revise the scoring formula to reduce the cost of some of these errors in the performance calculation.

- **Dutch**: The Dutch reading score (56%) is low but might be slightly enhanced given a possible lack of consistency regarding the phonemes used in the Dutch sub-dataset.

- **Russian**: The Russian writing score (41%) may seem low. However, Russian has strong stress-related vowel reduction, which makes it hard to know how to write a word without knowing the morphemes involved. Nevertheless, future work should either study their sub-dataset more in depth or use a different data source like wikipron[11] to possibly improve its scores.

- **Chinese**: The results indicated a low writing score (20%), which is not surprising given

[11] https://pypi.org/project/wikipron/

than some phonemes can have multiple corresponding graphemes and that there are thousands of graphemes (Hanzis) to be learnt. However, it turns out that its reading score is much higher (79%).

- **French**: With a low writing score (28%), the results showed that the chances of correctly writing a French word on the sole basis of its pronunciation were rare, as anticipated given the high number of phoneme-to-grapheme possibilities. Without being able to access a broader context than the word itself, the ANN was not able to reliably predict how to write a French word. With a much higher reading score (80%), the ANN obtained good reading results. As a comparison, for the same language, the alternative 'fro' orthography obtained excellent writing score (99%) and reading score (90%). Recall that the difference between its two scores is due to the fact that the 'fro' orthography is not bijective. For instance, in the reading direction, the <o> letter can be translated into /o/ or /ɔ/).

- **English**: With a low writing score (36%) and a low reading score (31%), the results showed that English orthography is also highly opaque, which is consistent with most studies. As a reminder, a phonemic reading of an English word often does not work because of its high number of grapheme-to-phoneme possibilities. For instance the grapheme <u> can either correspond to /ʌ/ (as in "hug"), to /juː/ (as in "huge"), to /ɜːr/ (as in "cur") or /jʊəː/ as in "cure". As for Russian, additional work should be dedicated to check the English sub dataset and possibly enhance it if necessary, which could improve 'en' scores by a few percent.

Observing the detailed result of each prediction also made it possible to study the phonemic correspondences learned or not learned by the OTEANN model.

- For task-orthographies with a high transparency score, the model successfully predicted most pronunciations or spellings even when the correspondences involved more than one letter. For instance, OTEANN predicted that the Italian word "cerchia" should be pronounced /ʧerkja/, hence showing that the model had successfully learned that <c>, when followed by <e>, should be pronounced as /ʧ/ and also that <c>, when followed by <h>, should be pronounced as /k/.

- For task-orthographies with a low transparency score, the model generally failed on letters involved in ambiguous correspondences (recall Figure 2). For instance, it incorrectly predicted that the pronunciation of the English word "level" was "livəl" instead of "lɛvəl", which might be a bad generalization from words like "lever" learned at training time. OTEANN also incorrectly predicted that the spelling of the French word /ale/ was "allez" when the expected target was "aller" (another French homophone); this type of error is inevitable since the OTEANN model intentionally use single word input samples and therefore cannot rely on neighboring words as additional context to discriminate between homophones with different spelling.

- Surprisingly, the model also predicted spellings that do not exist but who could have existed, in the same vein as *ThisWordDoesNotExist.com*[12]. For instance, OTEANN predicted that the spelling of the French word /swaʁe/" was "soirer", which does not exist but looks like a French infinitive verb that would mean "to celebrate at a party".

In addition, the results in Table 3 also showed that the ANN has less than a 30% chance of correctly writing a word in French or Chinese after training on 10000 samples while Figure 9 shows that the same ANN has more than a 85% chance of correctly writing a word in Finnish, Italian, Serbo-Croatian or Turkish after training only on 1000 samples. Such a discrepancy highlights the enormous additional cost in terms of time and energy for learning a non-transparent orthography.

4 Discussion and Conclusion

Among the tested orthographies, some shared the grapheme inventory. Given that they are all trained together, there might be an impact on performance. Although some of our preliminary experiments with a single ANN instance per orthography did not seem to lead to significant differences, it could be interesting to formally compare both approaches.

[12]https://www.thisworddoesnotexist.com

The accuracy metric we used is all or nothing. Additional work could also study alternative accuracy metrics and compare their results on the different orthographies.

Although Wiktionary data may be inconsistent in quality and therefore positively or negatively impact the measured metric, the results obtained for Dutch, English and French orthographies reasonably extended those of van den Bosch et al. (1994) while the other results reflected the perception of several other studies. Consequently, our OTEANN model showed that an ANN can convincingly estimate a level of phonemic transparency for multiple orthographies both for the phoneme-to-grapheme and grapheme-to-phoneme directions.

This method should be easily applicable to other orthographies beyond those tested in this study. However, since the superfluous IPA symbols slightly influence the score results, future work should closely examine and discuss the phonemes to use depending on the orthography to be tested.

As OTEANN also points out some possible grapheme or phoneme errors when writing or reading phonemically, it could also be used to detect possible errors in the dictionaries of transparent orthographies; it could also be used to evaluate proposals for improving opaque orthographies.

Finally, it would be beneficial to investigate if our ANN and its artificial neural units somehow imitate the way a beginner learns to write and read a language. If so, it might suggest that a transparent orthography would be easier and faster to learn than an opaque orthography.

References

Mikko Aro. 2004. *Learning to read: The effect of orthography*. 237. Jyväskylän yliopisto.

Dzmitry Bahdanau, Kyunghyun Cho, and Yoshua Bengio. 2014. Neural machine translation by jointly learning to align and translate. *arXiv preprint arXiv:1409.0473*.

Elisabeth Borleffs, Ben AM Maassen, Heikki Lyytinen, and Frans Zwarts. 2017. Measuring orthographic transparency and morphological-syllabic complexity in alphabetic orthographies: a narrative review. *Reading and writing*, 30(8):1617–1638.

Sylvia Defior, Francisco Martos, and Luz Cary. 2002. Differences in reading acquisition development in two shallow orthographies: Portuguese and spanish. *Applied Psycholinguistics*, 23(1):135–148.

Jacob Devlin, Ming-Wei Chang, Kenton Lee, and Kristina Toutanova. 2018. Bert: Pre-training of deep bidirectional transformers for language understanding.

Andrej Karpathy. 2020. mingtp. Available at `https://github.com/karpathy/minGPT`, MIT licence.

Banu Öney and Aydin Yücesan Durgunoğlu. 1997. Beginning to read in turkish: A phonologically transparent orthography. *Applied psycholinguistics*, 18(1):1–15.

Daniel W Otter, Julian R Medina, and Jugal K Kalita. 2018. A survey of the usages of deep learning in natural language processing. *arXiv preprint arXiv:1807.10854*.

A. Radford. 2018. Improving language understanding by generative pre-training.

Philip HK Seymour, Mikko Aro, Jane M Erskine, and Collaboration with COST Action A8 Network. 2003. Foundation literacy acquisition in european orthographies. *British Journal of psychology*, 94(2):143–174.

Ilya Sutskever, Oriol Vinyals, and Quoc V. Le. 2014. Sequence to sequence learning with neural networks. *CoRR*, abs/1409.3215.

MT Turvey, Laurie B Feldman, and G Lukatela++. 1984. The serbo-croatian orthography constrains the reader to a phonologically analytic strategy. *Status Report on Speech Research: A Report on the*, page 17.

Antal van den Bosch, Alain Content, Walter Daelemans, and Beatrice de Gelder. 1994. Analysing orthographic depth of different languages using data-oriented algorithms.

Ashish Vaswani, Noam Shazeer, Niki Parmar, Jakob Uszkoreit, Llion Jones, Aidan N. Gomez, Lukasz Kaiser, and Illia Polosukhin. 2017. Attention is all you need.

Yu-Chun Wang and Richard Tzong-Han Tsai. 2009. Rule-based korean grapheme to phoneme conversion using sound patterns. In *Proceedings of the 23rd Pacific Asia Conference on Language, Information and Computation, Volume 2*, pages 843–850.

A Additional Experiments and Results

In addition to testing our OTEANN model trained on $10,000$ samples, we also tested the same OTEANN model but trained with fewer samples ($1,000$, $2,000$, $3,000$, and $5,000$), each time following the methodology described in section 2. We then aggregated the results to summarize them in Figure 9, which shows the learning curve of the studied orthographies as a function of the number of training samples.

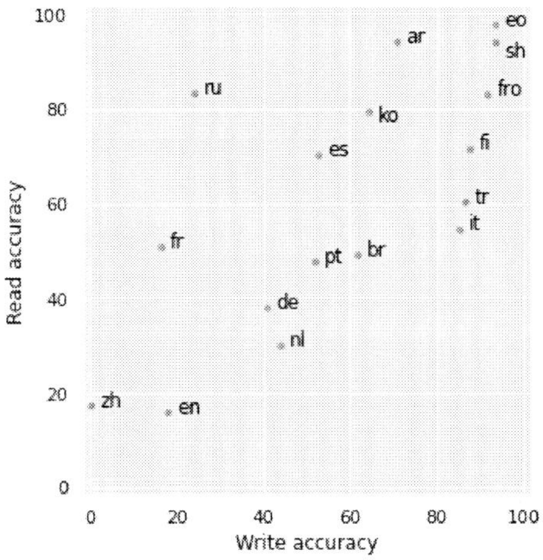

Figure 4: Scores with 1, 000 training samples.

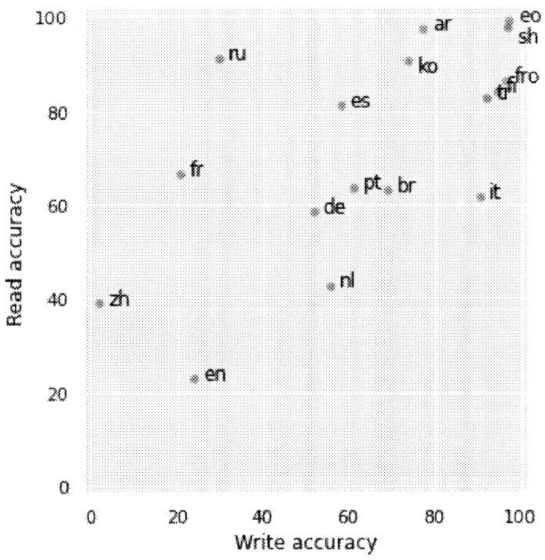

Figure 5: Scores with 2, 000 training samples.

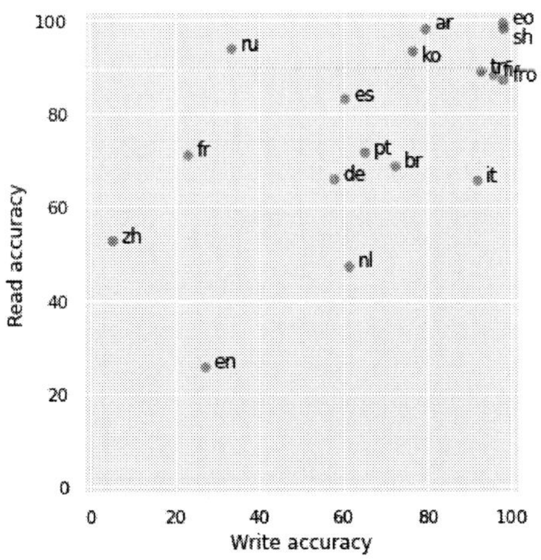

Figure 6: Scores with 3, 000 training samples.

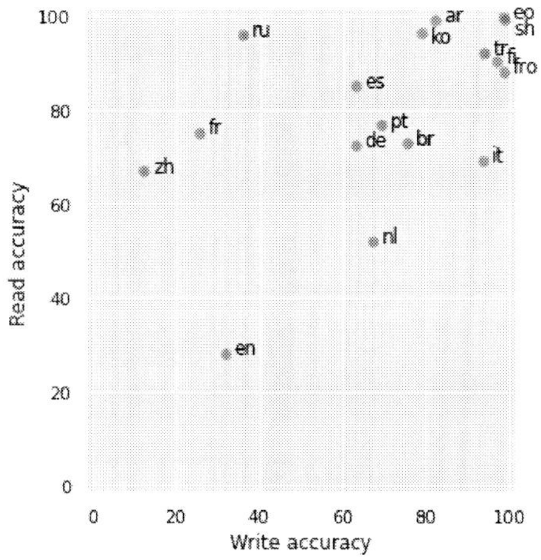

Figure 7: Scores with 5, 000 training samples.

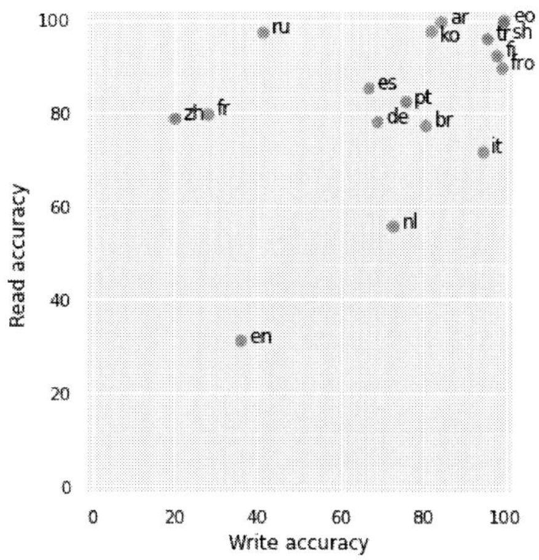

Figure 8: Scores with 10, 000 training samples.

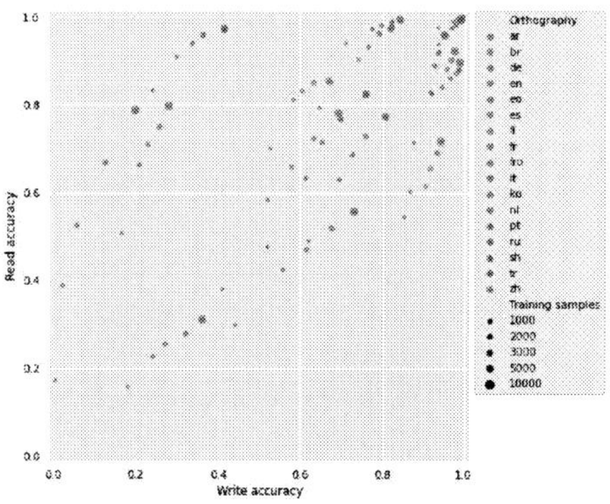

Figure 9: Scores according to the number of training samples

Inferring morphological complexity from syntactic dependency networks: a test

Luca Brigada Villa (Università degli Studi di Pavia) & Guglielmo Inglese (KU Leuven – FWO)

Abstract

Research in linguistic typology has shown that languages do not fall into the neat morphological types (synthetic vs. analytic) postulated in the 19th century. Instead, analytic and synthetic must be viewed as two poles of a continuum and languages may show a mix analytic and synthetic strategies to different degrees. Unfortunately, empirical studies that offer a more fine-grained morphological classification of languages based on these parameters remain few. In this paper, we build upon previous research by Liu & Xu (2011) and investigate the possibility of inferring information on morphological complexity from syntactic dependency networks.

1 Introduction

Language classification based on morphological profiles has prominently featured in the linguistic typology research agenda since the earliest days of the discipline.

Earlier 19th century classifications essentially focused on morphological complexity in terms of the number of morphemes per word and the number of meanings per morpheme, and proposed that languages may be typologized into neatly discrete type, e.g. 'isolating', 'agglutinative', 'inflectional' (see Schwegler 1990).[1] However, it soon became clear that such a holistic approach does not adequately capture the variation of natural languages (already Sapir 1921). Instead, morphological complexity should be viewed as an empirically measurable "multidimensional typological space" (Arkadiev & Klamer 2018: 444), in which languages can be arranged based on a number of parameters.[2]

Based on this line of reasoning, scholars have variously tried to measure morphological complexity by means of quantitative methods and classify languages accordingly. In this paper, we build upon a proposal by Liu & Xu (2011) and investigate whether syntactic dependency networks can be effectively used as tools for measuring (at least some aspects of) morphological complexity.

The paper is structured as follows: in Section 2 we review previous research on quantitative approaches to morphological typology. Section 3 briefly introduces syntactic dependency networks and network analysis. Section 4 is devoted to our own analysis. We first illustrate our data and methods (Section 4.1 and 4.2), and then present and discuss our results (Section 4.3 and 4.4). Section 5 contains a summary of our findings.

2 Quantitative morphological typology: previous research

Scholars generally agree that a more accurate and realistic morphological typology can only be achieved through empirical investigations of naturalistic (corpus) data, but how this measurement is to be carried out remains a matter of debate. To our knowledge, there exist two main approaches that have so far been pursued in the quantitative study of morphological typology.[3]

[1] We use the term *morphological complexity* in the narrow sense of *enumerative complexity*, that is, "the number of elements of which a given morphological entity consists, mainly inventory size and string length" (Arkadiev & Gardani 2020: 8).

[2] For the large scale cross-linguistic investigation of some of these parameters see e.g. Bickel & Nichols (2013a; 2013b; 2013c).

[3] By quantitative study, we intend here typological studies based on corpus data, that is, what Levshina (2019) refers to

Proceedings of the Third Workshop on Computational Typology and Multilingual NLP, pages 10–22
June 10, 2021.

The first approach stems from Greenberg (1960). Greenberg proposes that morphological complexity be decomposed in a few easily measurable indexes, e.g. the number of morphemes per word and the number of meanings expressed by each morpheme. To test this approach, Greenberg calculated each index by looking at 100-word stretches of texts in 8 different languages.

Siegel et al. (2014) follow a similar approach and focus on two morphological indexes, that is, the analyticity and the syntheticity indexes. They measure these by taking into account several parameters, including e.g. number of morphemes per words, in randomized samples of 1000 manually annotated token for 19 languages (4 languages plus 13 varieties of English and two English-based creoles).

The main advantage of the approach pursued by Greenberg (1960) and Siegel et al. (2014) is that they employ indexes that are theoretically well-grounded and offer an accurate morphological typology of the languages investigated. However, previous studies of this type present two major shortcomings. The first one concerns the data: both studies focus on a relatively narrow set of languages. The second one concerns the methodology: the indexes must be calculated by manually annotating (a sample of) tokens in each of the languages under investigation. While this methodology undoubtedly results in high quality and reliable data, it is a labor-intensive and time-consuming task, less suitable to investigate morphological complexity on a large cross-linguistic scale.

As an alternative, Liu & Xu (2011) propose to use syntactic dependency networks to explore morphological typology. The main assumption behind this approach is that network structure can be used as a proxy of morphological complexity, which can thus be measured by means of topological indexes of networks (see Section 3). The main advantage of this approach is that it allows to compare a potentially large number of languages for which annotated corpora are available, without the need to manually code each token for its morphological features.

Liu & Xu (2011) results suggest that networks can indeed be a useful tool to explore morphological typology, but their work may be improved in a number of respects. First, the methodology needs to be tested on a wider set of languages (Liu and Xu's sample includes only 15 languages, with a significant overrepresentation of Indo-European languages). Secondly, the authors partly leave open the question of which network measure best captures morphological complexity.

3 Syntactic dependency networks

In this section, we describe syntactic dependency networks and their properties (Section 3.1), and we illustrate various indexes that can be used to interpret network structure (Section 3.2), with a focus on those indexes that we use in our own analysis in Section 4.

3.1 Defining syntactic dependency networks

A network is a structure consisting of a set of objects, called vertices or nodes, and a set of links, called edges. Edges connect two nodes and may be directed, if two nodes are involved in a hierarchical structure, or undirected. Directed and undirected networks differ based on whether they feature directed or undirected edges, respectively.[4]

Networks have been shown to be a suitable tool to represent syntactic relations (Liu 2008; Čech & Mačutek 2009; Čech, Mačutek & Žabokrtský 2011; Passarotti 2014; Čech, Mačutek & Liu 2016). This holds particularly true for dependency grammars, which view syntactic structures as binary and hierarchical relations between lexical nodes (Robinson 1970), thereby allowing the representation of sentences as rooted trees.[5] In Figure 1, we illustrate the representation of the sentences 'John calls Mary', 'John eats an apple', 'The apple is red' and 'Mary buys some apples' as dependency trees.

as *token-based typology* and Gerdes et al. (2021) as *typometrics*. This contrasts with e.g. the classifications proposed by Bickel & Nichols (2013a; 2013b; 2013c), which are based on a sample of few formatives per language (Bickel & Nichols 2013d) and thus fall within the more traditional *type-based* typology (Levshina 2019).

[4] For the purpose of this work, we treat dependencies as undirected.

[5] A tree is a graph in which no cycle can be found. A rooted tree is a tree in which one node is designated as the root of the tree.

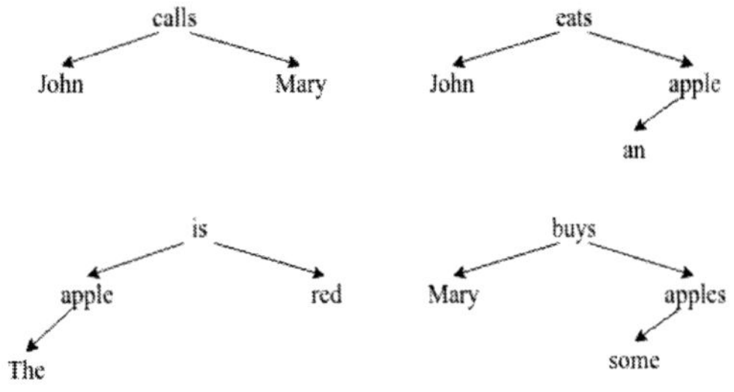

Figure 1: Dependency trees

A syntactic dependency network is a network representing dependency relations. We follow the definition of syntactic dependency network given by Ferrer i Cancho et al. (2004), that is, a set of words *V*, consisting of the vocabulary of a language, and an adjacency matrix *A*. If it happens in at least one sentence that two elements of *V*, let us call them *x* and *y*, are syntactically related, then the value in *A*, corresponding to column *x* and row *y*, will be equal to 1, otherwise it will be 0. The network is then induced from the matrix. This means that syntactic dependency networks built from treebanks actually consist of the combination of all networks that can be drawn from individual dependency trees. Taking the trees in Figure 1 as representing our treebank, the corresponding network has the structure shown in Figure 2.

Dependency networks can be further differentiated into word-based and lemma-based networks (see Čech & Mačutek 2009). The former feature words occurring in sentences as nodes, while in the latter the nodes consist of lemmas. The difference between word- and lemma-based networks is shown in Figure 2 and 3.

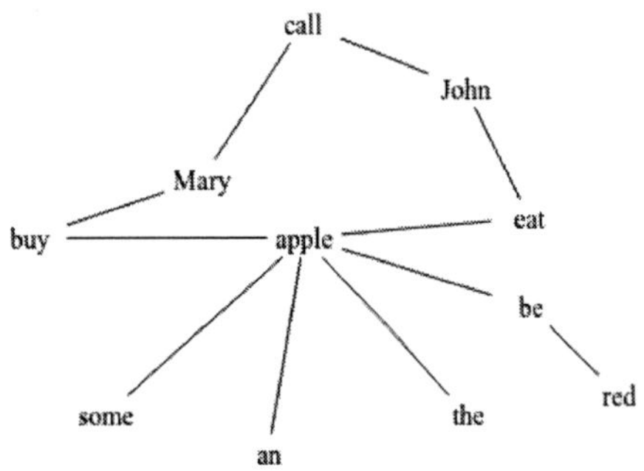

Figure 3: Lemma-based dependency network

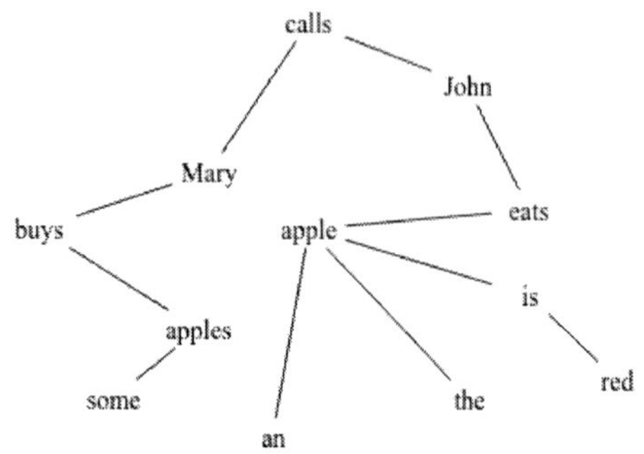

Figure 2: Word-based dependency network

3.2 Network indexes

The structure of networks can be analyzed by taking into account a number of parameters, or indexes. Here, we briefly illustrate the network topological indexes that we employ in our analysis (we refer to Albert & Barabasi 2002; Liu & Xu 2011 for extensive discussion on how the indexes are measured).

Number of edges and nodes: this is the total count of all nodes and edges featured in a network.

Average degree: the count of the links in which a node is involved is called *degree*. The average of the degrees of a network is the simplest measure that can be calculated.

Average path length: in a connected network, it is always possible to find a path between two given nodes. If two nodes are connected, the path length between them is 1, if they are not directly connected, then the path length is computed 'jumping' from one node to another starting from the source node until the target node is reached. The distance is calculated by considering the shortest possible path. The average path length refers to the average of the distances between each pair of nodes in the network.

Clustering coefficient: syntactic dependency networks have the tendency to form clusters in which groups of three elements are completely connected. Clustering coefficient measures the proportion of fully connected triplets of nodes over the number of all the possible groups of three nodes in the network.

Diameter: the diameter of a network is the maximal distance between any pair of its nodes.

Network centralization (Horvath & Dong 2008): network centralization (NC) is a measure to find the most central nodes in a network.

Gamma: according to Albert & Barabási (2002), in so-called real networks the degree distribution follows a power-law. It has been shown that syntactic dependency networks are real networks and likewise follow a power-law $P(k) \sim k^{-\gamma}$ (thus Ferrer i Cancho et al. 2004).

In particular, based on data discussed by (Ferrer i Cancho 2005), it seems that syntactic dependency networks share a common behavior: their degree distributions follow a power-law, their average path length is similar to average path length in random graphs (Erdös-Rényi graphs) and their clustering coefficient is significantly higher than clustering coefficient in random graphs. These features allow us to consider syntactic dependency networks as *small-world* and *scale-free* networks (see further Albert & Barabási 2002; Ferrer i Cancho et al. 2004; Liu & Xu 2011 for discussion).

4 Using networks to measure morphological complexity

Studies by Liu & Xu (2011) and Čech & Mačutek (2009) make a strong case that dependency networks may be used to infer morphological complexity. In this paper, we focus on the networks' potential to explore one component of morphological complexity, that is, the analyticity/syntheticity index. This index reflects the prevalence of synthetic vs. analytic strategies in individual languages. Based on Greenberg's (1960) insights, our assumption is that the index is a gradient, and languages may vary from highly synthetic (prevalence of synthesis) to highly analytic (prevalence of analysis), with several intermediate types.

Following Siegel et al. (2014: 52–53), we distinguish analytic vs. synthetic strategies based on how they convey grammatical information: analytic strategies use free markers, whereas synthetic strategies use bound markers (see also Bickel & Nichols 2013a for discussion).

Dependency treebanks are well suited to explore analyticity/syntheticity for a number of reasons. First, treebanks are already tokenized, which makes it straightforward to single out free vs. bound markers. [6] Moreover, the number of dependencies in a sentence can be indirectly taken as a sign of higher/lower analyticity.

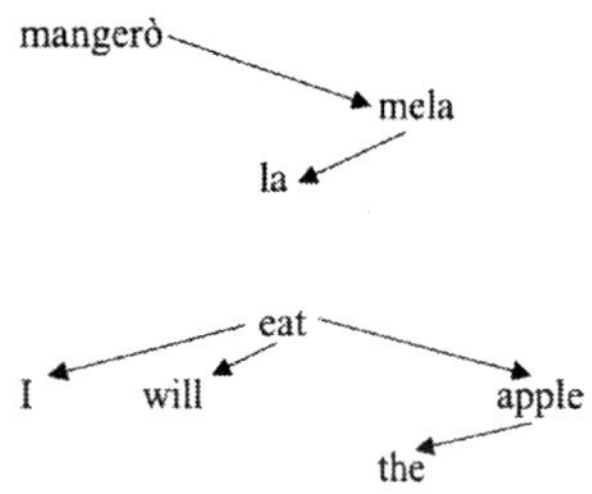

Figure 4: Italian vs. English dependency trees

To illustrate these points, let us compare the dependency trees of the sentence 'I will eat the apple' in Italian and English, as in Figure 4. The main difference between English and Italian is that in Italian grammatical information concerning verbal person/number and TAM is packed by a single form, i.e. *mangerò* 'eat.FUT.1SG', while the same content must be expressed by three free forms *I will eat* in English. In other words, to express future tense, Italian resorts to a more synthetic strategy than English. This is reflected in the number of nodes and links in the trees: the English tree features more nodes and hence more dependencies. This information easily translates into different network structures, in the sense that in principle the more analytic the construction the more edges and nodes the corresponding network will show.

In the reminder of this section, we put Liu & Xu's (2011) intuitions about the connection between analyticity and network structure to a test.

4.1 Data sampling

This study is based on a sample of 42 languages (Appendix A). The sampling procedure has been essentially practical in nature. First, we have only included languages for which treebanks are available in Universal Dependencies (UD) (Nivre et al. 2016; Croft et al. 2017). The reason to work with UD is both practical and theoretical. In the first place, UD allows to easily access already

[6] Clearly, the reliability of tokenization is a potential issue, especially considering problematic items such as clitics. In this study, we work with UD treebanks, which share a uniform tokenization schema. This limits the risk of biases induced by different tokenization styles across treebanks.

annotated data from a variety of languages. From a theoretical viewpoint, the UD annotation schema, which maximizes consistency of annotation across languages, makes UD treebanks particularly well suited for typological studies (see e.g. Levshina 2019; Gerdes et al. 2021).

To maximize diversity among the available UD treebanks, we have picked out one treebank for each language family represented in UD (and one for each branch in each family, where available). Moreover, we have also included historical varieties within the same branch where possible (e.g. Classical Chinese and Mandarin Chinese, Ancient Greek and Modern Greek).

In addition, we have split the treebanks into two groups. The first group features a set of six treebanks that we use to set up our control group. These are languages that can be reasonably taken as instantiating two poles of higher analyticity vs. higher syntheticity. [7] The former include Vietnamese (vie), Mandarine Chinese (zho), and Classical Chinese (lzh). The latter are Russian (rus), Finnish (fin), and Uyghur (uig). The second group includes all the other languages in the sample, whose degree of analyticity/syntheticity we seek to measure.

4.2 Methods

Our study diverges from Liu & Xu (2011) in a number of significant methodological respects. In the first place, Liu & Xu (2011) calculated for each of the 15 languages in their sample several topological indexes and then performed a cluster analysis to classify languages accordingly. In this study, we do not apply clustering techniques. The reason is that clustering analysis may force languages into "hierarchically organized groups" even in absence of a real underlying motivation (Cysouw 2007: 63–64). In our case, we do not in principle expect languages to cluster into neatly defined groups based on their degree of analyticity. Instead, as we have already mentioned, we conceive analyticity/syntheticity as a one-dimension continuum (cf. Gerdes et al. 2021: 13–19).

Abandoning clustering techniques also means that we need to independently single out among the topological indexes those that most likely reflect the difference between the prevalence of analytic vs. synthetic strategies. Moreover, we need take into consideration the different size of the treebanks in our sample (ranging from 955 tokens to 473.881 tokens), as treebank size could lead to potential biases when measuring network indexes.

To overcome these issues, we first established which network indexes perform well in distinguishing analytic vs. synthetic languages irrespective of treebank size. To do so, we set 7 arbitrary sizes (1.000, 5.000, 10.000, 20.000, 30.000, 50.000 and 75.000 tokens) and we extracted one random sub-treebank for each of the above sizes for the languages in the control group.

From each sub-treebank, we induced the corresponding word-based dependency network excluding punctuation marks, symbols and elliptical dependency relations. We calculated the topological indexes described in Section 3 using the python package *igraph* (Csárdi & Nepusz 2006).[8] For the purpose of this paper, we have focused on word-based networks, as these have been claimed to better represent morphological variation than lemma-based networks (Liu & Xu 2011; Čech & Mačutek 2009).

We then carried out a Welch *t*-test (Welch 1947) to establish which indexes are more reliable to separate the two groups, and have picked out only those indexes that perform significantly better across all sub-treebanks' sizes.[9] The Welch *t*-test is used to test the hypothesis that two groups have equal means. The null hypothesis, in our case, was that the two groups means were equal. If a *t*-test performed on a topological index resulted to discard null hypothesis (significance level=0.05), then we consider it as a metric able to separate the two groups, hence possibly reflecting the analytic vs. synthetic distinction.

Once the significant metrics have been singled out, the second step was to measure these indexes for the rest of the languages in our sample and compare them with those of the control group. For

[7] We are aware that the choice of these languages is in part arbitrary, but these are languages (or belong to language families) that have been repeatedly pointed out in the literature as instantiating prototypically analytic vs. synthetic languages.

[8] The code and data used for this study are freely available at https://github.com/bavagliladri/tb2net.

[9] The test was carried out using the python library SciPy (Virtanen et al. 2020)

Table 1: Results of the *t*-test on the control group per size

Variable	1k	5k	10k	20k	30k	50k	75k
n_edges	0.46654	0.29684	0.23868	0.23032	0.20536	0.36893	0.36173
n_nodes	0.04801	0.02542	0.02413	0.02402	0.02458	0.17776	0.17076
av_degree	0.00219	0.03466	0.05941	0.06613	0.07789	0.30949	0.31478
avg_path_length	0.02765	0.0017	0.0028	0.0026	0.00441	0.10372	0.09932
clus_coeff	0.2025	0.0186	0.02495	0.03039	0.03114	0.23311	0.22447
diam	0.04674	0.03303	0.06705	0.0083	0.06032	0.08439	0.21913
nc	0.35234	0.0197	0.01896	0.01642	0.00805	0.04418	0.10778
gamma	0.26583	0.12827	0.03547	0.03731	0.0401	0.26701	0.21379

the other languages we extracted only one treebank for the largest possible size (up to 30k, see Section 4.3), in order to make the best use of the available data. [10] For example, for the UD_Wolof-WTB treebank, whose size is 38.937 tokens, we produced a sub-treebank of 30.000 tokens. From these treebanks, we induced the corresponding dependency networks and calculated the relevant network indexes following the procedure outlined above. The results of our analysis are discussed in the next section.

4.3 Results

Let us first discuss the results of the *t*-test performed on the control group. Table 1 reports the p-value for each index across all treebank sizes (with 3 languages per group in the 1k-30k and 2 languages per group in 50-70k; see Appendix B for the raw data). As the results show, the indexes that consistently give a p-value of less than 0.05 are number of nodes and average path length.

The other indexes give a mixed picture. Number of edges is never significant. However, the other indexes are significant for some specific sub-size(s). For example, unlike Liu & Xu (2011: 4), we do not find network centrality (nc) to be a consistently significant index. This index performs well for treebank size 5k-30k, but not for the smallest size of 1k, and we found a similar result for clustering coefficient. By contrast, average degree gives consistent results only for the smallest sizes 1k and 5k. Nevertheless, since none of these indexes performs consistently well for size 1k-30k, for this preliminary study we have decided to leave these aside and focus only on number of nodes and average path length. More research is needed to fully understand the interplay between treebank size and topological indexes of the corresponding networks, also adopting other statistical tests.

In addition, note that none of the indexes yields significant results when the treebank size is 50k tokens or higher. It may be possible that the significant results obtained from the networks induced from the smaller treebanks are due to chance. However, it must be mentioned that only 4 out of the 6 treebanks of the control group have more than 50k tokens and the reduced size of the control group may have affected the statistical testing. For these reasons, for treebanks more than 30k tokens, we have randomly created 30k size sub-treebanks and have only analyzed the corresponding networks, since beyond this size the indexes appear to be less reliable.

We have then measured number of nodes and average path length for the networks induced from the rest of the languages in our sample. The results are reported in Appendix C. In Figure 5 and 6 we visualize the results for 5k and 30k treebanks respectively. Data is visualized as a one-dimension continuum for each index (see Gerdes et al. 2021: 13–19).

[10] An anonymous reviewer suggests that, as an alternative, one could also place each treebank in the uppermost allowable group and then, for treebanks with more than 5k, sample smaller sub-sets for each of the smaller sizes. While we see the potential for this approach, we have not pursued it in this paper. The reason is that based on the control group, we establish which network indexes perform well irrespective of treebank size. Once treebank size becomes irrelevant, this means that for the rest of the sample we can safely look one treebank of the largest possible size.

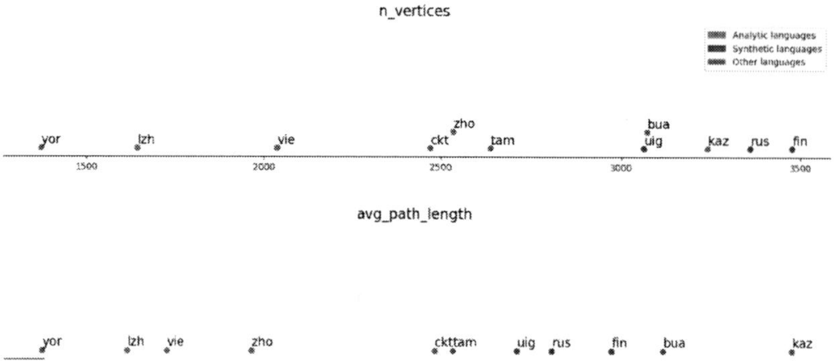

Figure 5: average path length and number of nodes for 5k treebanks

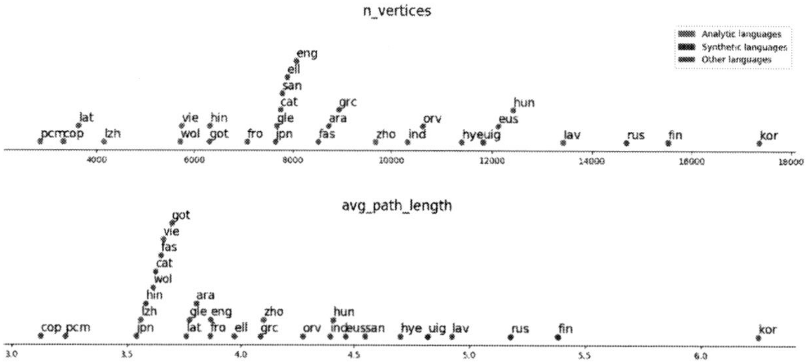

Figure 6: average path length and number of nodes for 30k treebanks

4.4 Discussion

Let us first comment upon the results of the *t*-test on the control group. Our hypothesis that average path length and number of nodes might be taken as proxies for the analyticity index can be linguistically motivated by the nature of networks.

Average path length represents the average distance between any pair of nodes and therefore reflects connectivity in the network. The more highly connected the nodes are, the easier it will be to reach any node in the network starting from any arbitrary point. In particular, the occurrence of hub nodes, that is, highly connected nodes, will result in a generally lower average path length, because hub nodes frequently serve as bridge between nodes which would otherwise be connected by longer paths. As shown by Passarotti (2014), in the case of syntactic dependency networks, hub nodes are often grammatical words like determiners, adpositions, and auxiliaries. Notably, these are as a general rule preferably used in analytic languages, which by definition tend to express grammatical information by means of independent words as opposed to bound morphology (see Siegel et al. 2014: 52–53). The prediction is thus that analytic languages will have a lower average path length than synthetic languages.

Number of nodes also indirectly reflects morphological complexity. In particular, in word-based networks, languages with inflectional morphology will feature more nodes per lexeme, one for each inflected form, than analytic languages. This can clearly be observed in Figure 1, where *apple* and *apples* are two distinct nodes. The prediction is thus that analytic languages will have a lower number of nodes than synthetic languages.[11]

[11] One anonymous reviewer suggests that the same result, i.e. higher number of nodes correlates with higher synthesis, could also be extracted by simply measuring the ratio of different word forms per lemma in treebanks, without the need to resorting to networks. However, a higher number of word forms per lemma does not necessarily mean that a language is more synthetic, but simply that it has larger inflectional paradigms. To achieve a more fine-grained

Both predictions are fully borne out by data from the control group (see Appendix B): networks induced from synthetic languages have higher average path length and higher number of nodes than those from analytic languages.

Turning to the rest of the languages in the sample, for treebanks with size lower than 30k, in most cases the results seem to match our intuitions about the relationship between the indexes under analysis and the analyticity/syntheticity index. Consider Figure 5. First, languages are indeed placed along a continuum, and do not seem to cluster into neatly defined groups. This matches our assumption that analyticity is a continuum. Languages of the control group indeed seem to occupy different regions of the continuum. The other languages also pattern accordingly. For example, Chukchi (ckt) and Buryat (bua), both rich inflectional language (see Dunn 1999; Skribnik 2003), show an average path length comparable to that of synthetic languages. By contrast, Yoruba, which shows a marked analytic profile (Awobuluyi 1978), shows an average path degree even lower than that of the control group analytic languages.

Unfortunately, the picture is not as neat for the rest of the languages in the sample. This is particularly true for the group of treebanks with 30k size (recall that this group also includes reduced versions of all treebanks with size over 30k in our sample). The results shown in Figure 6 can hardly reflect underlying morphological complexity of the languages under analysis. For example, it is not clear why most languages, even highly inflectional ones such as Latin and Ancient Greek, seem to pattern with the analytic languages in the control group. Further study is needed to understand why we get less reliable results with treebanks of higher size. Note that there seems to be a cluster of languages whose dependency networks have average path length between 3.5 and 4.0. This result has previously not been discussed in the literature, and more research is needed to investigate whether this is accidental or not.

Another limitation of the methodology pursued in this paper is that other indexes of morphological complexity cannot be inferred from network structure alone. For example, syntactic dependency networks do not allow to extrapolate more fine-grained information about the internal structure of words in term of cumulation. This means that distinctions that are crucial to morphological typology, such as the distinction between cumulative vs. agglutinative strategies, cannot be measured with this methodology.

5 Conclusions

In this paper, we have put to an empirical test the proposal advanced by Liu & Xu (2011) that syntactic dependency networks can be exploited to investigate cross-linguistic variation in morphological complexity.

Our findings only partly support the validity of this methodology. While we are sympathetic with the underlying assumptions, we must conclude, against Liu & Xu's (2011) more optimistic view, that when applied to larger cross-linguistic datasets, network indexes do not yet yield consistently interpretable results as to morphological complexity.

This means that more research is needed to fully ascertain the suitability of networks to explore morphological complexity. In particular, more attention needs to be paid to the role of treebank size and to the potential impact of annotation schemas. Another potentially confounding factor is that we have worked on networks directly extracted from treebanks as a whole. It needs to be tested whether better results may be achieved by working with networks that operate a finer-grained distinction for e.g. parts of speech.

Finally, we must stress that even for neat data such as that in Figure 5, the proposed correlation between network indexes and the language's analyticity index must remain at this stage tentative. While there might well be a linguistic motivation to link higher number of nodes and average path length to higher syntheticity, the validity of these assumptions needs to be tested against a finer-grained qualitative assessment such as that

result, one would need to calculate and compare the ratio of word forms per lemma for various lemmas and various parts of speech. This is a more complex procedure than simply exploring the number of nodes in a network, which is therefore in principle a more efficient procedure. Notably, variation in paradigm size in inflectional languages can also be explored with networks, by comparing word-based with corresponding lemma-based networks (see Čech & Mačutek 2009).

proposed by Greenberg (1960) and Siegel et al. (2014).

Acknowledgments

We would like to express our gratitude to three anonymous reviewers, whose comments have greatly contributed to improve this paper. The remaining shortcomings are our own. Guglielmo Inglese acknowledges the financial support of the FWO – Research Foundation Flanders (grant n. 12T5320N). The paper is the result of close collaboration between the two authors. For academic purposes, Luca Brigada Villa is responsible of Sections 3, 4.1, 4.2, 5 and Guglielmo Inglese is responsible of Sections 1, 2, 4, 4.3 and 4.4.

References

Albert, Reka & Albert-László Barabási. 2002. Statistical mechanics of complex networks. *Reviews of Modern Physics* 74(1). 47–97. https://doi.org/10.1103/RevModPhys.74.47.

Arkadiev, Peter & Francesco Gardani. 2020. Introduction: Complexities in morphology. In Peter Arkadiev & Francesco Gardani (eds.), *The Complexities of Morphology*, 1–19. Oxford: Oxford University Press.

Arkadiev, Peter & Marian Klamer. 2018. Morphological theory and typology. In Jenny Audring & Francesca Masini (eds.), *The Oxford Handbook of Morphological Theory*, 436–454. Oxford: Oxford University Press.

Awobuluyi, Oladele. 1978. *Essentials of Yoruba Grammar.* Ibadan: Oxford University Press Nigeria.

Bickel, Balthasar & Johanna Nichols. 2013a. Inflectional Synthesis of the Verb. In Matthew S. Dryer & Martin Haspelmath (eds.), *The World Atlas of Language Structures Online.* Leipzig: Max Planck Institute for Evolutionary Anthropology. (Available online at http://wals.info).

Bickel, Balthasar & Johanna Nichols. 2013b. Fusion of Selected Inflectional Formatives. In Matthew S. Dryer & Martin Haspelmath (eds.), *The World Atlas of Language Structures Online.* Leipzig: Max Planck Institute for Evolutionary Anthropology.

Bickel, Balthasar & Johanna Nichols. 2013c. Exponence of Selected Inflectional Formatives. In Matthew S. Dryer & Martin Haspelmath (eds.), *The World Atlas of Language Structures Online.* Leipzig: Max Planck Institute for Evolutionary Anthropology.

Bickel, Balthasar & Johanna Nichols. 2013d. Sampling Case and Tense Formatives. In Matthew S. Dryer & Martin Haspelmath (eds.), *The World Atlas of Language Structures Online.* Leipzig: Max Planck Institute for Evolutionary Anthropology.

Čech, Radek & Ján Mačutek. 2009. Word form and lemma syntactic dependency networks in Czech: A comparative study. *Glottometrics* 19. 85–98.

Čech, Radek, Ján Mačutek & Haitao Liu. 2016. Syntactic Complex Networks and Their Applications. In Alexander Mehler, Andy Lücking, Sven Banisch, Philippe Blanchard & Barbara Job (eds.), *Towards a Theoretical Framework for Analyzing Complex Linguistic Networks*, 167–186. Berlin, Heidelberg: Springer. https://doi.org/10.1007/978-3-662-47238-5_8.

Čech, Radek, Ján Mačutek & Zdeněk Žabokrtský. 2011. The role of syntax in complex networks: Local and global importance of verbs in a syntactic dependency network. *Physica A: Statistical Mechanics and its Applications* 390(20). 3614–3623. https://doi.org/10.1016/j.physa.2011.05.027.

Croft, William, Dawn Nordquist, Katherine Looney & Michael Regan. 2017. Linguistic Typology meets Universal Dependencies. In *TLT*, 63–75.

Csárdi, Gábor & Tamas Nepusz. 2006. The igraph software package for complex network research. *InterJournal Complex Systems* 1695.

Cysouw, Michael. 2007. New approaches to cluster analysis of typological indices. In Peter Grzybek & Reinhard Köhler (eds.), *Exact Methods in the Study of Language and Text*, 61–76. Berlin & New York: de Gruyter. https://doi.org/10.1515/9783110894219.61.

Dunn, Michael John. 1999. *A Grammar of Chukchi.* PhD Dissertation, Australian National University.

Ferrer i Cancho, Ramon. 2005. The structure of syntactic dependency networks: insights from recent advances in network theory. *Problems of quantitative linguistics* 60–75.

Ferrer i Cancho, Ramon, Ricard V. Solé & Reinhard Köhler. 2004. Patterns in syntactic dependency networks. *Physical Review E.* American Physical Society 69(5). 051915. https://doi.org/10.1103/PhysRevE.69.051915.

Gerdes, Kim, Sylvain Kahane & Xinying Chen. 2021. Typometrics: From Implicational to Quantitative Universals in Word Order Typology. *Glossa: a journal of general linguistics* 6(1). 17. https://doi.org/10.5334/gjgl.764.

Greenberg, Joseph H. 1960. A Quantitative Approach to the Morphological Typology of Language. *International Journal of American Linguistics* 26(3). 178–194.

Horvath, Steve & Jun Dong. 2008. Geometric Interpretation of Gene Coexpression Network Analysis. *PLOS Computational Biology* 4(8).

e1000117. https://doi.org/10.1371/journal.pcbi.1000117.

Levshina, Natalia. 2019. Token-based typology and word order entropy: A study based on Universal Dependencies. *Linguistic Typology* 23(3). 533–572. https://doi.org/10.1515/lingty-2019-0025.

Liu, Haitao. 2008. The complexity of Chinese syntactic dependency networks. *Physica A: Statistical Mechanics and its Applications* 387(12). 3048–3058. https://doi.org/10.1016/j.physa.2008.01.069.

Liu, Haitao & Chunshan Xu. 2011. Can syntactic networks indicate morphological complexity of a language? *EPL (Europhysics Letters)* 93(2). 28005. https://doi.org/10.1209/0295-5075/93/28005.

Nivre, Joakim, Marie-Catherine de Marneffe, Filip Ginter, Yoav Goldberg, Jan Hajicˇ, Christopher D Manning, Ryan McDonald, et al. 2016. Universal Dependencies v1: A Multilingual Treebank Collection. In *Proceedings of the Tenth International Conference on Language Resources and Evaluation (LREC'16)*, 1659–1666.

Passarotti, Marco. 2014. The importance of being sum : network analysis of a Latin dependency treebank. In Roberto Basili, Alessandro Lenci & Bernardo Magnini (eds.), *Proceedings of the First Italian Conference on Computational Linguistics CLiC-it 2014: 9-11 December 2014, Pisa*, 291–295. Pisa: Pisa University Press.

Robinson, Jane J. 1970. Dependency Structures and Transformational Rules. *Language* 46(2). 259–285. https://doi.org/10.2307/412278.

Sapir, Edward. 1921. *Language. An Introduction to the Study of Speech*. New York: Harcourt, Brace & World.

Schwegler, Armin. 1990. *Analyticity and Syntheticity: A Diachronic Perspective with Special Reference to Romance Languages*. Berlin & New York: de Gruyter.

Siegel, Jeff, Benedikt Szmrecsanyi & Bernd Kortmann. 2014. Measuring analyticity and syntheticity in creoles. *Journal of Pidgin and Creole Languages* 29(1). 49–85. https://doi.org/10.1075/jpcl.29.1.02sie.

Skribnik, Elena. 2003. Buryat. In Juha Janhunen (ed.), *The Mongolic Languages*, 102–128. London & New York: Routledge.

Welch, B. L. 1947. The Generalization of `Student's' Problem when Several Different Population Variances are Involved. *Biometrika* 34(1/2). 28–35. https://doi.org/10.2307/2332510.

Appendix A: Language sample

Language*	**ISO code**	**Treebank**	**Token size**
Akkadian	akk	UD_Akkadian-RIAO	21961
Arabic	ara	UD_Arabic-PADT	242383
Bambara	bam	UD_Bambara-CRB	11873
Buryat	bua	UD_Buryat-BDT	8333
Catalan	cat	UD_Catalan-AnCora	473881
Chukchi	ckt	UD_Chukchi-HSE	4740
Coptic	cop	UD_Coptic-Scriptorium	45496
Greek	ell	UD_Greek-GDT	56145
English	eng	UD_English-GUM	97979
Basque	eus	UD_Basque-BDT	101444
Persian	fas	UD_Persian-PerDT	457439
Finnish	fin	UD_Finnish-TDT	171836
Old French	fro	UD_Old_French-SRCMF	170740
Irish	gle	UD_Irish-IDT	104547
Gothic	got	UD_Gothic-PROIEL	55317
Ancient Greek	grc	UD_Ancient_Greek-PROIEL	213980
Mbyá Guaraní	gun	UD_Mbya_Guarani-Thomas	1070
Hindi	hin	UD_Hindi-HDTB	328101
Hungarian	hun	UD_Hungarian-Szeged	36212
Armenian	hye	UD_Armenian-ArmTDP	42213
Indonesian	ind	UD_Indonesian-GSD	103238
Japanese	jpn	UD_Japanese-GSD	172209
Kazakh	kaz	UD_Kazakh-KTB	8316
Korean	kor	UD_Korean-Kaist	310205
Komi Zyrian	kpv	UD_Komi_Zyrian-Lattice	4060
Latin	lat	UD_Latin-LLCT	206859
Latvian	lav	UD_Latvian-LVTB	179744
Classical Chinese	lzh	UD_Classical_Chinese-Kyoto	232188
Erzya	myv	UD_Erzya-JR	13038
Old Russian	orv	UD_Old_Russian-TOROT	149484
Naija	pcm	UD_Naija-NSC	100557
Russian	rus	UD_Russian-GSD	78200
Sanskrit Vedic	san	UD_Sanskrit-Vedic	27117
Nort Sami	sme	UD_North_Sami-Giella	22702
Tamil	tam	UD_Tamil-TTB	8580
Tagalog	tgl	UD_Tagalog-Ugnayan	955
Thai	tha	UD_Thai-PUD	21916
Uyghur	uig	UD_Uyghur-UDT	32401
Vietnamese	vie	UD_Vietnamese-VTB	33887
Wolof	wol	UD_Wolof-WTB	38937
Yoruba	yor	UD_Yoruba-YTB	7119

Chinese	zho	UD_Chinese-GSD	105195

*Languages of the control group are in bold.

Appendix B: number of nodes and average path length for the control group

Size[12]	**Index**	**ISO code**					
		fin	**rus**	**uig**	**lzh**	**vie**	**zho**
1k	avg_path_length	7,0926602	7,1181678	8,3712409	5,1750507	5,7376548	5,729498
	n_nodes	822	783	801	549	650	692
5k	avg_path_length	6,4890935	6,2090146	6,0436406	4,1943988	4,3817425	4,7894008
	n_nodes	3477	3359	3063	1642	2037	2534
10k	avg_path_length	6,0495081	5,8471496	5,5202574	3,8458437	4,0076761	4,4870999
	n_nodes	6309	6125	5306	2362	3050	4300
20k	avg_path_length	5,6139062	5,4378837	5,0921595	3,7027029	3,7923894	4,217152
	n_nodes	11174	10715	8888	3513	4588	7255
30k	avg_path_length	5,3847064	5,1784228	4,8219065	3,5586503	3,6615379	4,1005896
	n_nodes	15535	14699	11828	4154	5753	9682
50k	avg_path_length	5,0969112	4,95705	-	3,428777	-	3,9497258
	n_nodes	23451	22020	-	5273	-	13379
75k	avg_path_length	4,9043123	4,7678429	-	3,3602782	-	3,8341283
	n_nodes	31823	29734	-	6330	-	17393

Appendix C: network indexes for the sample languages

ISO code	**Size**	**avg_path_length**	**n_nodes**
gun	1k	4,3342128	410
kpv	1k	7,5279103	765
tgl	1k	3,8475797	383
bua	5k	6,7303552	3072
ckt	5k	5,6628477	2471
kaz	5k	7,3374322	3241
tam	5k	5,7456242	2637
yor	5k	3,7964219	1375
bam	10k	3,1309446	1063
myv	10k	5,6029887	5137
akk	20k	4,0322794	2802
sme	20k	4,4667009	7750
tha	20k	3,5982284	4076
ara	30k	3,8098087	8732

[12] For reasons of space, in Appendix B and C we only report data on average path lengths and number of nodes. Data on the other indexes can be consulted at https://github.com/bavagliladri/tb2net.

cat	30k	3,6261545	7752
cop	30k	3,1254	3341
ell	30k	3,973389	7892
eng	30k	3,8710204	8076
eus	30k	4,463648	12130
fas	30k	3,6510337	8517
fro	30k	3,8691324	7066
gle	30k	3,7789008	7670
got	30k	3,7018547	6311
grc	30k	4,0874524	8941
hin	30k	3,5812191	6320
hun	30k	4,4091939	12430
hye	30k	4,704363	11406
ind	30k	4,3958122	10332
jpn	30k	3,5393915	7644
kor	30k	6,2509272	17359
lat	30k	3,7646329	3645
lav	30k	4,9259688	13437
orv	30k	4,2763492	10635
pcm	30k	3,2327011	2876
san	30k	4,5486621	7785
wol	30k	3,6142526	5720

A Universal Dependencies Corpora Maintenance Methodology Using Downstream Application

Ran Iwamoto[*], **Hiroshi Kanayama**[†], **Alexandre Rademaker**[†‡], **Takuya Ohko**[†]
[*] Keio University, [†] IBM Research, [‡] FGV/EMAp
raniwamoto@gmail.com, hkana@jp.ibm.com
alexrad@br.ibm.com, ohkot@jp.ibm.com

Abstract

This paper investigates updates of Universal Dependencies (UD) treebanks in 23 languages and their impact on a downstream application. Numerous people are involved in updating UD's annotation guidelines and treebanks in various languages. However, it is not easy to verify whether the updated resources maintain universality with other language resources. Thus, validity and consistency of multilingual corpora should be tested through application tasks involving syntactic structures with PoS tags, dependency labels, and universal features. We apply the syntactic parsers trained on UD treebanks from multiple versions (2.0 to 2.7) to a clause-level sentiment extractor. We then analyze the relationships between attachment scores of dependency parsers and performance in application tasks. For future UD developments, we show examples of outputs that differ depending on version.

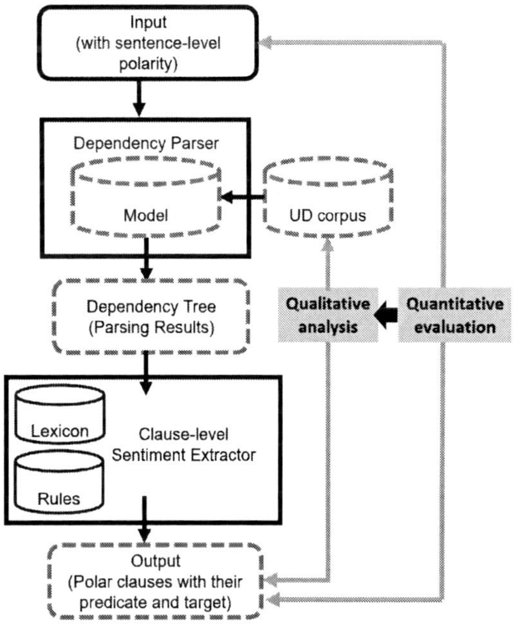

Figure 1: Our methodology to get insights from the difference of the corpora on the flow of the multilingual sentiment annotator. The components in red dashed lines are variable, while solid ones are fixed.

1 Introduction

Universal Dependencies (UD) (Nivre and Fang, 2017; Zeman et al., 2020) is a worldwide project that provides cross-linguistic treebank annotations. UD defined 17 PoS tags and 37 dependency labels to annotate multilingual sentences in a uniform manner, allowing language-specific extension to be represented by features. The resources and documents are updated every six months. The latest version 2.7, as of November 2020, consists of 183 treebanks in 104 languages.

The UD corpora are consistently annotated in multiple languages and are extensively used to train and evaluate taggers and parsers (Zeman et al., 2017). Kondratyuk and Straka (2019) trained a single dependency model for many languages relying on UD corpora. Schwenk and Douze (2017) used universal PoS (UPOS) labels to evaluate multilingual sentence representations. However, few studies have focused on the contributions of syntactic parsers trained by UD corpora to real-world applications.

Extrinsic evaluation of dependency parser has been already studied in a series of shared tasks (Oepen et al., 2017; Fares et al., 2018) using tasks of event extraction, negation detection and opinion analysis for English documents. In addition to extrinsic evaluation of parsers, Kanayama and Iwamoto (2020) established a method for evaluating the universality of UD-based parsers and UD corpora by using a clause-level sentiment extractor, which detects positive and negative predicates and targets on top of UD-based syntactic trees. They showed that language-universal syntactic structures

Proceedings of the Third Workshop on Computational Typology and Multilingual NLP, pages 23–31
June 10, 2021. ©2021 Association for Computational Linguistics

lang	name	# sentence
ar	PADT	7,664
ca	AnCora	16,678
cs	PDT	87,913
de	GSD	15,590
en	EWT	16,622
es	Ancora	17,680
fa	Seraji	5,997
fr	GSD	16,341
he	HTB	6,216
hi	HDTB	16,647
hr	SET	9,010
id	GSD	5,593
it	ISDT	14,167
ja	GSD	8,071
ko	GSD	6,339
nl	Alpino	13,578
no	Bokmaal	20,044
pl	LFG	17,246
pt	Bosque	9,364
ru	SynTagRus	61,889
sv	Talbanken	6,026
tr	IMST	5,635
zh	GSD	4,997

Table 1: UD corpora used in this study and their sizes. Sizes are based on sentence numbers in v2.7.

and features are effective in their multilingual systems.

In this paper we investigate how the UD corpora and underlying guidelines are updated and how they contribute to the parser and sentiment extractor which consumes the output of the parser. We compared UD versions 2.0 to 2.7 [1] in 23 languages from diverse language families.

Figure 1 shows the proposed methodology. The idea is to use corpora with sentence-level sentiment annotations (SA) in two ways: 1) we can compare SA results considering different syntactic models; 2) we can compare the SA annotation with the golden sentiment annotation. The first one is useful for qualitative analysis. The second one is useful for quantitative analysis, given that we can measure the SA efficiency.

First, we trained a dependency parsing model for each UD corpora version (UD release) using a fixed syntactic parser. Using the models, we produce as many syntactic analyses as models for each corpus with sentence-level sentiment annotations. Later, we applied a deterministic rule-based sentiment annotator for each syntactic tree. The advantage of this methodology is that it is much easier to find sentiment annotation errors than syntactic annotation errors, and those errors often show the essential aspects of syntax. Comparing the gold sentiment annotation of input and final output, we can quantitatively estimate the usefulness of parsing models, moreover, a qualitative analysis of system outputs provides practical insights for corpora maintainers. In particular, inspecting the output of a sentiment analysis system for discovering possible annotation inconsistencies is one important additional advantage.

We found examples where improvements in the corpus have led to improvements in the output of the sentiment annotator (reducing the number of uses of the `dep` relation and minimizing the errors reported by the UD validator). But some examples can be also found where change in the corpus had made a negative impact in the sentiment analysis (Section 5). We use a different measure (F_2) to extrinsically evaluate the UD corpora. It is not directly related to the intrinsic UD measures such as star rating for UD corpora and LAS for the dependency parser.

Section 2 summarizes the changes of the UD corpora in versions 2.0–2.7. Section 3 describes the sentiment analysis methodology which is used for benchmarking dependency parsers. In Section 4 we show how to evaluate multilingual systems, and in Section 5, we discuss the differences of multiple versions of UD corpora with multilingual instances of changes in syntactic structures and downstream results.

2 Universal Dependencies

Universal Dependencies is a framework for designing and maintaining consistent syntactic annotations across multiple languages. The UD corpora are updated every six months by numerous contributors.

However, few studies have focused on the changes in outputs of UD-trained parsers used for application tasks. Labeled Attachment Score (LAS) and the UD star rating are two commonly used metrics to evaluate the update of the UD corpora. LAS is a measure of the performance of dependency parsers, where the universal dependency labels are taken into account in the measurement. The star rating is a measure designed by UD organizers, which quantifies the qualities of the corpora themselves, such as usability of corpora and variety of genres. While the UD corpora and the parsers have been evaluated, there is a need for an external evaluation of UD in application tasks.

To explore the impacts caused by updates of UD

[1] In this paper we skipped v2.1 and v2.3 to more focus on the recent releases.

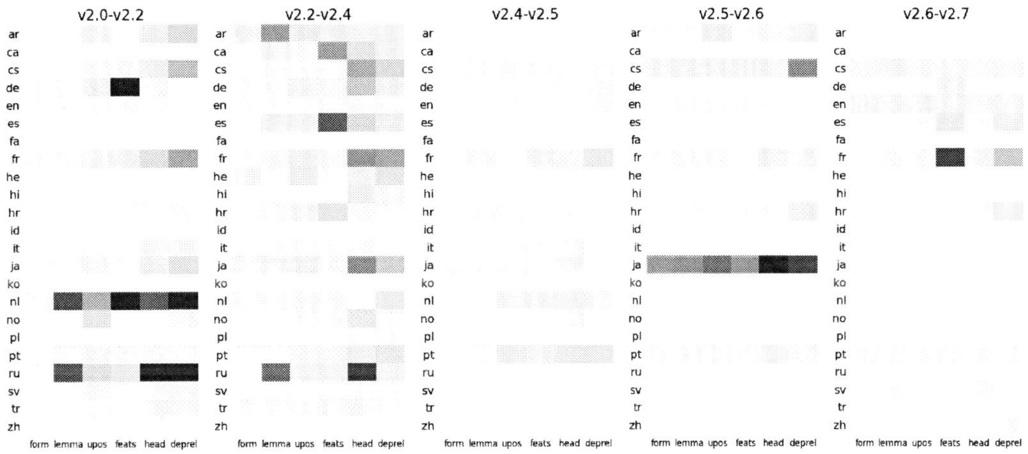

Figure 2: UD corpora version updates. The color of each cell represents the rate of change from the previous version. When a corpus has been significantly updated, the cell is dark in color.

corpora on the sentiment analysis task, we first investigate the changes in the UD corpora listed in Table 1 with versions 2.0–2.7. One treebank was selected per language on the basis of the following conditions: texts are included in the corpus, the corpus is sufficiently large, the updates are frequent so a long term comparisons can be made across versions 2.0–2.7.

Figure 2 shows the UD treebanks updates for versions 2.0 (March 2017) to 2.7 (November 2020) in 23 languages. Inspecting the amount of changes between versions for each treebank was done regarding six out of the ten fields in the CoNLL-U files (form, lemma, upostag, feats, head, and deprel). Most languages have been actively updated in versions 2.0–2.7. In versions 2.0–2.4, most of the modifications in the UD corpora focused on fundamental syntactic elements such as PoS tags and dependency labels, and universal features were incrementally appended. On the other hand, in versions 2.4–2.6, the major updates shifted towards language-specific features.

Through discussion across languages, the UD's annotation policy is gradually becoming more consistent among close languages. PoS tags for copulas and auxiliary verbs are one typical examples of this: "be" in "have been" and "will be" were changed from VERB to AUX in English v2.5, as well as "hebben" in Dutch v2.4. In addition, there is a movement to make AUX a closed set. In Portuguese v2.5, many AUX were changed to VERB, *e.g.,* "continuar" ('continue'), "deixar" ('leave'). Similarly, French v2.1 and onward limit AUX to "être", "avoir" and "faire,". "Pouvoir" ('can') and other words in the same category are tagged as VERB, even though English modal verbs are tagged as AUX.

3 Multilingual Clause-level Sentiment Analysis

We investigate changes in UD corpora and their impact on an application task. We use clause-level sentiment analysis designed for fine-grained sentiment detection with high precision. Kanayama and Iwamoto (2020) demonstrated that a system which fully utilizes UD-based syntactic structures can easily handle many languages, making it an effective platform for evaluating UD corpora and parsing models trained on them.

The main objective of clause-level sentiment analysis is to detect polar clauses associated with a predicate and a target. For example, the sentence (1) below conveys two polarities: (1a) a positive polarity regarding the hotel (which is loved) and (1b) a negative polarity about the waiters (who are *not* friendly).

(1) I love the hotel but she said none of the waiters were friendly.
(1a) + love (hotel)
(1b) − not friendly (waiter)

Figure 3 illustrates the top-down process of detecting sentiment clauses in the dependency tree. The main clause is headed by the `root` node of the dependency tree. When the node has child nodes labeled `conj` and `parataxis`, those nodes are

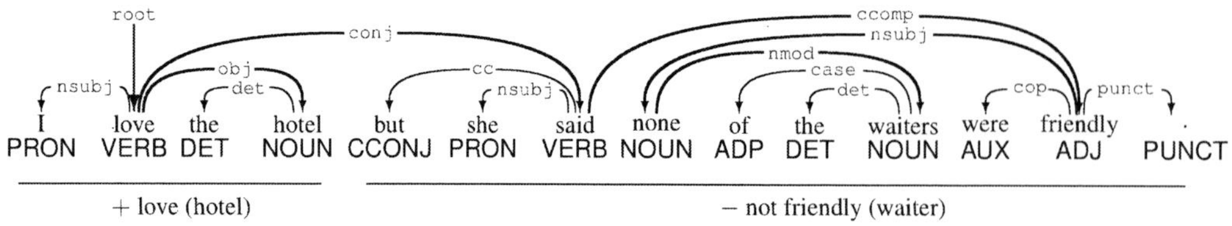

Figure 3: Dependency tree for sentence (1). The dependencies in bold lines from the `root` node are traversed to detect two sentiment clauses (predicates and targets).

	lemma	PoS tag	polarity	case frame
(a)	love	VERB	+	nsubj, <u>obj</u>
(b)	friendly	ADJ	+	<u>nsubj</u>
(c)	unhappy	ADJ	−	nsubj, <u>with</u>

Table 2: Examples of lexical entries. '+' is positive and '−' is negative. Underline denotes the target case.

recursively scanned as potential sentiment clauses. When a node is a verb that takes a `ccomp` (clausal compliment) child, *e.g.*, "say", the child node is also examined. In example (1), two clauses, headed by "love" and "friendly" are detected. After detecting the clauses, the predicates are compared with lexical entries associated with a lemma, a PoS tag and its polarity and the case frame, as exemplified in Table 2. Entry (a) is for the verb "love", which is positive and takes a subject and an object; the target (which is positive) is its object. For most adjectives, the target is in the subject, as in (b), but (c) "unhappy" specifies the target as "with" to detect "breakfast" as the target in (2).

(2) [−] I was **unhappy** with the <u>breakfast</u>.

In all of the languages, detecting negation is the key to detecting polarities with high precision. The basic types of negation are direct negation of the verb and noun in (3) and (4).

(3) [−] The hotel was *not* **good**.

(4) [+] It was *no* **problem**.

To multilingualize the clause-level sentiment detector, the English polarity lexicon shown in Table 2 was transferred to other languages as described in previous paper (Kanayama and Iwamoto, 2020).

4 Experimental Settings

To extrinsically evaluate the UD corpora, we combine a UD-compliant dependency parser trained with multiple versions of UD corpora to the sentiment extractor. Since the syntactic structure is the only factor that changes the output of sentiment detection, we can easily find the effects of parsing to the downstream application.

4.1 Dependency parser

In our experiments, we have used two UD-compliant dependency parsers: UDPipe and Stanza. UDPipe (Straka and Straková, 2017) is the standard pipeline which performs sentence segmentation, tokenization, PoS tagging, lemmatization and dependency parsing, can be trained given annotated CoNLL-U format. Though a prototype of UDPipe 2.0 is released with improved morphosyntactic performance compared to UDPipe 1.2, we use UDPipe 1.2 because the resources for training UDPipe 2.0 was not available at this moment.

Since pretrained models are provided for most of treebanks, we used the distributed models trained on UD versions 2.0, 2.2, 2.4, and 2.5[2]. For UD v2.6 and v2.7, we trained the models using the same parameters and word embeddings as those of v2.5. The models for Chinese v2.0 and v2.2 were not included since a simplified Chinese corpus was not available in those versions[3], and Polish for v2.0 is missing as well.

We also used Stanza, an open-source Python natural language processing toolkit that supports 66 languages. In this study we trained the Stanza models using each version of the UD corpora.

4.2 Datasets

To our knowledge, there is no *multilingual* clause-level sentiment annotation such as the Stanford Sentiment Treebank (Socher et al., 2013) for English. To compare output of various languages under the

[2]Downloaded from `http://ufal.mff.cuni.cz/udpipe`.

[3]UD_Chinese-GSDSimp did not exist in the official version of UD2.4 thus we trained the model for Chinese v2.4 by picking up the pre-release corpus from the development branch as of September 9, 2019.

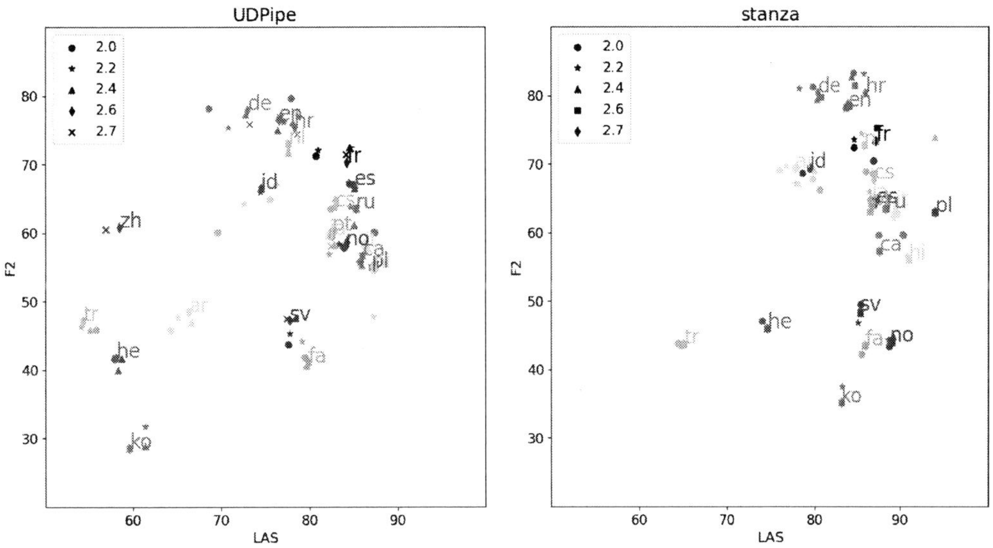

Figure 4: Relationship between parsing score (LAS) and sentiment detection performance (F_2) for each version in UDPipe and Stanza.

same conditions as possible, existing sentiment analysis datasets with clause-, aspect- or sentence-level annotations are simplified to sentence-level annotations by Kanayama and Iwamoto (2020). The reformatted dataset in each language consists of about 500 sentences, each with a positive or negative label. The percentage of those labels is equal and a sentence with a label does not contain a clause of the opposite polarity. Refer to the paper for more details.

4.3 Metrics

We evaluated the performance of the sentiment extractor using sentence-based metrics. Given a sentence, which is labeled either positive or negative in the datasets, our system detects an arbitrary number of sentiment clauses.

We calculate *recall* as the ratio of sentences for which the system detects one or more sentiment clauses that have the same polarity as the sentence-based polarity labeled in the gold data. *Precision* is the ratio of polarity coincidence between the system output (for a clause) and the gold label (for a sentence) for polar clauses detected by the system. A sentence that is labeled either positive or negative may have multiple clauses of opposite polarities, but for simplicity we just consider the sentence polarity in the gold data because we found that a simple evaluation is sufficient for relative comparison of parsers and syntactic operations.

To give precision more weight than recall for practical evaluation, we use the F_2 score in Equation (5), setting $\beta = 2$,

$$F_\beta = (1 + \beta^2)\frac{\text{prec} \cdot \text{rec}}{\text{prec} + \beta^2 \cdot \text{rec}} \quad (5)$$

We do not measure our system using the F_1 score because a naive word-spotting approach may result in a higher F_1 score where every sentence is classified positive or negative. The system is not for polarity classification, but to detect clauses that certainly express polarity. Therefore, non-syntactic sentiment clues (*e.g.* hashtags) or polar clauses with uncertain polarity to the target (*e.g.* subjunctive) are basically undetected.

5 Results and Analysis

5.1 Overall Quantitative Results

Figure 4 shows an overview of the relationship between dependency parsing and sentiment detection. The F_2 values calculated by switching the dependency parsing models trained on UD versions 2.0–2.7 in 23 languages and keeping the rest of the process (sentiment lexicon and tree-screening algorithms) consistent described in Section 3.

The figure shows that within a language, F_2 tend to increase as the LAS improves, and the latest version (v2.7) achieves better LAS and F_2 scores than the oldest one (v2.0) in many languages. The removing of bugs using UD validator and a variety of annotation changes in the corpus contributes to the improvement of both the LAS and the F_2, but other changes do not always improve the scores. For example, when annotations with complex and correct dependency relations are added, the learning of parsers become difficult and the LAS may decrease. No clear correlations between LAS and F_2 scores can be observed, and that is precisely the motivation for the qualitative analysis presented in next section. It means, F_2 (or our system, namely, evaluation in an application task) works as a different measure from the LAS or star rating.

Note that the F_2 score is difficult to compare in different languages because of diversity in complexity of datasets. The performance of the dependency parsers are determined not only by the training corpora but also by the parameter settings and external resources (*e.g.* word embeddings).[4]

5.2 Analysis of each language

We illustrate sentence pairs where dependency parsers changed the outputs of the sentiment extractor correspondingly. A label such as "(nl2.4U)" denotes the language, UD version and dependency parser (UDPipe or Stanza). For example, (nl2.4U) denotes a Dutch result parsed by UDPipe which was trained on UD v2.4. A highlighted box shows the predicate and an underlined word shows its target, with blue color for positive and red for negative.

First, we show the differences in parsing that can significantly affect the results of sentiment clause detection, although we cannot guarantee whether they are caused by changes in corpora. Correct detection of negation is important for a downstream task, especially polarity detection. The sentiment extractor detected a polar expression "groot" ('large') from Dutch sentences (nl2.4/2.5U). In (nl2.5U), the adjective "groot" is correctly negated by the adverb "niet" due to the direct link between two words and resulted in the correct extraction of negative sentiment, while in (nl2.4U) the system failed to change the polarity because "niet" was not directly attached to "groot".

[4]In some languages, different LAS scores were reported in different versions even when two corpora were identical.

(nl2.4U)

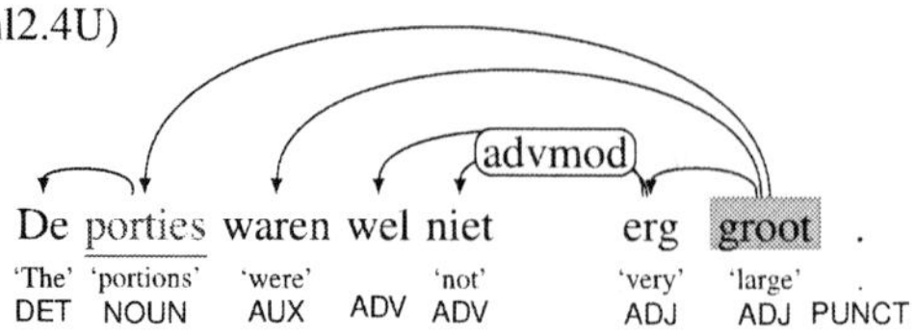

(nl2.5U)

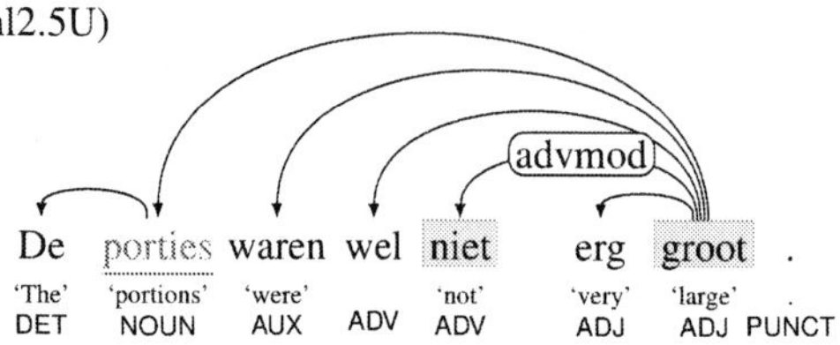

As shown in Section 3, a dependency label `conj` is heavily used for multiple clause detection; thus, it is the factor that significantly impacts the recall of the sentiment detector. For example, let us see (pt2.5U) and (pt2.6U) where the root node is "fácil" ('easy'). In (pt2.6U), the system correctly detected "fluente" as positive predicate, while it is regarded a conjunct of "fácil". In (pt2.5U), a predicate "fluente" ('fluent') is modifying the root node with a wrong label `amod` thus only one positive predicate "fácil" is detected.

(pt2.5U)

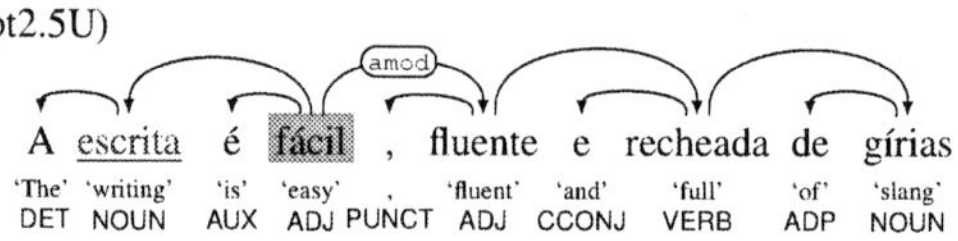

(pt2.6U)

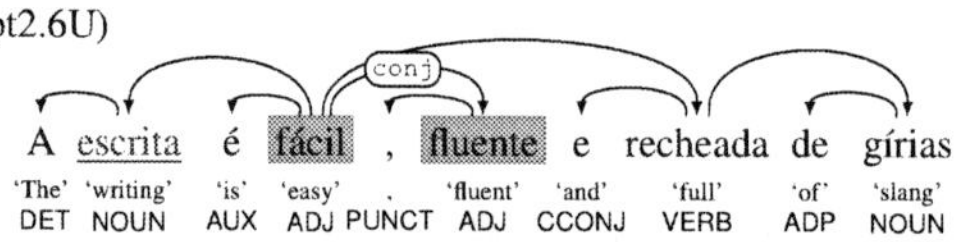

Giving correct annotations and removing inconsistencies within a corpora improve the performance of parsing, and output of the sentiment extractor as well. Reduction of unspecified labels, namely `dep` label, is still a challenge in a variety of UD corpora. In (cs2.5U), the parsing result was not correct with a `dep` label, but the parsing result was improved in (cs2.6U) and thus a positive predicate was extracted.

(cs2.5U)

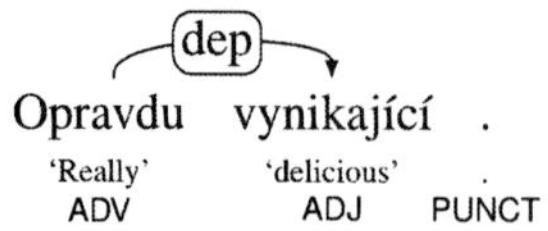

(cs2.6U)

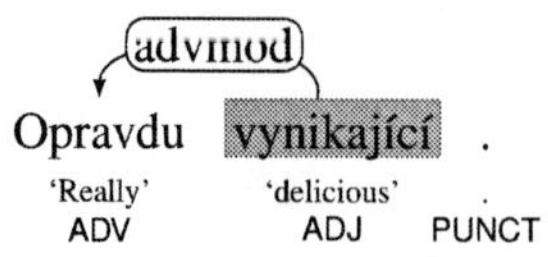

A similar change in parsing results was observed in Dutch. There were 1,471 `dep` labels in UD Dutch v2.0, but they were explicitly labeled in v2.2. That makes it possible to extract the polarity of the sentence in (nl2.2S) with the correct dependency labels.

(nl2.0S)

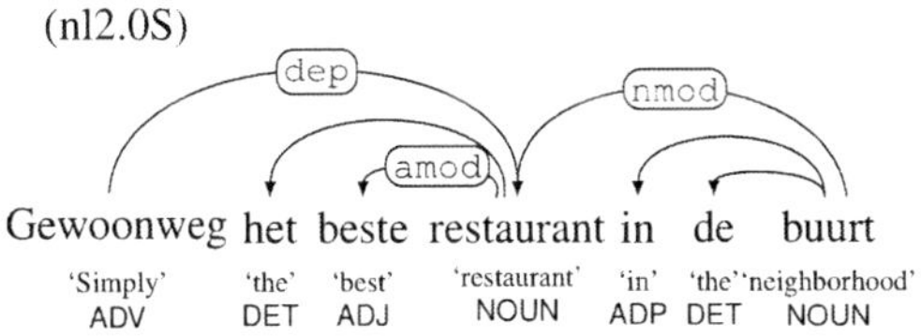

(nl2.2S)

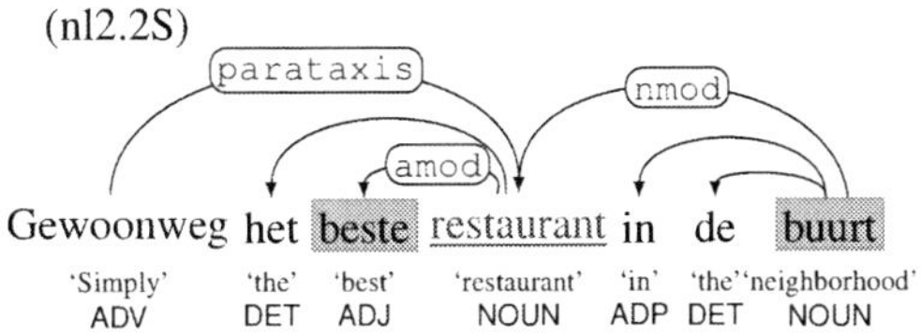

In the update of UD Arabic v2.4, various bugs were fixed which found by the new UD validation tool. In (ar2.2U)[5], the tokenizer did not correctly split a token "حياتي" ('my life'), and thus the parser wrongly duplicate the token. In addition, many words had been tagged as X in (ar2.2U). The usage of X tag should be limited to special cases such as foreign words. In (ar2.4U), all words were correctly tagged and helped the detection of negative polarity. These are typical examples where refinements of corpus improved the output of the sentiment extractor.

(ar2.2U)

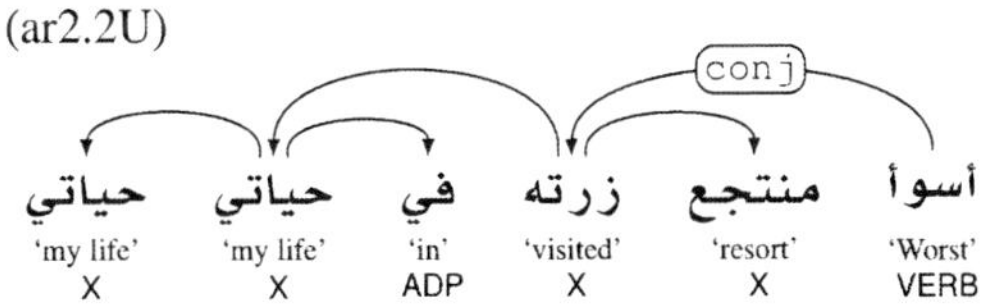

(ar2.4U)

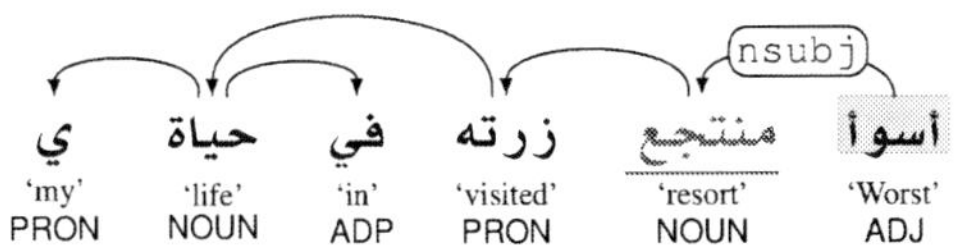

A lot of dependency labels and PoS tags were updated in UD French v2.4. In a noun phrase (fr2.4U), a negative adjective "méprisant" ('contemptuous') was successfully detected because its was correctly attached to the head noun "maître" ('master').

[5] Arabic tokens are written from right to left, based on the actual order of the sentences.

(fr2.2U)

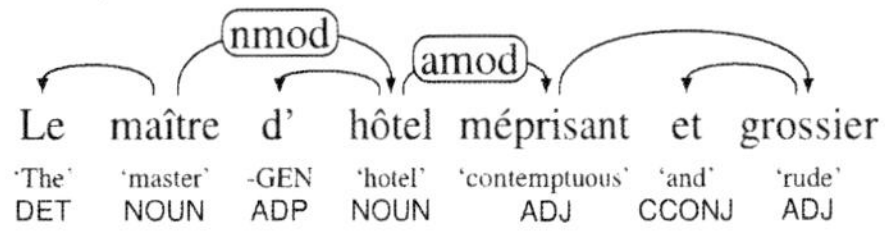

(fr2.4U)

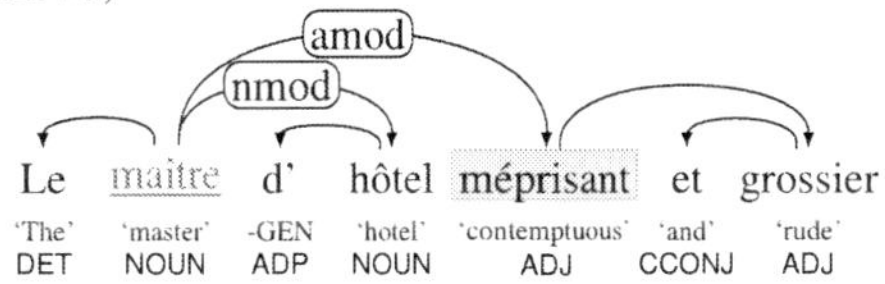

The PoS tagging error of "相当" ('very') in (zh2.4U) was fixed in (zh2.5U). Then the dependency structure was improved and a positive polarity was correctly detected.

(zh2.4U)

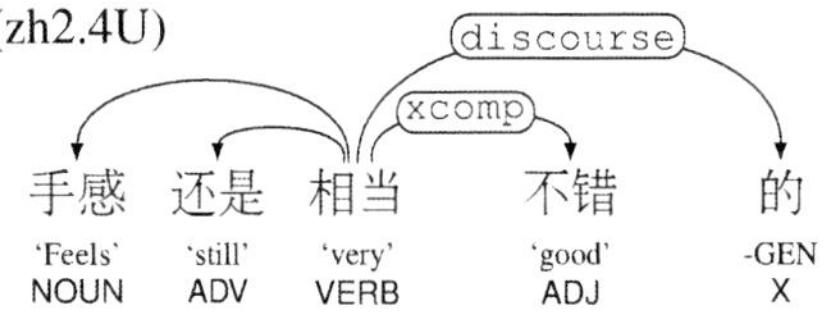

(zh2.5U)

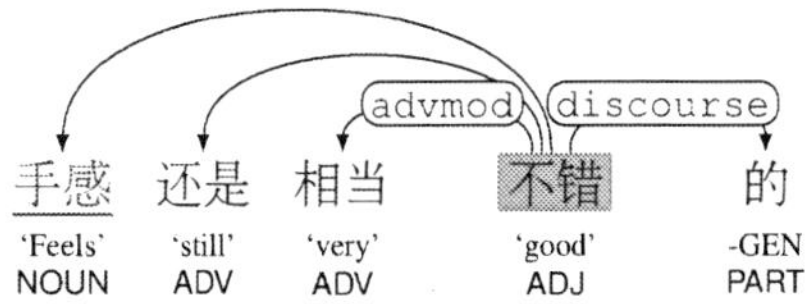

Major changes of tokenization policy or lemmatization significantly affect syntactic structures. The adjective "不自由" ('inconvenience') was regarded as a single word in (ja2.5U), which matched the sentiment lexicon, so the negative polarity was correctly detected. However, since UD Japanese v2.6 adopted short word units in its tokenization policy, "不自由" is divided into two words "不" + "自由" ('in-' + 'convenience') in (ja2.6U). The polarity was wrongly inversed because the system did not handle this type of negation. Meanwhile, this error can be easily fixed in future, by adding a rule to handle the negation by "不" to the sentiment extractor.

(ja2.5U)

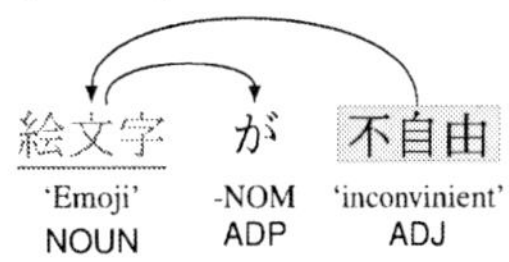

(ja2.6U)

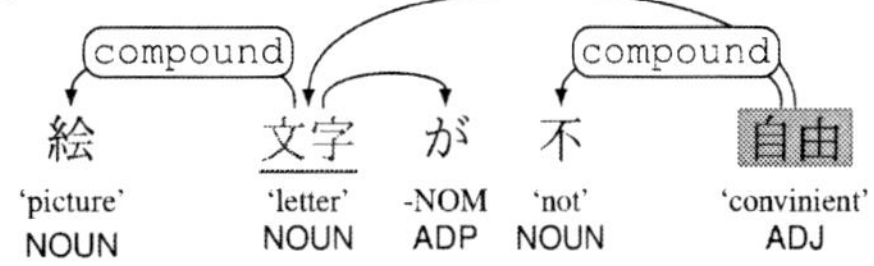

A similar example can be found in Dutch. In (nl2.0S), the lemma of "hadden" ('had') was "heb", but in (nl2.2S) the lemma was changed to "hebben". Since our system is based on the lemma of UD Dutch v2.4 (*e.g.*, for making dictionaries), parsers trained on corpora with different annotation policies result in worse performance.

If a dependency parser trained on UD is to be used for an application task, the user may consider whether the parser should be retrained for the new UD corpus. Detailed change logs of a corpus will help the system catch up the updated corpus.

(nl2.0S)

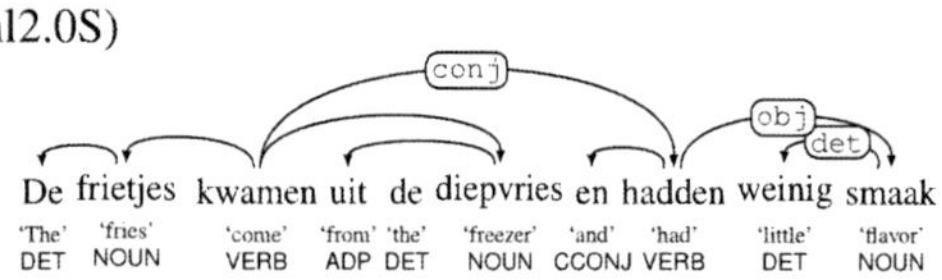

(nl2.2S)

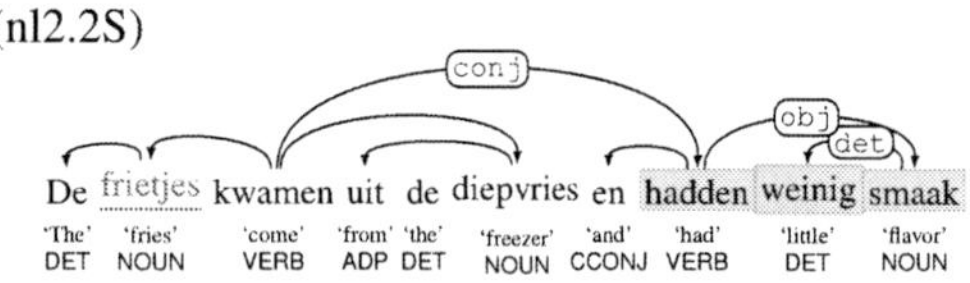

Next, we show an example where the updates in UD corpora have affected unintended parts of parsing results. In Arabic, the improvement of the MWT (multi-word token) labels has influenced other parts of the system. In UD Arabic v2.4, the labeling of MWTs containing " ف" ('and') has been improved. However, it caused overfitting; the model learned that words containing " ف " are always MWTs and increased parsing errors in the word "فندق" ('hotel') as shown in (ar2.4S).

(ar2.2S)

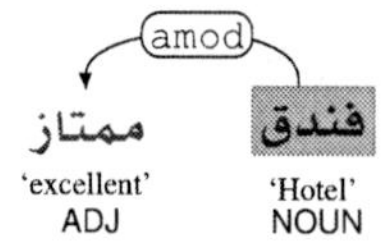

(ar2.4S)

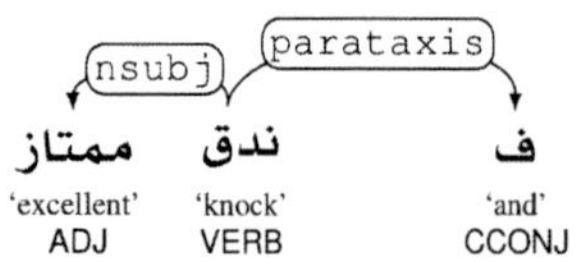

The change in the labels attached to verbs had an effect on the application task. In Catalan, many occurrences of AUX tag were changed to VERB in version 2.4. A PoS tag of "tornar" ('return') is changed from AUX to VERB, making the polar expression "segur" ('safe') being missed, because "segur" is the root node in (ca2.2S) but not in (ca2.4S).

(ca2.2S)

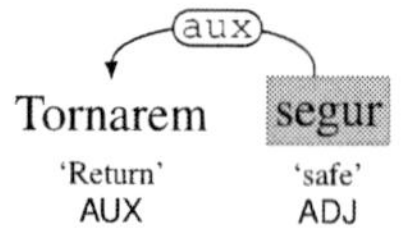

(ca2.4S)

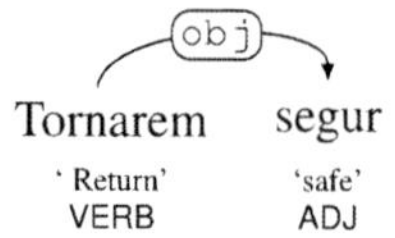

To utilize UD-trained parsers in application tasks, it is expected to be robust to a variety of inputs. In (en2.5U), PoS tagging was not robust enough for an upparcased writing "HIGHLY RECOMMEND", and the PoS tagging error was propagated to dependency parsing and sentiment extraction.

(en2.4U)

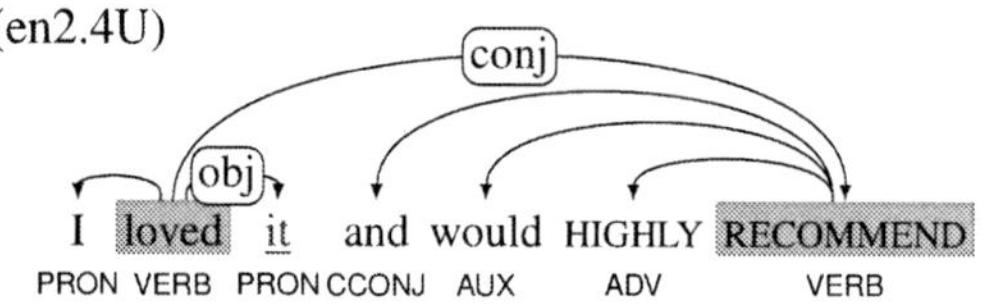

(en2.5U)

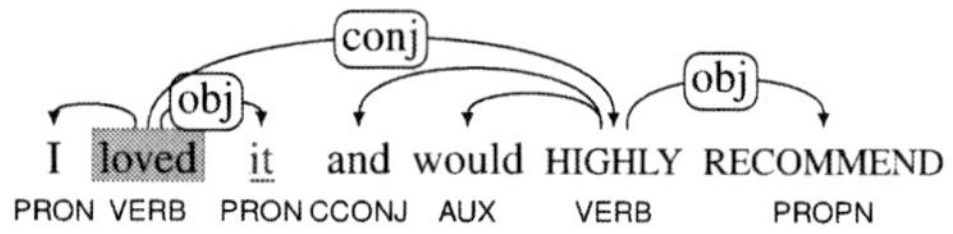

A similar issue can be found in German. Nouns should be always capitalized regardless of its position in a German sentence. In (de2.2U), a noun "Schneiden" ('blades') was wrongly tagged as VERB because it was not capitalized. Since real-world inputs such as reviews may contain such capitalizing errors and misspellings, robust PoS taggers to those errors are desired. It is important to use UD treebanks that is sufficiently large for the parser training and suitable genres for the downstream tasks.

(de2.0U)

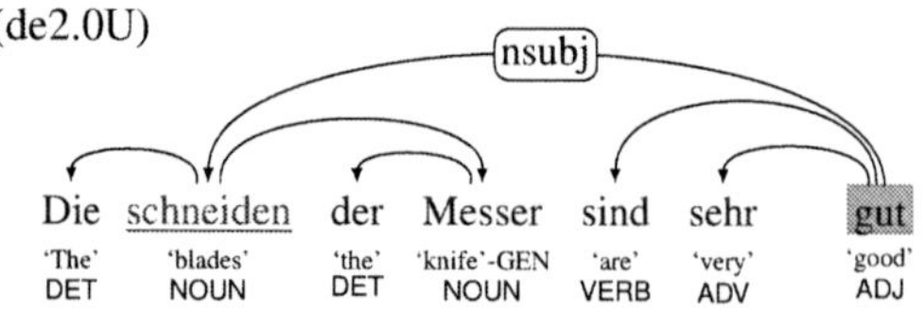

(de2.2U)

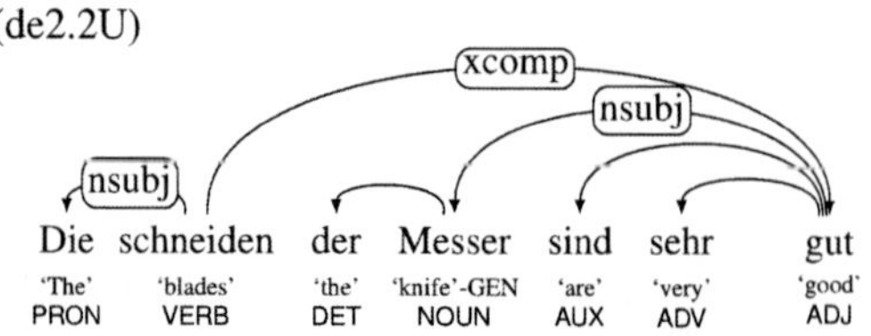

6 Conclusion

We observed updates of the UD corpora versions 2.0–2.7 in 23 languages and extrinsically evaluated the parsing models trained by the corpora in a real-world scenario. The evaluation using the sentiment extractor with UD-trained parsers do not correlate clearly with existing evaluations such as LAS and star rating, indicating that evaluation using an application task is useful to measure UD corpus from a new perspective.

We showed examples where the updates of UD corpora have either adversely or positively affected the output of dependency parsing and sentiment clause detection. Our methodology is easier to find the changes of sentiment detection. Those changes often show the important aspects of syntax.

We identified issues in multilingual applications of the UD platform. For example, some corpora have less diverse writing styles for informal sentences which are more common in review documents. In some languages, UD corpora updates have been slowed down after version 2.4 and shifted towards language-specific features and augmented dependencies, but there are still open problems in fundamental syntactic structures. We anticipate continuous improvements to multilingual corpora for UD communities worldwide. We hope the emergence of other applications that utilize UD's syntactic structures will lead to further discussions and enhancements of multilingual corpora.

References

Murhaf Fares, Stephan Oepen, Lilja Øvrelid, Jari Björne, and Richard Johansson. 2018. The 2018 shared task on extrinsic parser evaluation: On the downstream utility of English Universal Dependency parsers. In *Proceedings of the CoNLL 2018 Shared Task: Multilingual Parsing from Raw Text to Universal Dependencies*, pages 22–33.

Hiroshi Kanayama and Ran Iwamoto. 2020. How Universal are Universal Dependencies? Exploiting Syntax for Multilingual Clause-level Sentiment Detection. In *Proceedings of The 12th Language Resources and Evaluation Conference*, pages 4063–4073.

Daniel Kondratyuk and Milan Straka. 2019. 75 languages, 1 model: Parsing universal dependencies universally. In *Proceedings of the 2019 Conference on Empirical Methods in Natural Language Processing and the 9th International Joint Conference on Natural Language Processing*, pages 2779–2795.

Joakim Nivre and Chiao-Ting Fang. 2017. Universal dependency evaluation. In *Proceedings of the NoDaLiDa 2017 Workshop on Universal Dependencies*, 135, pages 86–95.

Stephan Oepen, Lilja Øvrelid, Jari Björne, Richard Jo-hansson, Emanuele Lapponi, Filip Ginter, and ErikVelldal. 2017. The 2017 shared task on extrinsic parser evaluation. towards a reusable community infrastructure. In *Proceedings of the 2017 Shared Task on Extrinsic Parser Evaluation at the Fourth International Conference on Dependency Linguistics and the 15th International Conference on Parsing Technologies*, pages 1–16.

Holger Schwenk and Matthijs Douze. 2017. Learning Joint Multilingual Sentence Representations with Neural Machine Translation. In *Proceedings of the 2nd Workshop on Representation Learning for NLP*, pages 157–167.

Richard Socher, Alex Perelygin, Jean Wu, Jason Chuang, Christopher D Manning, Andrew Ng, and Christopher Potts. 2013. Recursive deep models for semantic compositionality over a sentiment treebank. In *Proceedings of the 2013 conference on empirical methods in natural language processing*, pages 1631–1642.

Milan Straka and Jana Straková. 2017. Tokenizing, POS tagging, lemmatizing and parsing UD 2.0 with UDPipe. In *Proceedings of the CoNLL 2017 Shared Task: Multilingual Parsing from Raw Text to Universal Dependencies*, pages 88–99.

Daniel Zeman et al. 2017. CoNLL 2017 Shared Task: Multilingual Parsing from Raw Text to Universal Dependencies. In *Proceedings of the CoNLL 2017 Shared Task: Multilingual Parsing from Raw Text to Universal Dependencies*, pages 1–19.

Daniel Zeman et al. 2020. Universal Dependencies 2.6. LINDAT/CLARIAH-CZ digital library at the Institute of Formal and Applied Linguistics (ÚFAL), Faculty of Mathematics and Physics, Charles University.

Improving Cross-Lingual Sentiment Analysis via Conditional Language Adversarial Nets

Sai Hemanth Kandula
Tufts University
Sai_Hemanth.Kandula@tufts.edu

Bonan Min
Raytheon BBN Technologies
bonan.min@raytheon.com

Abstract

Sentiment analysis has come a long way for high-resource languages due to the availability of large annotated corpora. However, it still suffers from lack of training data for low-resource languages. To tackle this problem, we propose Conditional Language Adversarial Network (CLAN), an end-to-end neural architecture for cross-lingual sentiment analysis without cross-lingual supervision. CLAN differs from prior work in that it allows the adversarial training to be conditioned on both learned features and the sentiment prediction, to increase discriminativity for learned representation in the cross-lingual setting. Experimental results demonstrate that CLAN outperforms previous methods on the multilingual multi-domain Amazon review dataset. Our source code is released at https://github.com/hemanthkandula/clan.

1 Introduction

Recent success in sentiment analysis (Yang et al., 2019; Sun et al., 2019; Howard and Ruder, 2018; Brahma, 2018) is largely due to the availability of large-scale annotated datasets (Maas et al., 2011; Zhang et al., 2015; Rosenthal et al., 2017). However, such success can not be replicated to low-resource languages because of the lack of labeled data for training Machine Learning models.

As it is prohibitively expensive to obtain training data for all languages of interest, cross-lingual sentiment analysis (CLSA) (Barnes et al., 2018; Zhou et al., 2016b; Xu and Wan, 2017; Wan, 2009; Demirtas and Pechenizkiy, 2013; Xiao and Guo, 2012; Zhou et al., 2016a) offers the possibility of learning sentiment classification models for a target language using only annotated data from a different source language where large annotated data is available. These models often rely on bilingual lexicons, pre-trained cross-lingual word embeddings, or Machine Translation to bridge the gap between the source and target languages. CLIDSA/CLCDSA (Feng and Wan, 2019) is the first end-to-end CLSA model that does not require cross-lingual supervision which may not be available for low-resource languages.

In this paper, we propose Conditional Language Adversarial Network (CLAN) for end-to-end CLSA. Similar to prior work, CLAN performs CLSA without using any cross-lingual supervision. Differing from prior work, CLAN incorporates conditional language adversarial training to learn language invariant features by conditioning on both learned feature representations (or features for short) and sentiment predictions, therefore increases the features' discriminativity in the cross-lingual setting. Our contributions are three fold:

- We develop Conditional Language Adversarial Network (CLAN) which is designed to learn language invariant features that are also discriminative for sentiment classification.
- Experiments on the multilingual multi-domain Amazon review dataset (Prettenhofer and Stein, 2010) show that CLAN outperforms all previous methods for both in-domain and cross-domain CLSA tasks.
- t-SNE visualization of the held-out examples shows that the learned features align well across languages, indicating that CLAN is able to learn language invariant features.

2 Related Work

Cross-lingual sentiment analysis (CLSA): Several CLSA methods (Wan, 2009; Demirtas and Pechenizkiy, 2013; Xiao and Guo, 2012; Zhou et al., 2016a; Wan, 2009; Xiao and Guo, 2012) rely on Machine Translation (MT) for providing supervision across languages. MT, often trained from parallel corpora, may not be available for low-resource languages. Other CLSA methods (Barnes et al., 2018; Zhou et al., 2016b; Xu and Wan, 2017)

Proceedings of the Third Workshop on Computational Typology and Multilingual NLP, pages 32–37
June 10, 2021.

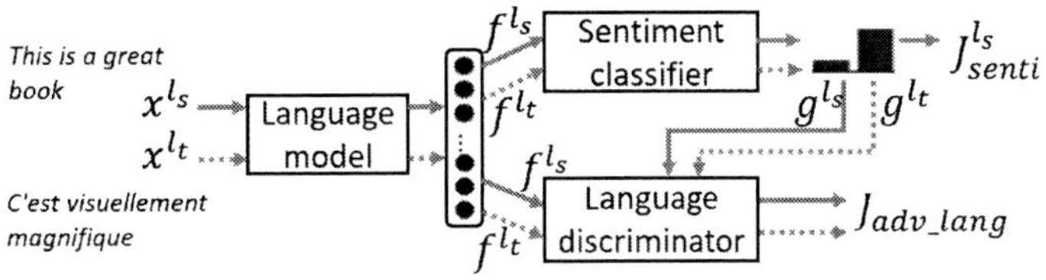

Figure 1: CLAN architecture. We illustrate with a source language l_s =English (solid line) and target language l_t =French (dotted line). x^{l_s}, x^{l_t} are sentences in l_s and l_t, f^{l_s}, f^{l_t} are features extracted by the language model for x^{l_s} and x^{l_t}, and g^{l_s}, g^{l_t} are the sentiment predictions for x^{l_s} and x^{l_t}, respectively. The sentiment classification loss $\mathcal{J}^{l_s}_{senti}$ is only trained on x^{l_s} for which the sentiment label is available, while the language discriminator is trained from both x^{l_s} and x^{l_t}.

uses bilingual lexicons or cross-lingual word embeddings (CLWE) to project words with similar meanings from different languages into nearby spaces, to enable training cross-lingual sentiment classifiers. CLWE often depends on a bilingual lexicon (Barnes et al., 2018) or parallel or comparable corpora (Mogadala and Rettinger, 2016; Vulić and Moens, 2016). Recently, CLWE methods (Lample and Conneau, 2019; Conneau et al., 2019) that rely on no parallel resources are proposed, but they require very large monolingual corpora to train. The work that is most related to ours is (Feng and Wan, 2019), which does not rely on cross-lingual resources. Different from the language adversarial network used in (Feng and Wan, 2019), our work performs cross-lingual sentiment analysis using conditional language adversarial training, which allows the language invariant features to be specialized for sentiment class predictions.

Adversarial training for domain adaptation Our approach draws inspiration from Domain-Adversarial Training of Neural Networks (Ganin et al., 2016) and Conditional Adversarial Domain Adaptation (CDAN) (Long et al., 2018). DANN (Ganin et al., 2016) trains a feature generator to minimize the classification loss, and a domain discriminator to distinguish the domain where the input instances come from. It attempts to learn domain invariant features that deceive the domain discriminator while learning to predict the correct sentiment labels.CDAN (Long et al., 2018) additionally makes the discriminator conditioned on both extracted features and class predictions to improve discriminativity.

3 Conditional Language Adversarial Networks for Sentiment Analysis

Figure 1 shows the architecture of CLAN. It has three components: a multilingual language model (LM) that extracts features from the input sentences, a sentiment classifier built atop of the features extracted by the LM, and a conditional language adversarial trainer to force the features to be language invariant. All three components are jointly optimized in a single end-to-end neural architecture, allowing CLAN to learn cross-lingual features and to capture multiplicative interactions between the features and sentiment predictions. The resulting cross-lingual features are specialized for each sentiment class.

CLAN aims at solving the cross-lingual multi-domain sentiment analysis task. Formally, given a set of domains $\mathcal{D}$ and a set of languages $\mathcal{L}$, CLAN consists of the following components:

- Sentiment classifier: train on (l_s, d_s) (sentiment labels are available) and test on (l_t, d_t) (no sentiment labels), in which $l_s, l_t \in \mathcal{L}, l_s \neq l_t$ and $d_s, d_t \in \mathcal{D}$. CLAN works for both variants of the CLSA problem: **in-domain CLSA** where $d_s = d_t$, and **cross-domain CLSA** where $d_s \neq d_t$.
- Language model: train on (l, d) in which $l \in \mathcal{L}, d \in \mathcal{D}$.
- Language discriminator: train on (l, d) in which $l \in \mathcal{L}$ and $d \in \mathcal{D}$. The language IDs are known.

Language Model (LM): For a sentence x, we compute the probability of seeing a word w_k given the previous words: $p(x) = \prod_{k=1}^{|x|} P(w_k|w_1, ..., w_{k-1})$: we first pass the input words through the embedding layer of language l parameterized by θ^l_{emb}. The embedding for word w_k is $\vec{w_k}$. We then pass the word embeddings to two LSTM layer parameterized by θ_1 and θ_2, that are shared across all languages and all domains, to generate hidden states $(z_1, z_2, ..., z_x)$ that can be considered as features for CLSA: $h_k = \text{LSTM}(h_{k-1}, \vec{w_k}; \theta_1)$, and $z_k = \text{LSTM}(z_{k-1}, h_k; \theta_2)$. We then use a linear decoding layer parameterized by θ^l_{dec} with a softmax for next word prediction. To summarize, the LM objective for l is:

$$\mathcal{J}^l_{lm}(\theta^l_{emb}, \theta_1, \theta_2, \theta^l_{dec}) = \mathbb{E}_{x\sim\mathcal{L}^l}[-\frac{1}{|x|}\sum_{k=1}^{|x|}\log p(w_k|w1, ..., w_{k-1})]$$

where $x \sim \mathcal{L}^l$ indicates that x is sampled from text in language l.

Sentiment Classifier We use a linear classifier that takes the average final hidden states $\frac{1}{|x|}\sum_{k=1}^{|x|} z_k$ as input features, and then a softmax to output sentiment labels. The objective is:

$$\mathcal{J}^l_{senti}(\theta^l_{emb}, \theta_1, \theta_2, \theta^l_{senti}) = \mathbb{E}_{(x,y)\sim\mathcal{C}_{senti}}[-\log p(y|x)]$$

where $(x, y) \sim \mathcal{C}^l_{senti}$ indicates that the sentence x and its label y are sampled from the labeled examples in language l, and θ^l_{senti} denotes the parameters of the linear sentiment classifier.

Conditional Language Adversarial Training To force the features to be language invariant, we adopted conditional adversarial training (Long et al., 2018): a language discriminator is trained to predict language ID given the features by minimizing the cross-entropy loss, while the LM is trained to fool the discriminator by maximizing the loss:

$$\mathcal{J}^l_{adv\_lang}(\theta_{emb}, \theta_1, \theta_2, \theta_{dis\_lang}) = \mathbb{E}_{(x,l)}[-\log p(l|f(x) \otimes g(x))]$$

where $f(x)$, $g(x)$ and $l \in L$ are features extracted by the LM for input sentence x, its sentiment prediction and its language ID respectively, $\theta_{emb} = \theta^1_{emb} \oplus \theta^2_{emb} \oplus ... \oplus \theta^{|\mathcal{L}|}_{emb}$ denotes the parameters of all embedding layers and θ_{dis_lang} denotes the parameters of the language discriminator. We use multilinear conditioning (Long et al., 2018) by conditioning l on the cross-covariance $f(x) \otimes g(x)$.

A key innovation is the conditional language adversarial training: the multilinear conditioning enables manipulation of the multiplicative interactions across features and class predictions. Such interactions capture the cross-covariance between the language invariant features and classifier predictions to improve discriminability.

The Full Model Putting all components together, the final objective function is the following:

$$\mathcal{J}(\theta_{emb}, \theta_{lstm}, \theta_{dec}, \theta_{senti}, \theta_{dis\_lang}) = \sum_{(l,d)} \mathcal{J}^l_{lm} + \alpha\mathcal{J}^l_{senti} - \beta\mathcal{J}^l_{adv\_lang}$$

where $\theta_{lstm} = \theta_1 \oplus \theta_2$ denotes parameters of the LSTM layers, $\theta_{dec} = \theta^1_{dec} \oplus \theta^2_{dec} \oplus ... \oplus \theta^{|\mathcal{L}|}_{dec}$ denotes the paramters of all decoding layers, α and β are hyperpameters controlling the relative importance of the sentiment classification and the language adversarial training objectives. Parameters θ_{dis_lang} is trained to maximize the full objective function while the others are trained to minimize it:

$$\hat{\theta}_{dis\_lang} = \arg\max_{\theta_{dis\_lang}} \mathcal{J}$$

$$(\hat{\theta}_{emb}, \hat{\theta}_{lstm}, \hat{\theta}_{dec}, \hat{\theta}_{senti}) = \arg\min_{\theta_{emb}, \theta_{lstm}, \theta_{dec}, \theta_{senti}} \mathcal{J}$$

4 Experiments

Datasets: We evaluate CLAN on the Websis-CLS-10 dataset (Prettenhofer and Stein, 2010) which consists of Amazon product reviews from 4 languages and 3 domains. Following prior work, we use English as the source language and other languages as the target languages. For each language-domain pair there are 2,000 training documents, 2,000 test documents, and 9,000-50,000 unlabeled documents depending on the language-domain pair (details are in Prettenhofer and Stein, 2010).

Implementation details: The models are implemented in PyTorch(Paszke et al., 2019). All models are trained on four NVIDIA 1080ti GPUs. We tokenized text using NLTK (Loper and Bird, 2002). For each language, we kept the most frequent 15000 words in the vocabulary since a bigger vocabulary leads to under-fitting and much longer training time. We set the word embedding size to 600 for the language model, and use 300 neurons for the hidden layer in the sentiment classifier. We set $\alpha = 0.02$ and $\beta = 0.1$ for all experiments. All weights of CLAN were trained end-to-end using Adam optimizer with a learning rate of 0.03. We train the models with a maximum of 50,000 iterations with early stopping (typically stops at 3,000-4,000 iterations) to avoid over-fitting.

Experiment results: We follow the experiment setting described in (Feng and Wan, 2019). Table 1a and 1b show the accuracy of CLAN comparing to prior methods for the in-domain CLSA and cross-domain CLSA tasks, respectively. We compare CLAN to the following methods: CL-SCL, BiDRL, UMM, CLDFA, CNN-BE (Ziser and Reichart, 2018), PBLM-BE (Ziser and Reichart, 2018), A-SCL (Ziser and Reichart, 2018) are methods that require cross-lingual supervision

	English-German				English-French				English-Japanese			
	B	D	M	AVG	B	D	M	AVG	B	D	M	AVG
CL-SCL (Prettenhofer and Stein, 2010)	79.5	76.9	77.7	78.0	78.4	78.8	77.9	78.3	73.0	71.0	75.1	73.0
BiDRL (Zhou et al., 2016a)	84.1	84.0	84.6	84.2	84.3	83.6	82.5	83.4	73.1	76.7	78.7	76.1
UMM (Xu and Wan, 2017)	81.6	81.2	81.3	81.3	80.2	80.2	79.4	79.9	71.2	72.5	75.3	73.0
CLDFA (Xu and Yang, 2017)	83.9	83.1	79.0	82.0	83.3	82.5	83.3	83.0	77.3	80.5	76.4	78.0
MAN-MoE (Chen et al., 2019)	82.4	78.8	77.1	79.4	81.1	84.2	80.9	82.0	62.7	69.1	72.6	68.1
MWE (Conneau et al., 2017)	76.1	76.8	74.7	75.8	76.3	78.7	71.6	75.5	-	-	-	-
CLIDSA (Feng and Wan, 2019)	86.6	**84.6**	85.0	85.4	87.2	87.9	87.1	87.4	79.3	81.9	84.0	81.7
CLAN	**88.2**	84.5	**86.3**	**86.3**	**88.6**	**88.7**	**87.7**	**88.3**	**82.0**	**84.1**	**85.1**	**83.7**

(a) Accuracy for in-domain CLSA.

	English-German							English-French						
$S \to T$	D→B	M→B	B→D	M→D	B→M	D→M	AVG	D→B	M→B	B→D	M→D	B→M	D→M	AVG
CNN-BE	62.8	63.8	65.3	68.7	71.6	72.0	67.3	69.5	59.7	63.7	65.7	65.9	67.0	65.2
DCI	67.1	60.6	66.9	66.7	68.9	68.2	66.4	71.2	65.4	69.1	67.5	66.7	71.4	68.6
CL-SCL	65.9	62.5	65.1	65.2	71.2	69.8	66.7	70.3	63.8	68.8	66.8	66.0	70.1	67.6
A-SCL	67.9	63.7	68.7	63.8	69.0	70.1	67.2	68.6	66.1	69.2	69.4	66.7	68.1	68.0
A-S-SR	68.3	62.5	69.4	69.9	70.2	69	67.4	69.3	68.9	70.9	70.7	67	71.4	69.7
PBLM+BE	78.7	78.6	80.6	79.2	81.7	78.5	79.5	81.1	74.7	76.3	75.0	75.1	76.8	76.5
CLCDSA	85.4	81.7	79.3	81.0	**83.4**	81.7	82.0	86.2	81.8	84.3	82.8	83.7	85.0	83.9
CLAN	**86.9**	**85.1**	**82.4**	**81.6**	83	**83.8**	**83.8**	**87.3**	**85.5**	**85.3**	**83.9**	**85.5**	**85.7**	**85.5**

(b) Accuracy for cross-domain CLSA. Six domain pairs were generated for each language pair. S and T refers to the source and target domains, respectively.

Table 1: Accuracy of CLSA methods on Websis-CLS-10. Top scores are shown in bold. D, M, B refers to DVD, music, and books, respectively. AVG refers to the average of scores per each language pair.

such as bilingual lexicons or Machine Translation. MAN-MoE and MWE use MUSE (Conneau et al., 2017) to generate cross-lingual word embeddings. CLIDSA/CLCDSA (Feng and Wan, 2019) uses language adversarial training. We refer readers to the corresponding papers for details of each model.

As shown in Table 1a and 1b, CLAN outperforms all prior methods in 11 out of 12 settings for cross-domain CLSA, and outperforms all prior methods in 8 out of 9 settings for in-domain CLSA. On average, CLAN achieves state-of-the-art performance on all language pairs for both in-domain and cross-domain CLSA tasks.

Analysis of results: To understand what features CLAN learned to enable CLSA, we probed CLAN by visualizing the distribution of features extracted from held-out examples from the language model through t-SNE (Maaten and Hinton, 2008). The plots are in Figure 2. The t-SNE plots show that the feature distributions for sentences in the source and target languages align well, indicating that CLAN is able to learn language-invariant features. To further look into what CLAN learns, we manually inspected 50 examples where CLAN classified correctly but the prior models failed: for example, in the books domain in German, CLAN classified *"unterhaltsam und etwas lustig"* (*"entertaining and a little funny"*) correctly as positive, also classified the following text correctly as positive: *"ein buch dass mich gefesselt hat...Dieses Buch ist absolut nichts für schwache Nerven oder Moralisten"* (*"a book that captivated me...this book is absolutely not for the faint of heart or moralists!"*). This indicates that CLAN is able to learn better lexical, syntactic and semantic features.

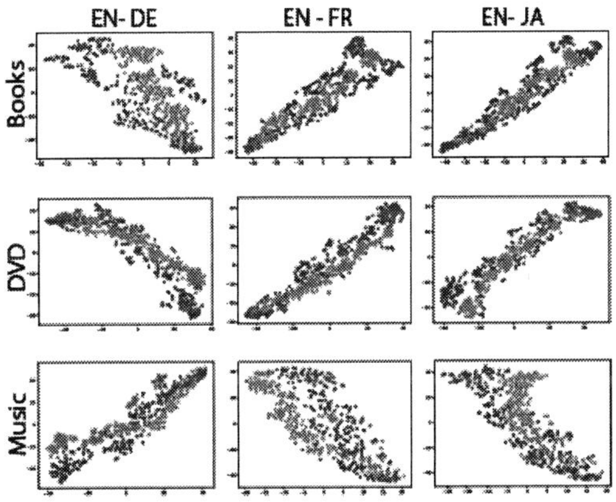

Figure 2: t-SNE plots of the distributions of features extracted from CLAN's language model, trained via the in-domain CLSA task. Red and blue dots represent features extracted from the source and target language held-out sentences, respectively. EN, DE, FR, JA refers to English, German, French and Japanese respectively.

5 Conclusion

We present Conditional Language Adversarial Networks for cross-lingual sentiment analysis, and show that it achieves state-of-the-art performance.

Acknowledgements

This work was supported by the Office of the Director of National Intelligence (ODNI), Intelligence Advanced Research Projects Activity (IARPA), via IARPA Contract No. 2019-19051600006 under the BETTER program. The views, opinions, and/or findings expressed are those of the author(s) and should not be interpreted as representing the official views or policies, either expressed or implied, of ODNI, IARPA, or the U.S. Government. The U.S. Government is authorized to reproduce and distribute reprints for governmental purposes notwithstanding any copyright annotation therein.

References

Jeremy Barnes, Roman Klinger, and Sabine Schulte im Walde. 2018. Bilingual sentiment embeddings: Joint projection of sentiment across languages. In *Proceedings of the 56th Annual Meeting of the Association for Computational Linguistics (Volume 1: Long Papers)*, pages 2483–2493, Melbourne, Australia. Association for Computational Linguistics.

Siddhartha Brahma. 2018. Improved sentence modeling using suffix bidirectional lstm. *arXiv preprint arXiv:1805.07340*.

Xilun Chen, Ahmed Hassan Awadallah, Hany Hassan, Wei Wang, and Claire Cardie. 2019. Multi-source cross-lingual model transfer: Learning what to share. In *Proceedings of the 57th Annual Meeting of the Association for Computational Linguistics*, pages 3098–3112, Florence, Italy. Association for Computational Linguistics.

Alexis Conneau, Kartikay Khandelwal, Naman Goyal, Vishrav Chaudhary, Guillaume Wenzek, Francisco Guzmán, Edouard Grave, Myle Ott, Luke Zettlemoyer, and Veselin Stoyanov. 2019. Unsupervised cross-lingual representation learning at scale. *arXiv preprint arXiv:1911.02116*.

Alexis Conneau, Guillaume Lample, Marc'Aurelio Ranzato, Ludovic Denoyer, and Hervé Jégou. 2017. Word translation without parallel data. *arXiv preprint arXiv:1710.04087*.

Erkin Demirtas and Mykola Pechenizkiy. 2013. Cross-lingual polarity detection with machine translation. In *Proceedings of the Second International Workshop on Issues of Sentiment Discovery and Opinion Mining*, pages 1–8.

Yanlin Feng and Xiaojun Wan. 2019. Towards a unified end-to-end approach for fully unsupervised cross-lingual sentiment analysis. In *Proceedings of the 23rd Conference on Computational Natural Language Learning (CoNLL)*, pages 1035–1044, Hong Kong, China. Association for Computational Linguistics.

Yaroslav Ganin, Evgeniya Ustinova, Hana Ajakan, Pascal Germain, Hugo Larochelle, François Laviolette, Mario March, and Victor Lempitsky. 2016. Domain-adversarial training of neural networks. *Journal of Machine Learning Research*, 17(59):1–35.

Jeremy Howard and Sebastian Ruder. 2018. Universal language model fine-tuning for text classification. *arXiv preprint arXiv:1801.06146*.

Guillaume Lample and Alexis Conneau. 2019. Cross-lingual language model pretraining. *arXiv preprint arXiv:1901.07291*.

Mingsheng Long, ZHANGJIE CAO, Jianmin Wang, and Michael I Jordan. 2018. Conditional adversarial domain adaptation. In S. Bengio, H. Wallach, H. Larochelle, K. Grauman, N. Cesa-Bianchi, and R. Garnett, editors, *Advances in Neural Information Processing Systems 31*, pages 1640–1650. Curran Associates, Inc.

Edward Loper and Steven Bird. 2002. Nltk: The natural language toolkit. In *Proceedings of the ACL-02 Workshop on Effective Tools and Methodologies for Teaching Natural Language Processing and Computational Linguistics - Volume 1*, ETMTNLP '02, page 63–70, USA. Association for Computational Linguistics.

Andrew L. Maas, Raymond E. Daly, Peter T. Pham, Dan Huang, Andrew Y. Ng, and Christopher Potts. 2011. Learning word vectors for sentiment analysis. In *Proceedings of the 49th Annual Meeting of the Association for Computational Linguistics: Human Language Technologies*, pages 142–150, Portland, Oregon, USA. Association for Computational Linguistics.

Laurens van der Maaten and Geoffrey Hinton. 2008. Visualizing data using t-sne. *Journal of machine learning research*, 9(Nov):2579–2605.

Aditya Mogadala and Achim Rettinger. 2016. Bilingual word embeddings from parallel and non-parallel corpora for cross-language text classification. In *Proceedings of the 2016 Conference of the North American Chapter of the Association for Computational Linguistics: Human Language Technologies*, pages 692–702, San Diego, California. Association for Computational Linguistics.

Adam Paszke, Sam Gross, Francisco Massa, Adam Lerer, James Bradbury, Gregory Chanan, Trevor Killeen, Zeming Lin, Natalia Gimelshein, Luca Antiga, Alban Desmaison, Andreas Kopf, Edward Yang, Zachary DeVito, Martin Raison, Alykhan Tejani, Sasank Chilamkurthy, Benoit Steiner, Lu Fang, Junjie Bai, and Soumith Chintala. 2019. Pytorch: An imperative style, high-performance deep learning library. In H. Wallach, H. Larochelle, A. Beygelzimer, F. dAlché-Buc, E. Fox, and R. Garnett, editors, *Advances in Neural Information Processing Systems 32*, pages 8024–8035. Curran Associates, Inc.

Peter Prettenhofer and Benno Stein. 2010. Cross-language text classification using structural correspondence learning. In *Proceedings of the 48th Annual Meeting of the Association for Computational Linguistics*, pages 1118–1127, Uppsala, Sweden. Association for Computational Linguistics.

Sara Rosenthal, Noura Farra, and Preslav Nakov. 2017. SemEval-2017 task 4: Sentiment analysis in twitter. In *Proceedings of the 11th International Workshop on Semantic Evaluation (SemEval-2017)*, pages 502–518, Vancouver, Canada. Association for Computational Linguistics.

Chi Sun, Xipeng Qiu, Yige Xu, and Xuanjing Huang. 2019. How to fine-tune bert for text classification? In *China National Conference on Chinese Computational Linguistics*, pages 194–206. Springer.

Ivan Vulić and Marie-Francine Moens. 2016. Bilingual distributed word representations from document-aligned comparable data. *Journal of Artificial Intelligence Research*, 55:953–994.

Xiaojun Wan. 2009. Co-training for cross-lingual sentiment classification. In *Proceedings of the Joint Conference of the 47th Annual Meeting of the ACL and the 4th International Joint Conference on Natural Language Processing of the AFNLP*, pages 235–243, Suntec, Singapore. Association for Computational Linguistics.

Min Xiao and Yuhong Guo. 2012. Multi-view AdaBoost for multilingual subjectivity analysis. In *Proceedings of COLING 2012*, pages 2851–2866, Mumbai, India. The COLING 2012 Organizing Committee.

Kui Xu and Xiaojun Wan. 2017. Towards a universal sentiment classifier in multiple languages. In *Proceedings of the 2017 Conference on Empirical Methods in Natural Language Processing*, pages 511–520, Copenhagen, Denmark. Association for Computational Linguistics.

Ruochen Xu and Yiming Yang. 2017. Cross-lingual distillation for text classification. *arXiv preprint arXiv:1705.02073*.

Zhilin Yang, Zihang Dai, Yiming Yang, Jaime Carbonell, Russ R Salakhutdinov, and Quoc V Le. 2019. Xlnet: Generalized autoregressive pretraining for language understanding. In *Advances in neural information processing systems*, pages 5753–5763.

Xiang Zhang, Junbo Zhao, and Yann LeCun. 2015. Character-level convolutional networks for text classification. In *Advances in neural information processing systems*, pages 649–657.

Xinjie Zhou, Xiaojun Wan, and Jianguo Xiao. 2016a. Attention-based LSTM network for cross-lingual sentiment classification. In *Proceedings of the 2016 Conference on Empirical Methods in Natural Language Processing*, pages 247–256, Austin, Texas. Association for Computational Linguistics.

Xinjie Zhou, Xiaojun Wan, and Jianguo Xiao. 2016b. Cross-lingual sentiment classification with bilingual document representation learning. In *Proceedings of the 54th Annual Meeting of the Association for Computational Linguistics (Volume 1: Long Papers)*, pages 1403–1412, Berlin, Germany. Association for Computational Linguistics.

Yftah Ziser and Roi Reichart. 2018. Deep pivot-based modeling for cross-language cross-domain transfer with minimal guidance. In *Proceedings of the 2018 Conference on Empirical Methods in Natural Language Processing*, pages 238–249, Brussels, Belgium. Association for Computational Linguistics.

Improving the performance of UDify with Linguistic Typology Knowledge

Chinmay Choudhary
National University of Ireland, Galway
c.choudhary1@nuigalway.ie

Colm O'Riordan
National University of Ireland, Galway
colm.oriordan@nuigalway.ie

Abstract

UDify is the state-of-the-art language-agnostic dependency parser which is trained on a polyglot corpus of 75 languages. This multilingual modeling enables the model to generalize over unknown/lesser-known languages, thus leading to improved performance on low-resource languages. In this work we used linguistic typology knowledge available in URIEL database, to improve the cross-lingual transferring ability of UDify even further.

1 Introduction

State-of-the-art approaches to dependency parsing are supervised approaches that require large manually annotated dataset to be trained on, thus limiting their utility to only few high-resource languages. Multilingual modeling which involves training a model on a mixed polyglot corpus of high-resource source-languages and applying it on a low resource target-language, is an effective way to circumvent this issue of data-sparsity.

In a similar way, as the proficiency of a speaker's previous languages can enhance his/her ability to learn a new language (Abu-Rabia and Sanitsky, 2010), a model which is trained on multilingual dataset can learn to generalize over unknown or lesser-known languages.

UDify (Kondratyuk and Straka, 2019) is the state-of-the-art mBERT based language-agnostic dependency parser, which takes the advantage of multilingual modeling to improve its performance on low-resource languages. The authors of UDify (Kondratyuk and Straka, 2019) trained it on a joint polyglot corpus created by concatenating all training treebanks available in UDv2.3, and evaluated it on all test treebanks in UDv2.3 individually. Results outlined in (Kondratyuk and Straka, 2019) show that for dependency parsing task, the UDify outperforms its baseline monolingual UDPipe Future (Straka, 2018) model by a large margin especially for low-resource languages, as the model benefit significantly from the cross-lingual transfer learning which occurs due to joint polyglot training.

However, the performance of UDify model on the low-resource languages (less represented in the polyglot training corpus) is still much lower than the performance of it on the high-resource languages which are well represented within the training corpus.

In this work, we use linguistic typology knowledge to improve the cross-lingual transferring ability of UDify model even further, thereby significantly reducing this gap between model's performance on high-resource and low-resource languages.

We induce the linguistic typology knowledge available in URIEL (Littell et al., 2017) database into the UDify model by adding an auxiliary task of linguistic typology feature prediction to it, within the multitasking framework. Sections 3 and 4 will describe the model in more details.

2 Related Work

Cross-lingual *Model-transfer* approaches to Dependency Parsing such as (McDonald et al., 2011; Cohen et al., 2011; Duong et al., 2015; Guo et al., 2016; Vilares et al., 2015; Falenska and Çetinoğlu, 2017; Mulcaire et al., 2019; Vania et al., 2019; Shareghi et al., 2019) involve training a model on high-resource languages and subsequently adapting it to low-resource languages. Participants of CoNLL 2017 shared-task (Daniel et al., 2017) and CoNLL 2018 shared task (Zeman et al., 2018) also provide numerous approaches to dependency parsing of low-resource languages.

Some approaches such as (Naseem et al., 2012; Täckström et al., 2013; Barzilay and Zhang, 2015; Wang and Eisner, 2016a; Rasooli and Collins, 2017; Ammar, 2016; Wang and Eisner, 2016b) indeed used linguistic typology to facilitate the cross-lingual transfer between source and target languages. However, all these approaches directly

Proceedings of the Third Workshop on Computational Typology and Multilingual NLP, pages 38–60
June 10, 2021.

feed the linguistic typology features into the respective model, whereas we induce the linguistic typology knowledge into UDify model through Multitask learning.
Inducing typology knowledge through Multitask learning rather than directly feeding it along with word-embeddings have following advantages.

1. The model can also be applied to low-resource languages for which many typology feature values are unknown/missing.

2. The auxiliary task should help to improve the performance on the main dependency parsing task as well, since it would make the model give special emphasis on the syntactic typology (specially word-order typology) of language being parsed while predicting the dependency relations.

3 UDify

UDify is a multitasking multilingual BERT based model which performs four key language-processing tasks simultaneously namely *UPOS-tagging*, *UFeat-tagging*, *Lemmatization* and *Dependency Parsing*, in a multitasking framework. The model utilizes a single shared mBERT based encoder, and four individual task-specific decoders, for each of the four tasks respectively.
The *mBERT Encoder* takes in the entire sentence as input, tokenizes it using pre-trained WordPiece Tokenizer (Wu et al., 2016) and subsequently outputs mBERT (Wu and Dredze, 2019) based contextualized-embeddings for each word within the input-sentence. We refer to original UDify (Kondratyuk and Straka, 2019) paper for detailed description of mechanism of computing/fine-tuning such contextualized embeddings.
The decoders for both *UPOS-tagging* and *UFeat-tagging* tasks adopt standard sequence-tagging architecture with softmax layer on the top. These decoders accept the contextual embeddings generated from the mBERT Encoder for each word in the input sentence, and predicts its UPOS/Ufeats tag.
For *Lemmatization* task as well, the model uses a standard sequence-tagger which predicts a class-tag representing a unique edit script, for each word. An edit-script is simply the sequence of character operations to transform a word form to its lemma-form.
For dependency-parsing, the model adopts the popular deep biaffine architecture (Dozat and Manning, 2016) for graph-based parsing, with LSTM-encoder been replaced by the shared *mBERT Encoder*.

4 Linguistic Typology prediction

To improve the cross-lingual transferring ability of UDify model, we added a fifth auxiliary task of Linguistic Typology prediction to it.
Our *Typology-predictor* is a simple deep feed-forward neural network with *sigmoid* activation function, which predicts the values of all typology features provided by the URIEL database (Littell et al., 2017).
URIEL database is a collection of binary features extracted from multiple typological, phylogenetic, and geographical databases such as WALS (Haspelmath, 2009), PHOIBLE (Moran and Richard Wright, 2014), Ethnologue (M. Paul Lewis and Fennig, 2015) and Glottolog (Harald Hammarstrom and Bank, 2015). URIEL database can be accessed through Pyton PyPi library called *lang2vec*[1].
Let $\hat{N}$ be the number of typology features provided by URIEL database. Our *Typology predictor* would then output the probability vector $Pr_{ty} \in R^{\hat{N}}$ by applying equation 1.

$$Pr_{ty} = sigmoid(e_{</s>} * U + c) \qquad (1)$$

Here $e_{</s>} \in R^d$ is the contextual embedding from the shared *mBERT Encoder* for end-token $< /s >$ of the input-sentence. $U \in R^{d*\hat{N}}$ and $c \in R^{\hat{N}}$ are weights and biases respectively. Pr_{Ty} comprises of the probability of value of each URIEL binary feature being as 1, for the specific language being parsed.
The total-loss is computed by simply adding the *Typology Predictor* loss to *UDify* model's (as computed in (Kondratyuk and Straka, 2019))

5 Experiments

This section describes the details of experiments conducted to evaluate our proposed model.

5.1 Experimental Setup

Both baseline *UDify* and the proposed *UDify+Typology-predictor* models are trained on a single large joint-polyglot corpus, created by concatenating all training datasets available in

[1] https://pypi.org/project/lang2vec/

UDv2.5[2] together.
Before each training-epoch, we randomly shuffled all sentences in our polyglot training corpus, and subsequently fed mixed batches of sentences from this shuffled corpus into the model being trained, where each batch may contain sentences from any language or treebank (as done by authors of UDify (Kondratyuk and Straka, 2019)).
We used batch-size of 32, drop-out probability of 0.01 and the pre-trained mBERT model *cased_L-12_H-768_A-12* downloaded from tensorflow-hub[3]. We fine-tuned these hyper-parameters on *Dev* dataset for *English-EWT* treebank.

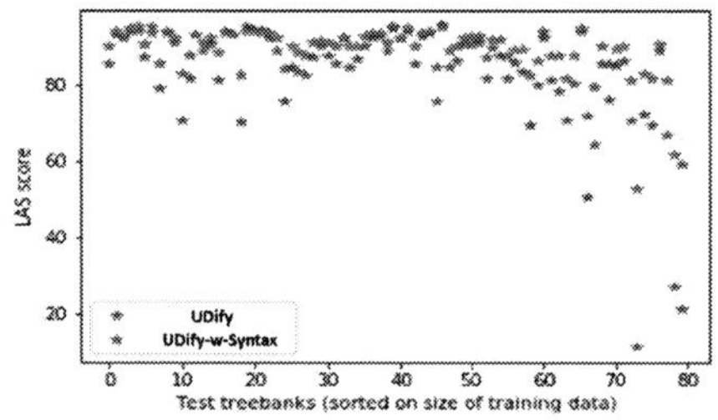

Figure 1: Trends in LAS achieved by *UDify* and *UDify-w-Syntax* models on all 80 test treebanks

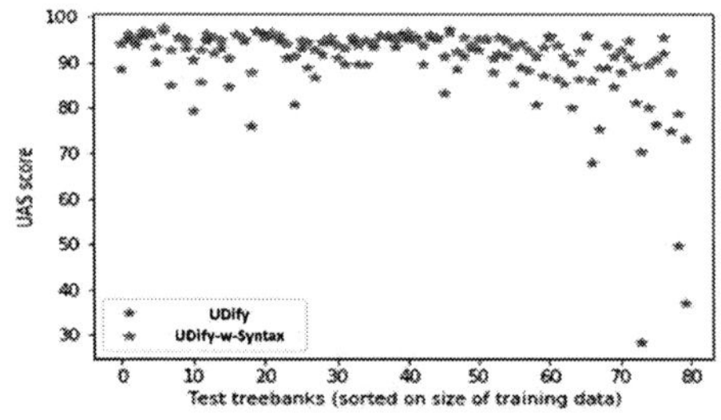

Figure 2: Trends in UAS achieved by *UDify* and *UDify-w-Syntax* models on all 80 test treebanks

6 Results

We evaluated our proposed model on 80 test treebanks available in UDv2.5 datasets individually. Appendix A provides the results achieved on each of these 80 test-treebanks, whereas table 1 outlines the average results on all these 80 treebanks. All scores are evaluated using the official CoNLL 2018 Shared Task evaluation script. We compared the performance of our model with two baselines namely *UDPipe Fututre*(Straka, 2018) and *UDify*. URIEL database comprises of three categories of typology features namely *Syntactic*, *Semantic* and *Phonological* features. In this work, we evaluated three variants of our proposed model, based on the categories of features predicted by the typology-predictor within the auxiliary task, namely *UDify-w-Syntax* (predicts only syntactic typology features), *UDify-w-Syntactic+Semantic* (predicts syntactic and semantic typology-features) and *UDify-w-All* (predicts all the URIEL typology-features). Furthermore, we evaluated the performance of *UDify-w-Lang_id* model. The architecture of it is identical to our proposed model but the linguistic-typology predictor is replaced by a simple language-id predictor.

7 Discussion

It is observed that the *UDify-w-Syntax* variant of our proposed model outperforms the other two variants of it, for most of the test-treebanks, despite the fact that the *UDify-w-Syntax+Semantic* and *UDify-w-All* variants utilizes more typology-features than the *UDify-w-Syntax* variant.
The reason being that since all four tasks performed by the UDify model namely *UPOS-tagging*, *UFeats-tagging*, *Lammelization* and *Dependency Parsing* are syntactic tasks, only the syntactic typology-features are relevant to these tasks.
(Henderson, 2004) proved that, having large number of unrelated features makes it difficult for a neural-network model to effectively learn from provided training-data, and thereby would lead to drop in performance.
Figures 1 and 2 depict the trends in LAS and UAS achieved by the *UDify* and *UDify-w-Syntax* models on all 80 test treebanks. The test-treebanks (as indexes) on the x-axises in these figures are inversely-sorted by the size of their corresponding train treebank, which is part of the training corpus. It is evident in the figures that the *UDify* model shows stronger performance on the high-resource languages which are well represented in the training corpus as compared to the low-resource languages. On the other hand, *UDify+Syntax* shows relatively uniform performance across all languages.
Overall the results in Appendix A, show that *UDify+Syntax* outperforms baselines *UDPipe Future*, *UDify* and *UDify+Lang_id* for almost all 80 test-treebanks. For high-resource languages, the *UD-*

[2]https://universaldependencies.org/

[3]https://tfhub.dev/tensorflow/bert$_{m}ulti_{c}ased_{L} - 12_{H} - 768_{A} - 12/3$

Corpus	Model	UPOS	UFeats	Lemmas	UAS	LAS	Typo F1
Overall (all UDv2.5 test-banks)	UDPipe	94.27	91.37	94.99	86.24	81.78	–
	UDify	94.03	89.33	90.92	87.84	82.83	–
	UDify-w-Lang_id	95.76	90.95	91.52	90.21	85.61	–
	UDify-w-Syntax	**95.89**	**92.05**	**91.87**	**93.18**	**88.4**	**74.6**
	UDify-w-Syntax+Semantic	94.04	88.06	87.09	89.26	83.84	73.33
	UDify-w-All	92.85	85.48	84.33	84.86	79.17	64.88

Table 1: Overall Results achieved by the baseline and all variants of our proposed model. These are average of all results outlayed in Appeandix A.

Corpus	Model	UPOS	UAS	LAS
English-EWT (size: 25377)	UDify	97.73	94.64	90.04
	UDify+	98.32	95.73	91.41
French-GSD (size: 33399)	UDify	98.14	94.74	92.77
	UDify+	99.24	96.19	92.84
Buryat-BDT (size: 19)	UDify	60.23	36.98	21.52
	UDify+	73.73	73.25	59.1
Lithuanian-HSE (size: 2494)	UDify	90.47	80.1	70.38
	UDify+	93.56	90.14	81.6

Table 2: Selected results from Appendix A. **UDify+** refers to *UDify+Syntax* model

Distrb 1	Distrb 2	t-value	p-value
Typo F1	Diff	84.23	3.24e-23
Typo F1	Size	6.98	7.36e-11
Typo F1	UDify	1.42	0.16
Typo F1	UDify+	3.49	6.26e-4

Table 3: Results of t-test for correlation between various performance parmeters. **Typo F1**: Its F1 score achieved by *UDify+Syntax* for auxiliary task.; **UDify, UDify+**:UAS achieved by *UDify* and *UDify+Syntax* models; **Diff**: Improvement in UAS of *UDify+* over *UDify*

Corpus	Model	UPOS	UAS	LAS
Breton-KEB	UDify	63.67	63.97	40.19
	UDify+	62.15	60.65	34.23
Tagalog-TRG	UDify	61.64	64.73	39.38
	UDify+	62.38	63.9	38.31
Faroese-OFT	UDify	77.86	69.28	61.03
	UDify+	77.46	65.57	54.11
Naija-NSC	UDify	56.59	47.13	33.43
	UDify+	55.06	46.61	27.94
Sanskrit-UFAL	UDify	40.21	41.73	19.8
	UDify+	38.08	43.14	15.48

Table 4: Results achieved in zero-shot learning scenario. **UDify+** refers to *UDify+Syntax* model

ify+Syntax model shows only marginal improvement in performance over *UDify* whereas for low-resource languages it shows strong improvement in performance. Such trends can also be observed in Table 2. Table 4 outlines results obtained on selected languages which are not represented in the training data at all (zero-shot learning). For such treebanks, *UDify+Syntax* under-performs *UDify*. Hence it can be inferred that the auxiliary task of linguistic typology prediction, does lead to significant improvement in performance of *UDify* within few-shot learning scenario, but does not lead to any improvement within zero-shot learning scenario. Furthermore, to ensure that the auxiliary task of linguistic typology-prediction is indeed responsible for the improvement in performance of *UDify*, we conducted numerous statistical t-tests to find the correlation between F1 scores achieved by the *UDify+Syntax* model for the auxiliary-task of typology-prediction, and various other performance parameters including the improvement in performance of *UDify+Syntax* over *UDify*. Table 3 outlays results of these t-tests.

8 Conclusion

In this work we used linguistic typology knowledge available in URIEL database to improve the cross-lingual transferring ability of the state-of-the-art language-agnostic UDify parser. We injected typology knowledge in UDify model through an auxiliary task, in multitasking settings.

References

Salim Abu-Rabia and Ekaterina Sanitsky. 2010. Advantages of bilinguals over monolinguals in learning a third language. *Bilingual Research Journal*, 33(2):173–199.

Waleed Ammar. 2016. *Towards a Universal Analyzer of Natural Languages*. Ph.D. thesis, Ph. D. thesis, Google Research.

Regina Barzilay and Yuan Zhang. 2015. Hierarchical low-rank tensors for multilingual transfer parsing. Association for Computational Linguistics.

Shay B Cohen, Dipanjan Das, and Noah A Smith. 2011. Unsupervised structure prediction with non-parallel multilingual guidance. In *Proceedings of the 2011 Conference on Empirical Methods in Natural Language Processing*, pages 50–61.

Zeman Daniel, Popel Martin, Straka Milan, Hajic Jan, Nivre Joakim, Ginter Filip, Luotolahti Juhani, Pyysalo Sampo, Petrov Slav, Potthast Martin, et al. 2017. Conll 2017 shared task: Multilingual parsing from raw text to universal dependencies. In *CoNLL 2017 Shared Task: Multilingual Parsing from Raw Text to Universal Dependencies*, volume 1, pages 1–19. Association for Computational Linguistics.

Timothy Dozat and Christopher D Manning. 2016. Deep biaffine attention for neural dependency parsing. *arXiv preprint arXiv:1611.01734*.

Long Duong, Trevor Cohn, Steven Bird, and Paul Cook. 2015. Low resource dependency parsing: Cross-lingual parameter sharing in a neural network parser. In *Proceedings of the 53rd Annual Meeting of the Association for Computational Linguistics and the 7th International Joint Conference on Natural Language Processing (Volume 2: Short Papers)*, pages 845–850.

Agnieszka Falenska and Özlem Çetinoğlu. 2017. Lexicalized vs. delexicalized parsing in low-resource scenarios. In *Proceedings of the 15th International Conference on Parsing Technologies*, pages 18–24.

Jiang Guo, Wanxiang Che, David Yarowsky, Haifeng Wang, and Ting Liu. 2016. A representation learning framework for multi-source transfer parsing. In *Thirtieth AAAI Conference on Artificial Intelligence*.

Martin Haspelmath Harald Hammarstrom, Robert Forkel and Sebastian Bank. 2015. Glottolog 2.6.

Martin Haspelmath. 2009. *The typological database of the World Atlas of Language Structures*. Berlin: Walter de Gruyter.

James Henderson. 2004. Discriminative training of a neural network statistical parser. In *ACL'04: Proceedings of the 42nd Annual Meeting of the Association for Computational Linguistics*, pages 95–102. Association for Computational Linguistics.

Dan Kondratyuk and Milan Straka. 2019. 75 languages, 1 model: Parsing universal dependencies universally. *arXiv preprint arXiv:1904.02099*.

Patrick Littell, David R Mortensen, Ke Lin, Katherine Kairis, Carlisle Turner, and Lori Levin. 2017. Uriel and lang2vec: Representing languages as typological, geographical, and phylogenetic vectors. In *Proceedings of the 15th Conference of the European Chapter of the Association for Computational Linguistics: Volume 2, Short Papers*, pages 8–14.

Gary F. Simons M. Paul Lewis and Charles D. Fennig. 2015. Ethnologue: Languages of the World, Eighteenth edition.

Ryan McDonald, Slav Petrov, and Keith B Hall. 2011. Multi-source transfer of delexicalized dependency parsers.

Daniel McCloy Moran, Steven and editors Richard Wright. 2014. PHOBIA Online.

Phoebe Mulcaire, Jungo Kasai, and Noah A Smith. 2019. Low-resource parsing with crosslingual contextualized representations. *arXiv preprint arXiv:1909.08744*.

Tahira Naseem, Regina Barzilay, and Amir Globerson. 2012. Selective sharing for multilingual dependency parsing. The Association for Computational Linguistics.

Mohammad Sadegh Rasooli and Michael Collins. 2017. Cross-lingual syntactic transfer with limited resources. *Transactions of the Association for Computational Linguistics*, 5:279–293.

Ehsan Shareghi, Yingzhen Li, Yi Zhu, Roi Reichart, and Anna Korhonen. 2019. Bayesian learning for neural dependency parsing. In *Proceedings of the 2019 Conference of the North American Chapter of the Association for Computational Linguistics: Human Language Technologies, Volume 1 (Long and Short Papers)*, pages 3509–3519.

Milan Straka. 2018. Udpipe 2.0 prototype at conll 2018 ud shared task. In *Proceedings of the CoNLL 2018 Shared Task: Multilingual Parsing from Raw Text to Universal Dependencies*, pages 197–207.

Oscar Täckström, Ryan McDonald, and Joakim Nivre. 2013. Target language adaptation of discriminative transfer parsers.

Clara Vania, Yova Kementchedjhieva, Anders Søgaard, and Adam Lopez. 2019. A systematic comparison of methods for low-resource dependency parsing on genuinely low-resource languages. *arXiv preprint arXiv:1909.02857*.

David Vilares, Carlos Gómez-Rodríguez, and Miguel A Alonso. 2015. One model, two languages: training bilingual parsers with harmonized treebanks. *arXiv preprint arXiv:1507.08449*.

Dingquan Wang and Jason Eisner. 2016a. The galactic dependencies treebanks: Getting more data by synthesizing new languages. *Transactions of the Association for Computational Linguistics*, 4:491–505.

Dingquan Wang and Jason Eisner. 2016b. The galactic dependencies treebanks: Getting more data by synthesizing new languages. *Transactions of the Association for Computational Linguistics*, 4:491–505.

Shijie Wu and Mark Dredze. 2019. Beto, bentz, becas: The surprising cross-lingual effectiveness of bert. *arXiv preprint arXiv:1904.09077*.

Yonghui Wu, Mike Schuster, Zhifeng Chen, Quoc V Le, Mohammad Norouzi, Wolfgang Macherey, Maxim Krikun, Yuan Cao, Qin Gao, Klaus Macherey, et al. 2016. Google's neural machine translation system: Bridging the gap between human and machine translation. *arXiv preprint arXiv:1609.08144*.

Daniel Zeman, Jan Hajic, Martin Popel, Martin Potthast, Milan Straka, Filip Ginter, Joakim Nivre, and Slav Petrov. 2018. Conll 2018 shared task: Multilingual parsing from raw text to universal dependencies. In *Proceedings of the CoNLL 2018 Shared Task: Multilingual parsing from raw text to universal dependencies*, pages 1–21.

A Results

This section outlines the results obtained by the three variants of our proposed models namely *UDify-w-Syntax* (predicts only syntactic typology features), *UDify-w-Syntactic+Semantic* (predicts syntactic and semantic typology-features) and *UDify-w-All* (predicts all the URIEL typology-features), as well as the baselines.

Table 1: Results achieved on all 80 test tree-banks

Begin of Table							
Corpus	**Model**	**UPOS**	**UFeats**	**Lemma**	**UAS**	**LAS**	**Typo F1**
Afrikaans-AfriBooms	UDPipe	98.25	97.66	97.46	91.26	88.46	–
(size: 1315)	UDify	95.31	91.34	94.5	88.79	85.17	–
	Multi-w-Lang_id	96.61	92.64	94.84	90.15	87.87	–
	Multi-w-Syntax	96.73	93.51	95.04	94.36	89.96	82.27
	Multi-w-Syntax+Semantic	94.8	90.51	88.31	83.91	90.63	74.82
	Multi-w-All	93.73	88.8	86.48	81.5	85.96	64.94
Arabic-PADT	UDPipe	96.83	94.11	95.28	88.29	83.69	–
(size: 21864)	UDify	95.35	99.35	99.97	88.6	84.42	–
	Multi-w-Lang_id	96.64	99.33	99.66	89.92	87.13	–
	Multi-w-Syntax	96.76	99.31	99.59	93.78	89.24	81.75
	Multi-w-Syntax+Semantic	96.41	92.77	94.39	90.83	84.12	74.5
	Multi-w-All	96.16	89.76	90.53	86.93	81.51	69.26
Armenian-ArmTDP	UDPipe	93.49	82.85	92.86	79.65	72.3	–
(size: 1975)	UDify	94.42	76.9	85.63	87.01	79.99	–
	Multi-w-Lang_id	96.02	80.58	86.62	89.06	84.3	–
	Multi-w-Syntax	96.15	83.06	87.19	93.43	86.23	83.55
	Multi-w-Syntax+Semantic	92.3	82.87	86.93	85.35	84.2	71.52
	Multi-w-All	91.5	81.24	85.22	79.53	81.21	60.95
Basque-BDT	UDPipe	96.11	92.48	96.29	86.8	83.55	–
(size: 5396)	UDify	95.45	86.8	90.53	85.47	81.5	–
	Multi-w-Lang_id	96.71	88.85	91.16	88.02	85.28	–
	Multi-w-Syntax	95.45	94.95	98.46	92.96	87.4	88.3

	Multi-w-Syntax+Semantic	95.58	87.18	82.9	88.37	81.11	79.26
	Multi-w-All	93.56	84.17	80.34	84.61	79.0	73.01
Belarusian-HSE (size: 319)	UDPipe	93.63	73.3	87.34	80.44	74.58	–
	UDify	96.12	88.36	93.97	91.08	88.59	–
	Multi-w-Lang_id	97.01	95.77	96.72	93.69	89.9	–
	Multi-w-Syntax	97.13	96.22	96.83	95.59	92.26	83.94
	Multi-w-Syntax+Semantic	96.64	92.73	89.73	91.63	92.88	73.98
	Multi-w-All	95.56	90.76	88.24	86.3	88.83	66.82
Bulgarian-BTB (size: 8907)	UDPipe	98.98	97.82	97.94	95.21	92.18	–
	UDify	96.7	96.57	95.1	95.7	92.58	–
	Multi-w-Lang_id	97.54	97.01	95.4	95.05	92.26	–
	Multi-w-Syntax	97.64	97.3	95.57	96.61	93.46	82.07
	Multi-w-Syntax+Semantic	95.06	93.48	87.06	98.7	94.63	74.77
	Multi-w-All	93.42	92.38	84.14	93.69	92.16	69.3
Buryat-BDT (size: 19)	UDPipe	40.34	32.4	58.17	34.07	20.3	–
	UDify	61.73	47.45	61.03	49.61	27.46	–
	Multi-w-Lang_id	73.25	47.9	61.09	56.98	41.08	–
	Multi-w-Syntax	73.73	54.74	62.8	74.42	58.5	82.69
	Multi-w-Syntax+Semantic	72.56	53.23	59.49	77.17	47.95	71.76
	Multi-w-All	70.76	49.35	56.68	73.23	44.38	63.12
Catalan-AnCora (size: 13123)	UDPipe	98.88	98.37	99.07	95.12	92.96	–
	UDify	98.89	98.34	98.14	95.61	93.69	–
	Multi-w-Lang_id	99.0	98.49	98.22	95.9	93.96	–
	Multi-w-Syntax	99.08	98.58	98.26	96.97	93.55	81.77
	Multi-w-Syntax+Semantic	97.47	95.05	95.29	91.97	90.02	71.06
	Multi-w-All	96.12	93.31	92.87	86.69	87.62	60.62
Chinese-GSD (size: 7994)	UDPipe	94.88	99.22	99.99	85.84	81.7	–
	UDify	93.48	99.31	100.0	92.98	84.66	–
	Multi-w-Lang_id	97.46	93.0	75.43	90.79	86.76	–
	Multi-w-Syntax	97.57	93.83	76.49	94.61	89.19	60.82

	Multi-w-Syntax+Semantic	95.17	93.62	70.49	86.34	91.08	49.85
	Multi-w-All	94.17	91.89	67.93	81.95	88.31	38.65
Coptic-Scriptorium (size: 792)	UDPipe	94.7	96.35	95.49	87.4	82.79	–
	UDify	27.17	52.85	55.71	28.29	11.53	–
	Multi-w-Lang_id	51.24	60.49	58.89	51.29	32.13	–
	Multi-w-Syntax	52.06	65.65	60.7	71.54	53.73	84.55
	Multi-w-Syntax+Semantic	50.62	59.7	59.62	71.52	49.73	75.59
	Multi-w-All	48.95	56.29	57.39	68.19	43.67	64.17
Croatian-SET (size: 6914)	UDPipe	98.13	92.25	97.27	92.45	88.13	–
	UDify	97.89	88.97	97.15	92.98	90.5	–
	Multi-w-Lang_id	98.33	90.66	97.3	94.29	92.07	–
	Multi-w-Syntax	98.42	91.8	97.38	95.65	92.08	81.92
	Multi-w-Syntax+Semantic	97.08	86.49	92.89	95.4	81.97	72.68
	Multi-w-All	96.44	83.45	90.91	90.35	75.32	61.19
Czech-CAC (size: 102993)	UDPipe	99.37	96.34	98.57	93.48	91.2	–
	UDify	98.14	96.55	97.18	94.74	92.77	–
	Multi-w-Lang_id	98.5	96.99	97.33	93.9	92.84	–
	Multi-w-Syntax	98.59	97.29	97.41	96.04	93.82	82.61
	Multi-w-Syntax+Semantic	96.63	94.17	94.72	97.75	87.74	76.35
	Multi-w-All	96.29	90.57	92.35	91.46	85.34	65.28
Czech-CLTT (size: 102993)	UDPipe	98.88	91.59	98.25	87.86	84.99	–
	UDify	99.17	93.66	98.86	93.7	91.97	–
	Multi-w-Lang_id	99.18	94.58	98.88	94.14	91.71	–
	Multi-w-Syntax	99.26	95.19	98.9	95.13	93.7	82.49
	Multi-w-Syntax+Semantic	98.64	91.41	91.24	86.51	89.79	74.57
	Multi-w-All	96.66	88.17	87.53	80.78	86.25	66.55
Czech-FicTree (size: 102993)	UDPipe	98.55	95.87	98.63	93.32	90.16	–
	UDify	98.18	96.36	97.33	95.77	93.98	–
	Multi-w-Lang_id	98.52	96.83	97.47	95.9	93.27	–
	Multi-w-Syntax	98.61	97.15	97.54	95.3	93.52	82.45

	Multi-w-Syntax+Semantic	97.04	95.16	88.41	89.48	94.11	75.34
	Multi-w-All	95.34	92.47	84.58	83.23	87.94	64.9
Czech-PDT (size: 102993)	UDPipe	99.18	97.23	99.02	94.94	92.92	–
	UDify	98.21	98.38	97.55	96.27	93.99	–
	Multi-w-Lang_id	98.54	98.52	97.67	96.08	93.1	–
	Multi-w-Syntax	98.63	98.61	97.74	95.69	94.8	81.59
	Multi-w-Syntax+Semantic	95.22	96.9	94.12	86.46	96.18	71.77
	Multi-w-All	93.41	93.3	91.73	83.01	92.49	65.57
Danish-DDT (size: 4383)	UDPipe	97.78	97.33	97.52	88.25	85.68	–
	UDify	96.02	89.78	91.0	89.76	85.52	–
	Multi-w-Lang_id	97.09	91.34	91.6	92.53	87.77	–
	Multi-w-Syntax	97.2	92.39	91.94	93.76	89.87	82.18
	Multi-w-Syntax+Semantic	96.56	90.73	85.33	93.11	83.86	73.52
	Multi-w-All	95.36	89.03	83.13	87.91	80.49	64.36
Dutch-Alpino (size: 18051)	UDPipe	96.83	96.33	97.09	93.13	90.14	–
	UDify	97.12	92.59	98.23	95.82	92.15	–
	Multi-w-Lang_id	97.82	93.69	98.3	96.25	92.69	–
	Multi-w-Syntax	97.92	94.42	98.34	96.59	93.22	82.11
	Multi-w-Syntax+Semantic	97.58	92.81	90.05	87.22	91.38	74.53
	Multi-w-All	96.59	91.16	88.05	82.43	87.64	64.24
Dutch-LassySmall (size: 18051)	UDPipe	96.5	96.42	97.41	91.82	88.01	–
	UDify	98.89	96.18	93.49	95.73	92.59	–
	Multi-w-Lang_id	99.0	96.68	93.91	96.14	93.95	–
	Multi-w-Syntax	99.08	97.02	94.14	96.05	94.27	82.29
	Multi-w-Syntax+Semantic	96.1	90.53	86.95	85.32	85.91	71.28
	Multi-w-All	94.1	89.36	84.08	82.57	80.57	60.34
English-EWT (size: 25377)	UDPipe	96.29	97.1	98.25	91.21	88.55	–
	UDify	97.73	96.12	95.84	94.64	90.04	–
	Multi-w-Lang_id	98.22	96.63	96.09	93.9	90.07	–
	Multi-w-Syntax	98.32	96.97	96.22	94.76	91.65	81.84

	Multi-w-Syntax+Semantic	95.0	96.22	92.23	88.32	81.7	72.3
	Multi-w-All	94.52	95.07	90.36	81.53	75.82	66.63
English-GUM (size: 25377)	UDPipe	96.02	96.82	96.85	88.4	85.25	–
	UDify	95.44	94.12	93.15	91.01	87.6	–
	Multi-w-Lang_id	96.7	94.96	93.59	92.8	89.74	–
	Multi-w-Syntax	96.82	95.53	93.84	93.3	91.27	82.38
	Multi-w-Syntax+Semantic	96.33	88.65	85.01	91.19	88.07	71.87
	Multi-w-All	95.15	87.52	83.36	88.24	85.02	66.05
English-LinES (size: 25377)	UDPipe	96.91	96.31	96.45	84.79	80.35	–
	UDify	94.55	90.43	94.42	89.56	85.34	–
	Multi-w-Lang_id	96.11	91.88	94.77	91.71	88.13	–
	Multi-w-Syntax	96.23	92.86	94.97	93.51	89.89	82.15
	Multi-w-Syntax+Semantic	92.8	88.52	86.98	83.74	87.1	72.22
	Multi-w-All	92.35	86.44	84.13	79.28	82.34	63.23
English-ParTUT (size: 25377)	UDPipe	96.1	95.51	97.74	91.53	88.51	–
	UDify	96.16	92.61	96.45	94.72	92.02	–
	Multi-w-Lang_id	97.18	93.7	96.65	94.19	92.97	–
	Multi-w-Syntax	97.29	94.43	96.76	94.66	93.07	82.21
	Multi-w-Syntax+Semantic	95.24	87.42	89.92	93.54	87.18	74.59
	Multi-w-All	94.78	84.1	86.6	90.09	82.66	65.91
Estonian-EDT (size: 25749)	UDPipe	97.64	96.23	95.3	88.52	85.7	–
	UDify	96.91	87.45	77.73	91.65	86.97	–
	Multi-w-Lang_id	97.68	89.39	79.3	92.51	87.78	–
	Multi-w-Syntax	98.16	97.34	95.68	93.24	89.49	94.0
	Multi-w-Syntax+Semantic	95.95	88.72	74.83	90.1	86.44	84.33
	Multi-w-All	93.85	85.02	72.23	84.23	84.05	76.18
Finnish-FTB (size: 27198)	UDPipe	96.65	96.62	95.49	90.89	88.1	–
	UDify	94.37	82.8	96.68	88.8	83.21	–
	Multi-w-Lang_id	95.99	85.51	96.86	90.97	85.49	–
	Multi-w-Syntax	96.12	87.33	96.97	94.4	89.35	82.17

	Multi-w-Syntax+Semantic	94.63	85.13	95.54	83.78	86.72	72.11
	Multi-w-All	94.1	83.61	93.65	79.29	82.58	66.5
Finnish-TDT (size: 27198)	UDPipe	97.45	95.43	91.45	90.67	88.25	–
	UDify	94.43	90.48	82.89	86.8	82.41	–
	Multi-w-Lang_id	96.03	91.92	84.08	89.67	85.5	–
	Multi-w-Syntax	96.16	92.89	84.76	92.58	89.15	82.76
	Multi-w-Syntax+Semantic	94.19	87.24	77.24	90.98	88.75	71.47
	Multi-w-All	93.01	83.9	75.86	87.38	83.01	65.01
French-GSD (size: 33399)	UDPipe	97.63	97.13	98.35	91.77	89.18	–
	UDify	99.14	95.42	98.32	94.77	92.85	–
	Multi-w-Lang_id	99.16	96.05	98.38	94.18	92.07	–
	Multi-w-Syntax	99.24	96.47	98.42	95.57	93.09	82.08
	Multi-w-Syntax+Semantic	98.52	93.7	97.28	91.49	92.14	71.13
	Multi-w-All	97.28	91.12	93.64	84.77	87.26	64.84
French-ParTUT (size: 33399)	UDPipe	96.93	94.43	95.7	93.97	91.43	–
	UDify	95.91	95.08	96.52	92.24	88.65	–
	Multi-w-Lang_id	97.8	91.27	92.16	93.67	90.63	–
	Multi-w-Syntax	97.91	92.33	92.47	94.05	91.75	78.07
	Multi-w-Syntax+Semantic	96.92	90.9	88.81	89.36	88.05	66.92
	Multi-w-All	95.29	89.88	84.99	85.83	86.02	58.57
French-Sequoia (size: 33399)	UDPipe	98.79	98.09	98.57	93.84	92.2	–
	UDify	98.11	95.92	95.5	93.15	90.27	–
	Multi-w-Lang_id	98.48	96.47	95.77	93.74	90.82	–
	Multi-w-Syntax	98.57	96.83	95.92	94.37	91.27	82.08
	Multi-w-Syntax+Semantic	95.2	90.06	86.83	88.32	86.32	75.4
	Multi-w-All	93.9	86.61	84.06	82.46	84.06	68.37
French-Spoken (size: 33399)	UDPipe	95.91	100.0	96.92	83.08	77.71	–
	UDify	96.23	98.67	96.59	86.42	81.19	–
	Multi-w-Lang_id	97.23	98.76	96.78	90.28	84.23	–
	Multi-w-Syntax	97.34	98.82	96.89	93.39	88.49	81.8

	Multi-w-Syntax+Semantic	94.08	94.21	87.61	82.96	81.89	75.73
	Multi-w-All	93.18	92.38	83.82	78.53	76.85	69.6
Galician-CTG (size: 2872)	UDPipe	97.84	99.83	98.58	86.66	84.04	–
	UDify	96.51	97.1	97.08	84.88	81.02	–
	Multi-w-Lang_id	97.41	97.45	97.23	88.55	83.49	–
	Multi-w-Syntax	97.52	97.68	97.32	92.77	88.59	82.22
	Multi-w-Syntax+Semantic	96.75	93.95	89.53	91.93	89.52	75.0
	Multi-w-All	95.31	92.51	85.92	87.76	83.59	69.39
Galician-TreeGal (size: 2872)	UDPipe	95.82	93.96	97.06	83.26	78.23	–
	UDify	94.59	80.67	94.93	85.52	78.21	–
	Multi-w-Lang_id	96.13	83.73	95.24	88.31	81.67	–
	Multi-w-Syntax	96.26	85.79	95.42	92.63	85.98	81.8
	Multi-w-Syntax+Semantic	94.16	84.84	88.28	89.43	84.42	69.56
	Multi-w-All	93.12	82.96	85.17	82.64	81.41	58.73
German-GSD (size: 166849)	UDPipe	94.48	90.68	96.8	87.17	82.71	–
	UDify	97.48	96.63	95.23	88.64	85.15	–
	Multi-w-Lang_id	98.06	97.06	95.52	91.49	86.49	–
	Multi-w-Syntax	97.78	90.7	80.19	93.92	89.53	69.14
	Multi-w-Syntax+Semantic	97.85	91.07	94.13	91.44	83.6	59.88
	Multi-w-All	96.76	89.17	90.6	87.22	80.87	54.63
Gothic-PROIEL (size: 3387)	UDPipe	96.61	90.73	94.75	86.61	80.93	–
	UDify	95.55	85.97	80.57	86.37	80.13	–
	Multi-w-Lang_id	96.77	88.16	81.93	88.24	84.09	–
	Multi-w-Syntax	97.7	92.18	92.64	91.62	87.82	90.23
	Multi-w-Syntax+Semantic	95.55	85.73	75.99	90.14	80.92	82.58
	Multi-w-All	93.8	82.53	71.99	84.73	78.59	71.71
Greek-GDT (size: 1662)	UDPipe	97.98	94.96	95.82	92.9	90.59	–
	UDify	97.08	99.97	98.8	95.91	93.62	–
	Multi-w-Lang_id	97.79	99.78	98.83	94.66	93.51	–
	Multi-w-Syntax	97.89	99.87	98.84	96.56	94.05	81.96

	Multi-w-Syntax+Semantic	97.69	92.93	97.88	96.65	87.99	70.44
	Multi-w-All	95.88	89.61	96.23	91.83	85.26	63.61
Hebrew-HTB (size: 5241)	UDPipe	97.02	95.87	97.12	90.4	87.56	–
	UDify	96.21	96.02	97.28	92.14	89.68	–
	Multi-w-Lang_id	97.21	96.55	97.42	93.99	91.55	–
	Multi-w-Syntax	97.32	96.9	97.5	94.2	92.59	82.29
	Multi-w-Syntax+Semantic	97.32	95.77	94.17	92.57	82.66	72.15
	Multi-w-All	96.81	92.77	91.51	87.58	76.24	66.3
Hindi-HDTB (size: 13304)	UDPipe	97.52	94.15	98.67	94.95	91.93	–
	UDify	98.3	92.22	95.86	95.93	92.2	–
	Multi-w-Lang_id	98.6	93.38	96.1	95.47	93.32	–
	Multi-w-Syntax	98.69	94.15	96.24	95.72	92.11	82.27
	Multi-w-Syntax+Semantic	98.5	91.25	87.06	85.1	94.9	76.16
	Multi-w-All	97.47	89.99	84.47	81.16	89.88	67.11
Hungarian-Szeged (size: 910)	UDPipe	95.76	91.75	95.05	84.17	79.86	–
	UDify	96.36	86.16	90.19	91.01	86.21	–
	Multi-w-Lang_id	97.31	88.31	90.85	91.8	88.59	–
	Multi-w-Syntax	97.42	89.76	91.22	94.65	90.96	82.35
	Multi-w-Syntax+Semantic	94.01	84.9	87.63	94.74	81.06	71.86
	Multi-w-All	93.46	81.98	86.48	91.43	74.44	65.56
Indonesian-GSD (size: 4477)	UDPipe	93.69	95.58	99.64	86.54	80.22	–
	UDify	93.36	93.32	98.37	87.75	81.4	–
	Multi-w-Lang_id	95.31	94.29	98.43	90.96	84.62	–
	Multi-w-Syntax	96.82	90.23	91.52	92.83	87.4	76.11
	Multi-w-Syntax+Semantic	92.65	87.9	93.12	88.35	85.84	64.79
	Multi-w-All	91.91	86.23	89.17	85.59	83.36	55.57
Irish-IDT (size: 858)	UDPipe	92.72	82.43	90.48	81.77	73.72	–
	UDify	90.96	82.09	81.08	79.38	70.65	–
	Multi-w-Lang_id	93.72	84.91	82.4	84.27	76.57	–
	Multi-w-Syntax	93.88	86.82	83.16	90.08	82.83	83.97

	Multi-w-Syntax+Semantic	90.39	83.34	81.23	82.63	73.14	76.57
	Multi-w-All	89.53	80.31	78.39	76.84	68.89	71.55
Italian-ISDT (size: 29685)	UDPipe	98.39	98.11	98.66	95.24	93.29	–
	UDify	98.51	98.01	97.72	96.15	94.3	–
	Multi-w-Lang_id	98.74	98.21	97.83	96.57	93.16	–
	Multi-w-Syntax	98.83	98.34	97.89	96.53	94.18	82.27
	Multi-w-Syntax+Semantic	95.14	93.4	94.91	94.87	92.56	71.28
	Multi-w-All	94.13	90.05	90.97	91.84	88.32	62.14
Italian-ParTUT (size: 29685)	UDPipe	98.38	97.77	98.16	93.62	91.45	–
	UDify	99.18	96.69	98.52	95.9	94.05	–
	Multi-w-Lang_id	99.19	97.11	98.57	95.38	94.85	–
	Multi-w-Syntax	99.27	97.39	98.6	96.97	94.76	81.61
	Multi-w-Syntax+Semantic	96.52	90.68	93.6	98.24	89.89	74.21
	Multi-w-All	94.83	88.46	91.05	94.28	87.47	65.06
Japanese-GSD (size: 47926)	UDPipe	98.13	99.98	99.52	95.99	94.66	–
	UDify	98.73	93.44	96.5	95.1	93.43	–
	Multi-w-Lang_id	98.22	94.27	90.14	94.89	93.71	–
	Multi-w-Syntax	98.31	94.93	90.55	95.15	94.23	76.72
	Multi-w-Syntax+Semantic	96.63	91.07	90.11	97.63	91.41	70.03
	Multi-w-All	95.98	90.07	87.13	95.22	88.14	63.07
Kazakh-KTB (size: 31)	UDPipe	55.84	40.4	63.96	55.12	35.2	–
	UDify	91.29	99.58	99.21	74.74	66.63	–
	Multi-w-Lang_id	93.94	99.52	99.21	81.92	72.97	–
	Multi-w-Syntax	94.1	99.48	99.21	88.58	80.55	82.36
	Multi-w-Syntax+Semantic	91.45	96.21	96.02	81.59	80.85	73.43
	Multi-w-All	90.23	93.96	93.1	75.99	74.65	62.45
Korean-GSD (size: 27410)	UDPipe	96.29	99.77	93.4	88.84	85.38	–
	UDify	91.98	99.89	100.0	83.24	75.73	–
	Multi-w-Lang_id	94.4	99.56	99.75	87.17	81.12	–
	Multi-w-Syntax	94.55	99.63	99.59	91.16	84.3	81.2

	Multi-w-Syntax+Semantic	92.58	94.34	92.28	90.01	85.69	68.82
	Multi-w-All	92.18	92.19	89.53	87.41	79.76	63.39
Korean-Kaist (size: 27410)	UDPipe	95.59	100.0	94.3	88.62	86.68	–
	UDify	94.67	99.98	85.89	87.9	84.85	–
	Multi-w-Lang_id	96.19	99.64	86.86	90.58	87.0	–
	Multi-w-Syntax	96.31	99.9	87.42	92.87	89.07	83.56
	Multi-w-Syntax+Semantic	94.16	97.98	81.44	94.07	80.1	75.91
	Multi-w-All	93.34	95.61	77.72	88.69	74.55	68.58
Kurmanji-MG (size: 20)	UDPipe	53.36	41.54	69.58	46.16	35.25	–
	UDify	60.23	37.78	58.08	36.98	21.52	–
	Multi-w-Lang_id	74.25	55.98	63.82	64.24	44.36	–
	Multi-w-Syntax	74.72	61.74	65.41	78.91	60.28	85.67
	Multi-w-Syntax+Semantic	72.44	60.99	58.85	72.01	61.32	73.28
	Multi-w-All	71.18	60.04	55.01	66.12	58.02	66.53
Latin-ITTB (size: 34060)	UDPipe	98.34	96.97	98.99	92.35	90.09	–
	UDify	97.71	88.63	94.0	93.22	90.69	–
	Multi-w-Lang_id	98.21	90.38	94.38	94.19	91.25	–
	Multi-w-Syntax	97.8	95.01	94.73	95.24	91.82	82.42
	Multi-w-Syntax+Semantic	97.18	87.84	85.95	88.24	92.54	75.68
	Multi-w-All	96.76	85.14	82.36	84.01	87.23	64.79
Latin-Perseus (size: 34060)	UDPipe	88.4	79.1	81.45	72.86	62.94	–
	UDify	91.5	83.21	80.84	80.24	72.19	–
	Multi-w-Lang_id	94.08	85.85	82.18	84.84	78.38	–
	Multi-w-Syntax	94.24	87.63	82.95	90.66	82.9	83.56
	Multi-w-Syntax+Semantic	90.67	84.65	78.08	91.71	84.56	73.65
	Multi-w-All	90.08	81.38	74.86	86.87	77.64	64.8
Latin-PROIEL (size: 34060)	UDPipe	97.01	91.53	96.32	84.97	80.29	–
	UDify	96.79	89.49	91.79	85.89	81.56	–
	Multi-w-Lang_id	97.6	91.1	92.33	87.94	85.54	–
	Multi-w-Syntax	96.89	89.63	82.71	93.14	88.1	74.65

	Multi-w-Syntax+Semantic	94.25	87.77	89.66	87.03	80.45	65.26
	Multi-w-All	93.56	84.81	86.89	83.26	77.58	56.93
Latvian-LVTB (size: 10156)	UDPipe	96.11	93.01	95.46	87.6	83.75	–
	UDify	97.5	95.41	94.6	88.94	85.68	–
	Multi-w-Lang_id	98.07	96.04	94.94	91.26	87.31	–
	Multi-w-Syntax	97.74	90.55	93.44	93.79	90.15	81.29
	Multi-w-Syntax+Semantic	97.47	91.74	86.86	87.64	79.88	71.0
	Multi-w-All	95.4	88.6	84.17	84.92	74.62	65.49
Lithuanian-HSE (size: 2494)	UDPipe	81.7	60.47	76.89	53.52	43.71	–
	UDify	90.49	71.84	81.27	81.15	70.38	–
	Multi-w-Lang_id	93.39	74.81	69.51	85.29	76.17	–
	Multi-w-Syntax	93.56	78.07	70.84	90.47	81.32	74.84
	Multi-w-Syntax+Semantic	91.27	77.81	65.57	83.26	80.25	64.85
	Multi-w-All	90.6	76.85	62.99	77.68	76.15	54.86
Maltese-MUDT (size: 1123)	UDPipe	95.99	100.0	100.0	86.18	81.24	–
	UDify	90.56	99.63	82.84	84.65	76.17	–
	Multi-w-Lang_id	93.45	99.48	84.04	88.21	80.22	–
	Multi-w-Syntax	93.62	99.4	84.72	92.02	85.5	82.93
	Multi-w-Syntax+Semantic	92.66	93.39	80.36	83.99	81.66	75.95
	Multi-w-All	92.39	90.17	77.56	77.68	78.32	65.6
Marathi-UFAL (size: 373)	UDPipe	80.1	67.23	81.31	71.59	62.37	–
	UDify	94.29	84.49	87.71	76.46	69.34	–
	Multi-w-Lang_id	95.93	86.92	88.55	82.65	76.35	–
	Multi-w-Syntax	96.06	88.56	89.03	88.99	82.35	82.7
	Multi-w-Syntax+Semantic	94.22	86.29	82.01	83.57	76.35	73.14
	Multi-w-All	93.6	82.85	80.63	77.5	73.46	66.84
Norwegian-Bokmaal (size: 33282)	UDPipe	98.31	97.14	98.64	93.07	91.17	–
	UDify	98.34	91.82	98.13	96.37	93.95	–
	Multi-w-Lang_id	98.63	93.04	98.21	95.16	93.86	–
	Multi-w-Syntax	98.72	93.86	98.25	95.93	92.85	82.54

	Multi-w-Syntax+Semantic	98.67	88.01	92.42	92.62	88.51	76.51
	Multi-w-All	97.17	86.85	89.65	87.88	83.47	66.37
Norwegian-Nynorsk (size: 33282)	UDPipe	98.14	97.02	98.18	93.71	91.63	–
	UDify	97.83	96.17	97.34	95.08	92.93	–
	Multi-w-Lang_id	98.29	96.68	97.48	94.66	92.82	–
	Multi-w-Syntax	98.38	97.01	97.55	96.47	93.01	82.47
	Multi-w-Syntax+Semantic	98.11	96.32	90.59	87.94	85.1	71.03
	Multi-w-All	96.65	95.16	88.84	85.59	79.94	64.62
Norwegian-NynorskLIA (size: 33282)	UDPipe	89.59	86.13	93.93	69.27	61.26	–
	UDify	95.01	93.36	96.13	75.8	70.0	–
	Multi-w-Lang_id	96.41	94.33	96.35	82.11	76.21	–
	Multi-w-Syntax	96.54	94.98	96.48	89.43	82.32	82.45
	Multi-w-Syntax+Semantic	96.47	91.97	93.68	84.95	71.57	75.39
	Multi-w-All	94.4	88.52	92.04	81.15	65.31	66.05
Persian-Seraji (size: 4798)	UDPipe	97.75	97.78	97.44	91.68	88.29	–
	UDify	96.22	94.73	92.55	91.21	87.46	–
	Multi-w-Lang_id	97.22	95.47	93.04	93.1	89.74	–
	Multi-w-Syntax	98.19	92.08	87.04	95.54	91.46	76.91
	Multi-w-Syntax+Semantic	95.33	89.81	89.63	85.58	88.76	65.78
	Multi-w-All	95.08	88.41	86.93	79.6	84.56	56.29
Polish-LFG (size: 31496)	UDPipe	98.8	95.49	97.54	96.77	94.95	–
	UDify	98.97	96.29	94.47	96.82	95.12	–
	Multi-w-Lang_id	99.05	96.78	94.82	96.24	94.76	–
	Multi-w-Syntax	99.13	97.1	95.01	96.58	94.42	82.34
	Multi-w-Syntax+Semantic	95.77	95.71	90.4	97.59	94.27	75.21
	Multi-w-All	95.55	92.96	88.51	92.51	90.71	64.28
Portuguese-Bosque (size: 17992)	UDPipe	97.07	96.4	98.46	91.48	89.16	–
	UDify	97.54	89.36	85.46	93.38	88.75	–
	Multi-w-Lang_id	98.1	90.99	86.46	92.93	90.17	–
	Multi-w-Syntax	97.33	95.97	93.31	93.61	91.43	88.42

	Multi-w-Syntax+Semantic	97.25	86.0	86.6	85.0	87.72	78.71
	Multi-w-All	96.86	83.66	85.4	82.64	85.66	72.05
Portuguese-GSD (size: 17992)	UDPipe	98.31	99.92	99.3	94.28	92.9	–
	UDify	98.04	95.75	98.95	96.21	94.53	–
	Multi-w-Lang_id	98.43	96.32	98.97	95.64	95.03	–
	Multi-w-Syntax	98.52	96.71	98.98	96.08	94.67	82.17
	Multi-w-Syntax+Semantic	94.99	90.1	91.69	89.47	84.48	74.26
	Multi-w-All	93.54	88.1	88.37	85.86	79.15	65.18
Romanian-Nonstandard (size: 21782)	UDPipe	96.68	90.88	94.78	90.07	85.15	–
	UDify	96.85	87.24	92.7	89.73	86.45	–
	Multi-w-Lang_id	97.64	89.22	93.17	92.32	89.02	–
	Multi-w-Syntax	98.17	96.46	95.13	94.02	90.33	84.2
	Multi-w-Syntax+Semantic	95.03	86.69	87.79	94.45	92.69	76.75
	Multi-w-All	94.77	84.06	84.24	89.51	86.1	67.56
Romanian-RRT (size: 21782)	UDPipe	97.96	97.53	98.41	92.72	88.15	–
	UDify	96.94	93.41	94.15	93.43	89.91	–
	Multi-w-Lang_id	97.7	94.37	94.52	93.95	91.22	–
	Multi-w-Syntax	98.31	91.55	94.59	94.39	91.86	82.46
	Multi-w-Syntax+Semantic	97.79	88.58	92.66	96.92	89.67	74.87
	Multi-w-All	96.92	85.79	91.08	91.81	85.74	63.73
Russian-GSD (size: 54099)	UDPipe	97.1	92.66	97.37	89.47	85.69	–
	UDify	97.44	95.13	86.56	89.8	86.94	–
	Multi-w-Lang_id	98.03	95.81	87.48	91.44	88.86	–
	Multi-w-Syntax	98.13	96.26	88.01	92.79	90.68	83.44
	Multi-w-Syntax+Semantic	97.55	90.07	87.88	94.22	88.19	73.55
	Multi-w-All	96.62	86.43	84.78	91.21	83.72	64.12
Russian-SynTagRus (size: 54099)	UDPipe	99.12	97.57	98.53	95.22	93.74	–
	UDify	97.46	89.3	93.8	97.35	95.3	–
	Multi-w-Lang_id	98.04	90.94	94.19	96.42	94.06	–
	Multi-w-Syntax	98.14	92.04	94.42	96.6	95.49	82.8

	Multi-w-Syntax+Semantic	96.47	91.56	85.24	97.58	95.59	73.68
	Multi-w-All	95.69	88.9	82.75	94.32	92.34	65.16
Russian-Taiga (size: 54099)	UDPipe	93.18	82.87	89.99	76.81	70.47	–
	UDify	95.39	88.47	90.19	85.05	78.83	–
	Multi-w-Lang_id	96.67	90.24	90.85	87.91	83.11	–
	Multi-w-Syntax	96.79	91.44	91.22	92.4	86.68	82.88
	Multi-w-Syntax+Semantic	94.62	84.64	81.78	93.23	76.18	74.81
	Multi-w-All	92.94	82.19	79.46	89.74	71.12	68.8
Serbian-SET (size: 3328)	UDPipe	98.33	94.35	97.36	93.68	90.25	–
	UDify	97.67	97.66	95.44	95.19	92.17	–
	Multi-w-Lang_id	98.18	97.92	95.71	94.34	93.51	–
	Multi-w-Syntax	98.28	98.09	95.87	95.15	92.72	81.84
	Multi-w-Syntax+Semantic	96.82	92.0	94.62	97.62	95.09	69.71
	Multi-w-All	96.12	90.24	91.3	93.18	88.4	62.96
Slovak-SNK (size: 8483)	UDPipe	96.83	90.82	96.4	90.77	87.85	–
	UDify	98.8	87.71	94.04	97.1	95.01	–
	Multi-w-Lang_id	98.94	89.61	94.42	96.52	94.48	–
	Multi-w-Syntax	99.02	90.89	94.63	97.19	94.18	82.57
	Multi-w-Syntax+Semantic	98.24	89.32	86.29	93.11	97.1	72.51
	Multi-w-All	96.77	86.76	82.84	87.17	90.83	61.05
Slovenian-SSJ (size: 8556)	UDPipe	98.61	95.92	98.25	93.75	91.95	–
	UDify	97.72	93.29	89.43	95.75	93.57	–
	Multi-w-Lang_id	98.89	94.4	96.7	94.78	93.36	–
	Multi-w-Syntax	98.97	95.03	96.81	96.14	93.33	88.09
	Multi-w-Syntax+Semantic	98.01	94.46	96.56	99.07	95.06	75.63
	Multi-w-All	96.0	92.62	92.86	93.82	92.85	66.03
Slovenian-SST (size: 8556)	UDPipe	93.79	86.28	95.17	74.89	68.89	–
	UDify	95.4	89.81	95.15	80.89	75.55	–
	Multi-w-Lang_id	96.67	91.36	95.45	86.08	79.37	–
	Multi-w-Syntax	96.79	92.41	95.61	90.85	84.94	82.51

	Multi-w-Syntax+Semantic	94.89	91.45	89.54	93.06	77.71	71.56
	Multi-w-All	93.25	89.92	87.1	89.35	72.92	66.05
Spanish-AnCora (size: 28492)	UDPipe	98.91	98.49	99.17	92.85	90.77	–
	UDify	98.53	97.89	98.07	94.72	92.23	–
	Multi-w-Lang_id	98.76	98.11	98.15	94.35	92.69	–
	Multi-w-Syntax	98.84	98.26	98.2	95.05	92.43	82.47
	Multi-w-Syntax+Semantic	98.49	94.01	90.46	86.57	82.26	74.49
	Multi-w-All	97.12	91.6	88.9	82.45	80.2	68.69
Spanish-GSD (size: 28492)	UDPipe	96.85	97.09	98.97	92.14	89.46	–
	UDify	97.1	89.7	91.6	92.22	88.69	–
	Multi-w-Lang_id	97.15	90.15	94.35	92.4	89.44	–
	Multi-w-Syntax	97.26	91.36	94.57	95.03	92.11	84.76
	Multi-w-Syntax+Semantic	96.27	88.24	86.95	88.19	90.98	77.8
	Multi-w-All	95.32	87.05	83.41	84.96	87.81	67.84
Swedish-LinES (size: 7479)	UDPipe	96.78	89.43	97.03	86.97	82.76	–
	UDify	96.83	88.89	89.33	91.31	86.21	–
	Multi-w-Lang_id	97.63	90.59	90.05	93.03	88.63	–
	Multi-w-Syntax	97.73	91.74	90.46	94.14	89.37	82.74
	Multi-w-Syntax+Semantic	96.32	85.52	88.97	95.04	81.05	72.38
	Multi-w-All	94.5	84.43	85.93	88.81	75.54	64.43
Swedish-Talbanken (size: 7479)	UDPipe	97.94	96.86	98.01	90.73	87.71	–
	UDify	98.48	95.81	98.08	92.92	90.61	–
	Multi-w-Lang_id	98.72	96.37	98.16	93.6	91.35	–
	Multi-w-Syntax	98.81	96.75	98.21	93.97	91.65	81.81
	Multi-w-Syntax+Semantic	97.59	91.2	95.15	85.2	88.69	72.94
	Multi-w-All	96.31	88.6	92.99	79.93	86.24	65.96
Tamil-TTB (size: 400)	UDPipe	91.05	87.28	93.92	74.37	66.63	–
	UDify	90.47	70.0	67.17	80.1	70.38	–
	Multi-w-Lang_id	93.4	76.35	82.58	86.07	75.59	–
	Multi-w-Syntax	93.57	79.4	83.33	89.93	83.32	91.56

	Multi-w-Syntax+Semantic	89.6	76.93	82.69	82.85	81.06	81.72
	Multi-w-All	89.4	75.18	81.16	78.94	77.48	71.06
Telugu-MTG (size: 1051)	UDPipe	93.07	99.03	100.0	92.74	86.5	–
	UDify	96.58	91.77	73.55	89.46	84.62	–
	Multi-w-Lang_id	95.39	99.3	99.72	94.52	87.82	–
	Multi-w-Syntax	95.53	99.28	99.93	95.94	90.11	98.97
	Multi-w-Syntax+Semantic	92.4	96.82	94.55	85.87	92.79	88.27
	Multi-w-All	91.8	93.97	90.45	80.01	86.46	81.44
Turkish-IMST (size: 3664)	UDPipe	96.01	92.55	96.01	75.11	68.48	–
	UDify	88.59	59.22	72.82	80.85	69.2	–
	Multi-w-Lang_id	92.14	65.81	74.75	84.77	76.11	–
	Multi-w-Syntax	92.33	70.26	75.85	89.8	81.3	84.15
	Multi-w-Syntax+Semantic	89.85	65.69	69.47	91.52	74.33	77.58
	Multi-w-All	88.44	64.48	65.52	89.05	71.95	71.7
Ukrainian-IU (size: 5496)	UDPipe	97.59	92.66	97.23	90.2	87.16	–
	UDify	98.02	89.67	95.34	95.3	91.01	–
	Multi-w-Lang_id	98.42	91.25	95.62	95.87	91.56	–
	Multi-w-Syntax	98.51	92.31	95.78	95.26	92.1	81.89
	Multi-w-Syntax+Semantic	96.75	91.34	94.79	96.5	81.13	75.05
	Multi-w-All	95.12	87.64	93.36	92.39	78.1	63.56
Urdu-UDTB (size: 4043)	UDPipe	93.66	81.92	97.4	89.41	83.53	–
	UDify	93.8	90.38	88.8	88.3	83.33	–
	Multi-w-Lang_id	95.61	91.84	89.56	89.56	86.99	–
	Multi-w-Syntax	95.74	92.82	89.99	93.24	89.31	83.37
	Multi-w-Syntax+Semantic	94.04	92.7	81.71	84.07	86.3	72.71
	Multi-w-All	93.4	90.32	79.35	80.98	83.0	61.73
Uyghur-UDT (size: 1656)	UDPipe	89.87	88.3	95.31	79.97	68.6	–
	UDify	75.88	70.8	79.7	67.78	50.69	–
	Multi-w-Lang_id	83.67	75.48	81.13	76.91	61.43	–
	Multi-w-Syntax	83.99	78.65	81.94	85.84	73.26	83.4

Corpus	**Model**	**UPOS**	**UFeats**	**Lemmas**	**UAS**	**LAS**	**Typo F1**
	Multi-w-Syntax+Semantic	83.15	72.27	79.1	76.14	74.65	77.17
	Multi-w-All	82.6	69.28	76.9	73.88	72.57	67.9
Vietnamese-VTB (size: 1400)	UDPipe	89.68	99.72	99.55	72.2	64.38	–
	UDify	85.59	65.49	77.18	75.29	64.18	–
	Multi-w-Lang_id	90.14	71.05	78.79	81.82	72.35	–
	Multi-w-Syntax	90.36	74.8	79.71	89.12	78.29	83.13
	Multi-w-Syntax+Semantic	88.68	68.43	71.27	91.0	70.24	73.17
	Multi-w-All	86.7	67.48	69.45	87.18	67.23	68.02

FrameNet and Linguistic Typology

Michael Ellsworth, Collin F. Baker, and **Miriam R. L. Petruck**
International Computer Science Institute
{infinity, collinb, miriamp}@ icsi.berkeley.edu

Abstract

FrameNet and the Multilingual FrameNet project have produced multilingual semantic annotations of parallel texts that yield extremely fine-grained typological insights. Moreover, frame semantic annotation of a wide cross-section of languages can provide information on the limits of Frame Semantics (Fillmore, 1982, 1985). Multilingual semantic annotation offers critical input for research on linguistic diversity and recurrent patterns in computational typology. Drawing on results from FrameNet annotation of parallel texts, this paper proposes frame semantic annotation as a new component to complement the state of the art in computational semantic typology.[1]

1 Introduction

For some time, typologists and cognitive linguists have explored and discovered recurring cross-linguistic semantic patterns of differences across languages. Talmy (2000) characterized languages as *verb framing* or *satellite framing*, depending on the locus of path information in descriptions of motion events. Nichols et al. (2004) studied basic verbs and their causative counterparts (*sit, seat*; *fall, drop*) in 80 languages, determining just four ways of treating the realization of intransitives/transitives as basic/derived. Croft's (2012) model of event structure for aspect and argument structure in diverse languages presents the *causal chain* as the primary semantic factor in argument realization of simple verbs.

How many such recurring patterns exist? How are such patterns related to each other? Because these and many other questions remain open, we suggest that annotation with **semantic frames** can help to find semantic universals and language-specific exceptions, just as syntactic annotation is useful for investigating syntactic typology. Such semantic frames may be very general or quite specific, depending on the nature of the research.

The goal of Computational Typology is "the development of robust language technology applicable across the world's languages" (Dubossarsky et al., 2019). As such, the computational linguistics world must exploit all resources that contribute to the community's understanding of typological phenomena in those languages. FrameNet (FN) and its related projects in diverse languages are underutilized resources that must be a part of an inclusive drive to model semantic typology.

The rest of this paper proceeds as follows here: Section 2 presents FrameNet and Multilingual FN; Section 3 describes a FN study showing typological differences across diverse languages; Section 4 describes another crosslinguistic annotation study; Section 5 discusses crosslinguistic comparability of frames and presents **ViToXF**, a frame alignment visualization tool; and finally, Section 6 concludes the paper.

2 Background

2.1 FrameNet

FrameNet (Ruppenhofer et al., 2016) is a research and resource development project in corpus-based computational lexicography grounded in the theory of **Frame Semantics** (Fillmore, 1985).

At the heart of the work is the **semantic frame**, a script-like knowledge structure that facilitates inferencing within and across events, situations, states-of-affairs, relations, and objects. FN defines a semantic frame in terms of its **frame elements**

[1]Frame Semantics is distinct from PropBank and Unified Meaning Representation (UMR), a typologically-informed annotation scheme, both only peripherally addressing representing predicate-specific roles analogous to FrameNet's frame-specific FEs. PropBank has a feature termed *framefiles* that UMR inherited. These *framefiles* are syntactic in nature, bearing no relation to FrameNet's semantic frames. As developers of UMR agree, Frame Semantics is not fully integrated into Computational Typology (Gysel et al., To Appear in *Künstliche Intelligenz*).

Proceedings of the Third Workshop on Computational Typology and Multilingual NLP, pages 61–66
June 10, 2021. ©2021 Association for Computational Linguistics

(FEs), or participants (and other concepts) in the scene that the frame captures; a **lexical unit** (LU) is a pairing of a lemma and a frame, characterizing that LU in terms of the frame that it evokes.

Example 1 illustrates annotation for the verb **BUY**, which FN defines in the `Commerce_buy` frame, with the FEs BUYER, SELLER, GOODS, and MONEY.[2]

1. Chuck BUYER **BOUGHT** a car GOODS from Jerry SELLER for $2,000 MONEY

Along with frames and their associated annotations, FN employs a set of **Frame-to-Frame Relations** to link semantically related frames into a set of frame hierarchies, including Inheritance, Subframe, Precedes, Perspective_on, Inchoative_of, and Causative_of. For instance, FN defines the frame `Commerce_buy` as Inheriting from `Getting` and holding a Perspective_on relation to `Commerce_goods_transaction`, which is a Subframe of `Commercial_transaction`. `Commerce_sell` has the same relations, but it inherits from `Giving` (not `Getting`). Table 1 lists FN's frame-to-frame relations.

Relation	Superframe	Subframe
Inheritance	Parent	Child
Subframe	Complex	Component
Precedes	Earlier	Later
Using	Parent	Child
Perspective_on	Neutral	Perspectivized
See_also	Main Entry	Referring Entry
Metaphor	Source	Target
Inchoative_of	Inchoative	State
Causative_of	Causative	Inchoative/State

Table 1: Frame-to-Frame Relations

2.2 Multilingual FrameNet (MLFN)

Do semantic frames represent universals of human language or are they language specific characterizations of the lexicon? Despite many and varied language-specific patterns of expression, the successful development of FN-type resources for typologically distinct languages leads to the conclusion that many frames constitute appropriate characterizations of events, situations, etc., across typologically diverse languages, especially frames for basic human experiences, like eating, drinking, and sleeping. Even frames for cultural practices are similar across languages; for instance, all commercial transactions, regardless of culture, involve the same participants (or frame elements) defined for English *buy*.[3]

Berkeley FrameNet (BFN) has inspired the development of numerous comparable resources for languages other than English.[4] While the methods to develop these resources have differed, each project creating frames based on its own linguistic data, all consider how they compare with BFN's frames for the lexicon of English (Boas, 2009). Table 2 lists the number of frames and LUs for languages available with the MLFN tool (Gilardi and Baker, 2018), **ViToXF** (Visualization Tool across Frames). The tool visualizes a comparison of BFN's English to frame resources for each of seven other languages (See Section 5).

Project	# Frames	# LUs
FrameNet (BFN)	1,224	13,675
Chinese FN	1,259	20,551
FN Brasil (PT)	1,092	2,896
French FN (Asfalda)	148	2,590
German FN (SALSA)	1,023	1,826
Japanese FN	984	3392
Spanish FN	1,196	11,352
Swedish FN	1,186	38,749

Table 2: Sizes of FrameNets accessible in **ViToXF**

3 Typology via Frames

Translations attempt meaning equivalence; so, expecting them to evoke the same frames as the original text seems reasonable. Yet, an analysis of frame mismatch (Ellsworth et al., 2006) reveals typological differences in motion and location vocabulary across languages. The annotation of Chapter 14 of *The Hound of the Baskervilles* (Doyle, 1902) in English, Japanese, Spanish, and German demonstrated that even a modest amount of annotation confirmed known typological differences between English and Ger-

[2]This paper uses these typographical conventions: Frame names are in `typewriter font`; FE Names are in SMALL CAPS; and lexical units are in **BOLD CAPS.**

[3]This point still allows the possibility of monotransitive predicates in giving events. In this cross-linguistically rare conceptualization of giving, recipients are encoded as possessors of the transferred object (as in English "gave his book", meaning "gave him a book")(Daniel, 2006). A recipient is semantically relevant, even if encoded monotransitively. Frame Semantics can encode the relationship in both types of giving events by creating a new frame with a Perspective_on relation to `Giving`.

[4]Global FrameNet serves as an umbrella for more than 12 such language resources.

man as satellite-framing languages vs. Spanish and (less so) Japanese as verb-framing ones.[5] The annotation also showed several patterns unrelated to these typologies. Consider example 2a, showing an original sentence; 2b is the text of one Japanese translation, and 2c is a (fairly literal) back-translation of the Japanese.[6] In this case, while the Japanese (2) does show a verb-framed clause ("這う" 'crawl on') compared to a satellite-framed clause with a manner verb in English ("came **crawling** round..."), it also profiles an entirely different concept of visibility, i.e. the extent to which a sentence shows that some focal part of a scene is visible to the speaker. We hypothesize that the cline of saliency of visibility may be comparable to the cline of saliency of manner (Slobin, 2004).

2. (a) As we watched it the fog-wreaths [came $_{\texttt{Motion}}$] [crawling $_{\texttt{Self\_motion}}$] [round $_{\texttt{Path}}$] both corners of the house and [rolled $_{\texttt{Moving\_in\_place}}$] slowly into one dense bank.

   (b) やがて [あたりは (all_around) $_{\texttt{Locative\_relation}}$] 一面にうす [ぼやけて (became_blurry) $_{\texttt{*Change\_visibility}}$]、しだいに霧のなかへ [まきこまれて (wrap_up) $_{\texttt{Filling}}$] いったが、ことに白い霧がひくく地を[這う (crawl on) $_{\texttt{Self\_motion}}$] ので

   (c) **Translation:** 'Eventually the whole area **became slightly blurry**, and was gradually wrapped up in the fog, especially as the white fog crept low along the ground.'

Japanese consistently makes visibility explicit when other languages leave visibility as an inference from the location and nature of objects (2b vs. 2a). A large sample would show whether this phenomenon is an artifact of the sample (due to stylistics of a particular translation or the nature of the text) or a regular difference between Japanese and the other languages. Still, these results are suggestive.

To the best of our knowledge, typologists have not proposed a feature to distinguish languages based on the preferential encoding of visibility in this way. The frames approach holds power in its ability to code for vastly different domains simultaneously within the same framework.

4 Parallel Annotation of TED Talk

Building on results from the *Hound* study and the expansion of FrameNet-related projects, Global FN teams each annotated their own language's version of a TED talk "Do Schools Kill Creativity?"[7] in English, Portuguese, Japanese, and French. Since annotations with different frame inventories are hard to compare (Section 5), the teams agreed only to use the frames and LUs from Berkeley FrameNet (BFN) Release 1.7. If annotators found an appropriate BFN frame, they annotated the target language text with the BFN frame. If not, they marked the phrase with the closest available BFN frame, recording the discrepancy.

However, this exercise had problems. The policy called for teams to annotate the text completely, yet each understood "complete annotation" differently. Also, although the English was a fairly exact transcription of the original talk, versions in other languages were briefer than a full translations would be, since they were intended as subtitles and had to match the video stream timing (Ohara, 2020).

The TED annotation reinforced a key finding of the *Hound* study: even with an available equivalent frame, the translated phrase may evoke a different target frame, a phenomenon known as a *frame shift*, analogous to *translation shift* (Čulo et al., 2012). Consider # 3, where two English sentences (3a) translate into a single sentence of Japanese (3b). (Partial annotation of this sentence appears in # 4 and # 5, below. As in example # 2, # 3c is a back-translation from the Japanese.)

3. (a) If you think of it, children starting school this year will be retiring in 2065. Nobody has a clue, despite all the expertise that's been on parade for the past four days, what the world will look like in five years' time.[8]

   (b) 今年小学校に入学する子供たちは２０６５年に定年を迎えます

[5] An experienced frame semanticist and native speaker of each language did the annotation.

[6] An asterisk (*) before a frame name indicates that the frame does not yet exist in published FrameNet.

[7] Ken Robinson, 2006, `https://www.ted.com/talks/sir_ken_robinson_do_schools_kill_creativity`

[8] In the audio, the word *five* has contrastive stress.

が、TEDに集まるあらゆる分野のエキスパートをもってしても５年先の世界ですらわかりません。

(c) **Translation:** 'Children enrolling in elementary school this year will reach retirement age in 2065, but even with the experts in every possible field gathered at TED, we don't even know about the world five years from now.'

This short passage includes several examples of frame shift. The first English sentence (roughly, the first Japanese clause) treats *school* as the activities that occur in the building, evoking `Activity_start`, while Japanese specifies that it is an elementary school, treating it as an organization of which *children* become a part, evoking `Becoming_a_member`. An alternative analysis treats the whole phrase 'enroll in elementary school' as a multiword expression, evoking `Activity_start`, as in English.[9]

4. (a) [children AGENT] [starting Activity start] [school ACTIVITY]

   (b) [小学校に (in elementary school) GROUP][入学する (enroll) Becoming a member] [子供たちは (children) NEW MEMBER]

The English verb phrase repeated in 5a uses the one word *retiring* that evokes the frame `Quitting`. The Japanese 5b uses 定年を迎えます, analyzable either as a multiword expression (also evoking `Quitting`) or separately as 定年 (*teinen*) 'fixed year' and 迎えます (*mukaemasu*) 'welcome/go to meet'. Since Japanese workers generally retire at age 60, *teinen* has come to mean 'fixed retirement age'. The highly entrenched collocation with *mukaemasu* can imply happiness about reaching one's goal, as if meeting with a friend. Analyzed as such, *mukaemasu* evokes a motion frame and a backgrounded emotion frame,[10] with *teinen* the (metaphorical) GOAL.

5. (a) [children starting school this year EMPLOYEE] will be [retiring Quitting] [in 2065 TIME]

   (b) [今年小学校に入学する子供たちは EMPLOYEE] [2065 年に TIME] [定年を迎えます Quitting]

Such data suggest that detecting frame shifts facilitates recognizing precise cultural and conceptual differences across languages. The examples above are quite specific, but form part of larger conceptual systems reflected in the lexicon of each language, such as the system of terms for older/younger classmates partially shared across Chinese, Japanese, and Korean (Davies and Ikeno, 2002). Frame annotation can help typologists take advantage of many such patterns. Work is also underway on a system to predict frame shifts, based on the TED annotation data.[11]

5 Frame Alignment

Comparing the annotations across FrameNet projects demands raising the question about the extent to which frames are universal. In the individual and joint projects, all FrameNet projects agreed on semantic frames and found BFN frames generally applicable to their language. For example, all languages have a `Self_motion` frame, with MOVER, SOURCE, PATH, and GOAL FEs. Thus, semantic frames provide useful generalizations both over LUs within a language and across languages. However, crosslinguistic frame relations are not limited to equivalence. A language's frames can be broader or narrower than the nearest BFN frame; it even might give a different point of view on a scene.[12]

For example, English *I **LIKE** X*, with its verb in the `Experiencer_focused_emotion` frame translates into Spanish *Me **GUSTA** X* - 'X pleases me' with its verb in the `Experiencer_object` frame. Moreover, as Section 4 indicates, cultural differences may preclude the existence of equivalent frames, e.g., for religious concepts or legal processes, which differ greatly across cultures.

[9]Of course, *school* itself can stand for the institution or organization, the place where this is located, the activity at the school, and for the people via metonymy.

[10]The Japanese *mukaemasu* is highly associated with happiness, which can be encoded in Frame Semantics by placing it in a frame that inherits from `Arriving` and uses `Experiencer_focused_emotion`, a frame that also contains *happily*.

[11]Zheng Xin Yong, personal communication.

[12]The frame-to-frame relation Perspective_on captures different views on a scene in a language (Petruck and de Melo, 2012).

To wit, *sign on* in `Get_a_job` and *hire* in `Hiring` have the Perspective_on relation to `Employment_start`; *sign on* takes the EMPLOYEE's perspective and *hire* takes that of the EMPLOYER.

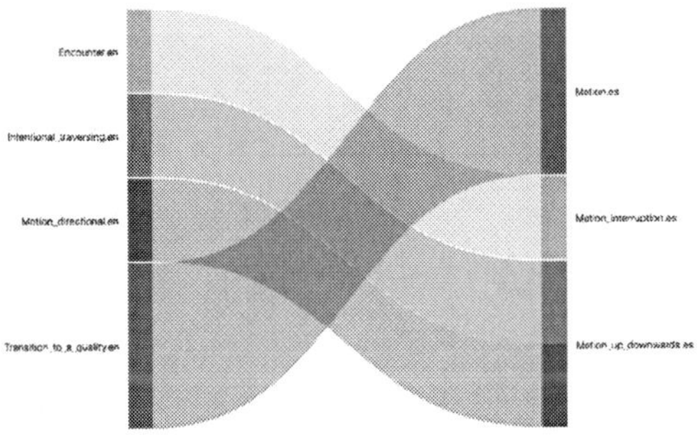

Figure 1: English ⇒ Spanish Motion Frames aligned by LU vector embeddings

The MLFN team developed several different approaches to provide quantitative measures of frame similarity across languages. Some of them rely on finding translation equivalents from the LUs in the BFN frame to those in the target language frame, using Open Multilingual Wordnet (Bond and Foster, 2013). Various measures of set overlap then give a value for the frame similarity. Other approaches use MUSE vector embeddings (Bojanowski et al., 2017); the metric can be either the mean vector similarity of all pairs of LUs in a pair frames in the two languages or the similarity between the mean vector for the LUs in a frame in one language and the same value for a frame in the other. Both approaches are beset with problems caused by the ambiguity of words taken out of context, but nevertheless reveal interesting differences in conceptualization between languages.

The MLFN team also developed a tool to facilitate visualizing cross-linguistic frame similarity, called **ViToXF** (Visualization Tool across FrameNets). The tool provides numerous parameter settings, such as the type of alignment algorithm and the minimum level of similarity to display. Figure 1 shows the tool displaying English and Spanish alignments of motion frames. Baker and Lorenzi (2020) provides details about the alignment algorithms and the parameters of the visualization tool. These data, the tool, and the TED parallel annotation will be available for the workshop.

6 Concluding Remarks

Crosslinguistic frame semantic annotation highlights the tension between language-specific meaning representations and the kind of generalizations that typology needs (Haspelmath, 2020). However, to be useful, the relationships between meanings must be structured to allow the recognition of commonalities and differences. FrameNet relations provide a sufficiently general framework to explore crosslinguistic semantic differences, without prejudging the nature of such relationships. Fine-grained analysis tied to an elaborate frame hierarchy of the sort available in FrameNet allows the viewing of linguistic structures at any level of abstraction from which computational typologists can confirm, refute, or add nuance to existing hypotheses, as well as discover previously unseen semantic patterns.

Acknowledgements

The authors thank Kyoko Ohara for her invaluable input about the Japanese data, Jessica Wong for her reliable annotation of the English TED transcript, Arthur Lorenzi for extracting the alignment data, as well as building the tool, ViToXF, and William Croft for his timely and informative consultation on UMR.

References

Collin F. Baker and Arthur Lorenzi. 2020. Exploring crosslinguistic frame alignment. In *Proceedings of the International FrameNet Workshop 2020: Towards a Global, Multilingual FrameNet*, pages 77–84, Marseille, France. European Language Resources Association.

Hans C. Boas. 2009. *Semantic frames as interlingual representations for multilingual lexical databases*, pages 59–100. Mouton de Gruyter, Berlin.

Piotr Bojanowski, Edouard Grave, Armand Joulin, and Tomas Mikolov. 2017. Enriching word vectors with subword information. *Transactions of the Association for Computational Linguistics*, 5:135–146.

Francis Bond and Ryan Foster. 2013. Linking and extending an Open Multilingual Wordnet. In *Proceedings of the 51st Annual Meeting of the Association for Computational Linguistics (Volume 1: Long Papers)*, pages 1352–1362, Sofia. Association for Computational Linguistics.

William Croft. 2012. *Verbs: Aspect and Causal Structure*. Oxford University Press.

M. Daniel. 2006. Monotransitivity in 'give'-constructions (exploring the periphery of ditransitives). In *Communication to the conference 'Rara and Rarissima'*, Leipzig. MPI.

Roger J. Davies and O. Ikeno. 2002. *The Japanese Mind: Understanding Contemporary Japanese Culture*, chapter Sempai-Kōhai: Seniority Rules in Japanese Relations. Tuttle Publishing.

Arthur Conan Doyle. 1902. *The Hound of the Baskervilles*. George Newnes Ltd, London.

Haim Dubossarsky, Arya D. McCarthy, Edoardo Maria Ponti, Ivan Vulić, Ekaterina Vylomova, Yevgeni Berzak, Ryan Cotterell, Manaal Faruqui, Anna Korhonen, and Roi Reichart, editors. 2019. *Proceedings of TyP-NLP: The First Workshop on Typology for Polyglot NLP*. Association for Computational Linguistics, Florence, Italy.

Michael Ellsworth, Kyoko Ohara, Carlos Subirats, and Thomas Schmidt. 2006. Frame-semantic analysis of motion scenarios in English, German, Spanish, and Japanese. Conference Presentation at the 4th International Conference on Construction Grammar.

Charles J. Fillmore. 1982. Frame semantics. In *Linguistics in the Morning Calm*, pages 111–138. Linguistics Society of Korea, Seoul.

Charles J. Fillmore. 1985. Frames and the semantics of understanding. *Quaderni di Semantica*, 6(2):222–254.

Luca Gilardi and Collin F. Baker. 2018. Learning to align across languages: Toward Multilingual FrameNet. In *Proceedings of the International FrameNet Workshop 2018: Multilingual FrameNets and Constructicons*, pages 13–22. LREC.

Jens E. L. Van Gysel, Meagan Vigus, Jayeol Chun, Kenneth Lai, Sarah Moeller, Jiarui Yao, Tim O'Gorman, Andrew Cowell, William Croft, Chu-Ren Huang, Jan Hajicˇ, James H. Martin, Stephan Oepen, Martha Palmer, James Pustejovsky, Rosa Vallejos, and Nianwen Xue. To Appear in *Künstliche Intelligenz*. Designing a Uniform Meaning Representation for natural language processing.

Martin Haspelmath. 2020. The structural uniqueness of languages and the value of comparison for language description. *Asian Languages and Linguistics*, 1(2):346–366.

Johanna Nichols, A. David Peterson, and Jonathan Barnes. 2004. Transitivizing and detransitivizing languages. *Linguistic Typology*, 8.2:149–211.

Kyoko Ohara. 2020. Finding corresponding constructions in English and Japanese in a TED talk parallel corpus using frames-and-constructions analysis. In *Proceedings of the International FrameNet Workshop 2020: Towards a Global, Multilingual FrameNet*, pages 8–12, Marseille, France. European Language Resources Association.

Miriam R.L. Petruck and Gerard de Melo. 2012. Precedes: A semantic relation in framenet. In *Proceedings of the LREC 2012 Workshop on Language Resources for Public Security Applications*, pages 45–49.

Josef Ruppenhofer, Michael Ellsworth, Miriam R. L. Petruck, Christopher R. Johnson, Collin F. Baker, and Jan Scheffczyk. 2016. *FrameNet II: Extended Theory and Practice*. ICSI: Berkeley.

Daniel Slobin. 2004. *Relating events in narrative, Vol. 2. Typological and contextual perspectives*, chapter The Many Ways to Search for a Frog: Linguistic Typology and the Expression of Motion Events. Lawrence Erlbaum Associates Publishers.

Leonard Talmy. 2000. *Toward a Cognitive Semantics, Vol 1: Concept Structuring Systems, Vol 2: Typology and Process in Concept Structuring*. MIT Press.

Oliver Čulo, Silvia Hansen-Schirra, Karin Maksymski, and Stella Neumann. 2012. Heuristic examination of translation shift. In Silvia Hansen-Schirra, Erich Steiner, Stella Neumann, Silvia Hansen-Schirra, Erich Steiner, and Stella Neumann, editors, *Cross-linguistic Corpora for the Study of Translations Insights from the language pair English—German*, pages 91–130. De Gruyter, Berlin.

Family of Origin and Family of Choice: Massively Parallel Lexiconized Iterative Pretraining for Severely Low Resource Text-based Translation

Zhong Zhou
Carnegie Mellon University
zhongzhou@cmu.edu

Alex Waibel
Carnegie Mellon University
alex@waibel.com

Abstract

We translate a closed text that is known in advance into a severely low resource language by leveraging massive source parallelism. In other words, given a text in 124 source languages, we translate it into a severely low resource language using only ~1,000 lines of low resource data without any external help. Firstly, we propose a systematic method to rank and choose source languages that are close to the low resource language. We call the linguistic definition of language family *Family of Origin* (FAMO), and we call the empirical definition of higher-ranked languages using our metrics *Family of Choice* (FAMC). Secondly, we build an *Iteratively Pretrained Multilingual Order-preserving Lexiconized Transformer* (IPML) to train on ~1,000 lines (~3.5%) of low resource data. To translate named entities correctly, we build a massive lexicon table for 2,939 Bible named entities in 124 source languages, and include many that occur once and covers more than 66 severely low resource languages. Moreover, we also build a novel method of combining translations from different source languages into one. Using English as a hypothetical low resource language, we get a +23.9 BLEU increase over a multilingual baseline, and a +10.3 BLEU increase over our asymmetric baseline in the Bible dataset. We get a 42.8 BLEU score for Portuguese-English translation on the medical EMEA dataset. We also have good results for a real severely low resource Mayan language, Eastern Pokomchi.

1 Introduction

We translate a closed text that is known in advance into a severely low resource language by leveraging massive source parallelism. In other words, we aim to translate well under three constraints: having severely small training data in the new target low resource language, having massive source language parallelism, having the same closed text across all languages. Generalization to other texts is preferable but not necessary in the goal of producing high quality translation of the closed text.

Eastern Pokomchi		English	
FAMD	*FAMP*	*FAMD*	*FAMP*
Chuj*	Dadibi	Danish*	Dutch*
Cakchiquel*	Thai	Norwegian*	Afrikaans*
Guajajara*	Gumatj	Italian	Norwegian*
Toba	Navajo	Afrikaans*	German*
Myanmar	Cakchiquel*	Dutch*	Danish*
Slovenský	Kanjobal	Portuguese	Spanish
Latin	Guajajara*	French	Frisian*
Ilokano	Mam*	German*	Italian
Norwegian	Kim	Marshallese	French
Russian	Chuj*	Frisian*	Portuguese

Table 1: Top ten languages closest to Eastern Pokomchi (left) and English (right) in ranking 124 source languages. *FAMD* and *FAMP* are two constructions of Family of Choice (*FAMC*) by distortion and performance metrics respectively. All are trained on ~1,000 lines. We star those in Family of Origin.

2020 is the year that we started the life-saving hand washing practice globally. Applications like translating water, sanitation, and hygiene (WASH) guidelines into severely low resource languages are very impactful in tribes like those in Papua New Guinea with 839 living languages (Gordon Jr, 2005; Simons and Fennig, 2017). Translating humanitarian texts like WASH guidelines with scarce data and expert help is key (Bird, 2020).

We focus on five challenges that are not addressed previously. Most multilingual transformer works that translate into low resource language limit their training data to available data in the same or close-by language families or the researchers' intuitive discretion; and are mostly limited to less than 30 languages (Gu et al., 2018; Zhou et al., 2018a; Zhu et al., 2020). Instead, we examine ways to pick useful source languages from 124 source languages in a principled fashion. Secondly, most works require at least 4,000 lines of low resource data (Lin et al., 2020; Qi et al., 2018; Zhou et al., 2018a); we use only ~1,000 lines of low resource data to simulate real-life situation of having ex-

Proceedings of the Third Workshop on Computational Typology and Multilingual NLP, pages 67–80
June 10, 2021. ©2021 Association for Computational Linguistics

tremely small seed target translation. Thirdly, many works use rich resource languages as hypothetical low resource languages. Moreover, most works do not treat named entities separately; we add an order-preserving lexiconized component for more accurate translation of named entities. Finally, many multilingual works present final results as sets of translations from all source languages; we build a novel method to combine all translations into one.

We have five contributions. Firstly, we rank the 124 source languages to determine their closeness to the low resource language and choose the top few. We call the linguistic definition of language family *Family of Origin* (FAMO), and we call the empirical definition of higher-ranked languages using our metrics *Family of Choice* (FAMC). They often overlap, but may not coincide.

Secondly, we build an *Iteratively Pretrained Multilingual Order-preserving Lexiconized Transformer* (IPML) training on $\sim$1,000 lines of low resource data. Using iterative pretraining, we get a +23.9 BLEU increase over a multilingual order-preserving lexiconized transformer baseline (MLc) using English as a hypothetical low resource language, and a +10.3 BLEU increase over our asymmetric baseline. Training with the low resource language on both the source and target sides boosts translation into the target side. Training on randomly sampled 1,093 lines of low resource data, we reach a 31.3 BLEU score testing on 30,022 lines of Bible. We have a 42.8 BLEU score for Portuguese-English translation on the medical EMEA dataset.

Thirdly, we use a real-life severely low resource Mayan language, Eastern Pokomchi, a Class 0 language (Joshi et al., 2020) as one of our experiment setups. In addition, we also use English as a hypothetical low resource language for easy evaluation.

We also add an order-preserving lexiconized component to translate named entities well. To solve the variable-binding problem to distinguish "Ian calls Yi" from "Yi calls Ian" (Fodor and Pylyshyn, 1988; Graves et al., 2014; Zhou et al., 2018a), we build a lexicon table for 2,939 Bible named entities in 124 source languages including more than 66 severely low resource languages.

Finally, we combine translations from all source languages by using a novel method. For every sentence, we find the translation that is closest to the translation cluster center. The expectated BLEU score of our combined translation is higher than translation from any of the individual sources.

2 Related Works

2.1 Information Dissemination

Interactive Natural Language Processing (NLP) systems are classified into information assimilation, dissemination, and dialogue (Bird, 2020; Ranzato et al., 2015; Waibel and Fugen, 2008). *Information assimilation* involves information flow from low resource to rich resource language communities while *information dissemination* involves information flow from rich resource to low resource language communities. Taken together, they allow *dialogue* and interaction of different groups at eye level. Most work on information assimilation (Bérard et al., 2020; Earle et al., 2012; Brownstein et al., 2008). Few work on dissemination due to small data, less funding, few experts and limited writing system (Östling and Tiedemann, 2017; Zoph et al., 2016; Anastasopoulos et al., 2017; Adams et al., 2017; Bansal et al., 2017).

2.2 Machine Polyglotism and Pretraining

Recent research on machine polyglotism involves training machines to be adept in many languages by adding language labels in the training data with a single attention (Johnson et al., 2017; Ha et al., 2016; Firat et al., 2016; Gillick et al., 2016; Zhou et al., 2018b). Some explores data symmetry (Freitag and Firat, 2020; Birch et al., 2008; Lin et al., 2019). Zero-shot translation in severely low resource settings exploits the massive multilinguality, cross-lingual transfer, pretraining, iterative back-translation and freezing subnetworks (Lauscher et al., 2020; Nooralahzadeh et al., 2020; Wang et al., 2020; Li et al., 2020; Pfeiffer et al., 2020; Baziotis et al., 2020; Chronopoulou et al., 2020; Lin et al., 2020; Thompson et al., 2018; Luong et al., 2014; Wei et al., 2020; Dou et al., 2020).

2.3 Linguistic Distance

To construct linguistic distances (Hajič, 2000; Oncevay et al., 2020), some explore typological distance (Chowdhury et al., 2020; Rama and Kolachina, 2012; Pienemann et al., 2005; Svalberg and Chuchu, 1998; Hansen et al., 2012; Comrie, 2005), lexical distance (Huang et al., 2007), Levenshtein distance and Jaccard distance (Serva and Petroni, 2008; Holman et al., 2008; Adebara et al., 2020), sonority distance (Parker, 2012) and spectral distance (Dubossarsky et al., 2020).

3 Methodology

3.1 Multilingual Order-preserving Lexiconized Transformer

3.1.1 Multilingual Transformer

In training, each sentence is labeled with the source and target language label. For example, if we translate from Chuj ("ca") to Cakchiquel ("ck"), each source sentence is tagged with `__opt_src_ca` `__opt_tgt_ck`. A sample source sentence is "`__opt_src_ca` `__opt_tgt_ck` Tec'b'ejec e b'a mach ex tzeyac'och Jehová yipoc e c'ool".

We train on Geforce RTX 2080 Ti using ~100 million parameters, a 6-layer encoder and a 6-layer decoder that are powered by 512 hidden states, 8 attention heads, 512 word vector size, a dropout of 0.1, an attention dropout of 0.1, 2,048 hidden transformer feed-forward units, a batch size of 6,000, "adam" optimizer, "noam" decay method, and a label smoothing of 0.1 and a learning rate of 2.5 on OpenNMT (Klein et al., 2017; Vaswani et al., 2017). After 190,000 steps, we validate based on BLEU score with early stopping patience of 5.

3.1.2 Star Versus Complete Configuration

We show two configurations of translation paths in Figure 1: *star* graph (multi-source single-target) configuration and *complete* graph (multi-source multi-target) configuration. The complete configuration data increases quadratically with the number of languages while the star configuration data increases linearly.

3.1.3 Order-preserving Lexiconized transformer

The variable binding problem issue is difficult in severely low resource scenario; most neural models cannot distinguish the subject and the object of a simple sentence like "Fatma asks her sister Wati to call Yi, the brother of Andika", especially when all named entities appear once or never appear in training (Fodor and Pylyshyn, 1988; Graves et al., 2014). Recently, researchers use order-preserving lexiconized Neural Machine Translation models where named entities are sequentially tagged in a sentence as `__NE`s (Zhou et al., 2018a). The previous example becomes "`__NE0` asks her sister `__NE1` to call `__NE2`, the brother of `__NE3`".

This method works under the assumption of translating a closed text known in advance. Its success relies on good coverage of named entities. To cover many named entities, we build on existing

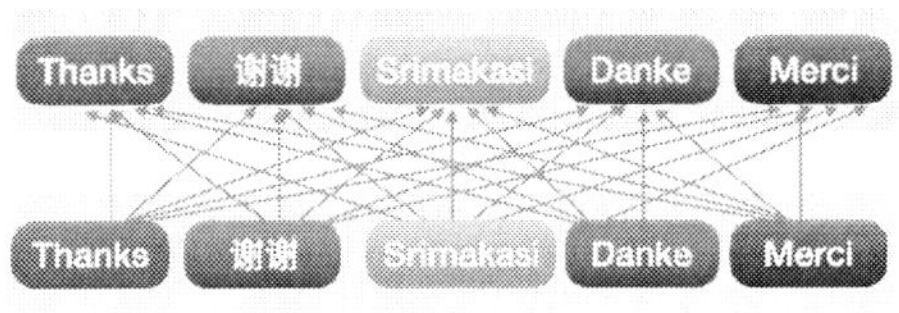

(a) Complete graph configuration

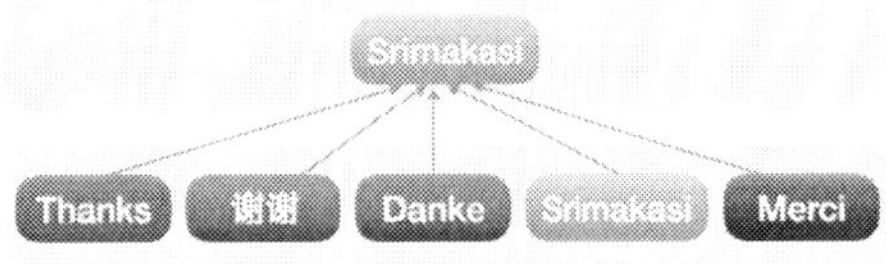

(b) Star graph configuration

Figure 1: (a) Complete graph configuration of translation paths (Many-to-many) in an example of multilingual translation. (b) Star configuration of translation paths (Many-to-one) using Indonesian as the low resource example.

research literature (Wu et al., 2018; Zhou et al., 2018a) to construct a massively parallel lexicon table that covers 2,939 named entities across 124 languages in our Bible database. Our lexicon table is an expansion of the existing literature that covers 1,129 named entities (Wu et al., 2018). We add in 1,810 named entities that are in the extreme end of the tail occurring only once. We also include 66 more real-life severely low resource languages.

For every sentence pair, we build a target named entity decoding dictionary by using all target lexicons from the lexicon table that match with those in the source sentence. In severely low resource setting, our sequence tagging is larged based on dictionary look-up; we also include lexicons that are not in the dictionary but have small edit distances with the source lexicons. In evaluation, we replace all the ordered `__NE`s using the target decoding dictionary to obtain our final translation.

Let us translate "Fatma asks her sister Wati to call Yi, the brother of Andika" to Chinese and German. Our tagged source sentence that translates to Chinese is "`__opt_src_en` `__opt_tgt_zh` `__NE0` asks her sister `__NE1` to call `__NE2`, the brother of `__NE3`"; and we use `__opt_tgt_de` for German. The source dictionary is "`__NE0`: Fatma, `__NE1`: Wati, `__NE2`: Yi, `__NE3`: Andika" and we create the target dictionaries. The Chinese output is "`__NE0`叫她的姐妹`__NE1`去打电话给`__NE3`的兄弟`__NE2`" and the German output is "`__NE0` bittet ihre Schwester `__NE1` darum, `__NE2`, den Bruder `__NE3`, anzurufen". We decode the named entities to get final translations.

3.2 Ranking Source Languages

Existing works on translation from multiple source languages into a single low resource language usually have at most 30 source languages (Gu et al., 2018; Zhou et al., 2018a; Zhu et al., 2020). They are limited within the same or close-by language families, or those with available data, or those chosen based on the researchers' intuitive discretion. Instead, we examine ways to pick useful source languages in a principled fashion motivated by cross-lingual impacts and similarities (Shoemark et al., 2016; Sapir, 1921; Odlin, 1989; Cenoz, 2001; Toral and Way, 2018; De Raad et al., 1997; Hermans, 2003; Specia et al., 2016). We find that using many languages that are distant to the target low resource language may produce marginal improvements, if not negative impact. Indeed, existing literature on zero-shot translation also suffers from the limitation of linguistic distance between the source languages and the target language (Lauscher et al., 2020; Lin et al., 2020; Pfeiffer et al., 2020). We therefore rank and select the top few source languages that are closer to the target low resource language using the two metrics below.

We rank source languages according to their closeness to the low resource language. We construct the Family of Choice (FAMC) by comparing different ways of ranking linguistic distances empirically based on the small low resource data.

Let S_s and S_t be the source and target sentences, let L_s be the source length, let $P(S_t = s_t | s_s, l_s)$ be the alignment probability, let F_s be the fertility of how many target words a source word is aligned to, let D_t be the distortion based on the fixed distance-based reordering model (Koehn, 2009).

We first construct a word-replacement model based on aligning the small amount of target low resource data with that of each source language using `fast_align` (Dyer et al., 2013). We replace every source word with the most probable target word according to the product of the alignment probability and the probability of fertility equalling one and distortion equalling zero $P(F_s = 1, D_t = 0 | s_t, s_s, l_s)$. We choose a simple word-replacement model because we aim to work with around 1,000 lines of low resource data. For fast and efficient ranking on such small data, a word-replacement model suits our purpose.

We use two alternatives to create our FAMCs. Our distortion measure is the probability of distortion equalling zero, $P(D_t = 0 | s_t, s_s, l_s)$, aggregated over all words in a source language. We use the distortion measure to rank the source languages and obtain the distortion-based FAMC (*FAMD*); we use the translation BLEU scores of the word-replacement model as another alternative to build the performance-based FAMC (*FAMP*). In Table 1, we list the top ten languages in FAMD and FAMP for Eastern Pokomchi and English. We use both alternatives to build FAMCs.

To prepare for transformer training, we choose the top ten languages neighboring our target low resource language in FAMD and FAMP. We choose ten because existing literature shows that training with ten languages from two neighboring language families is sufficient in producing quality translation through cross-lingual transfer (Zhou et al., 2018a). Since for some low resource languages, there may not be ten languages in FAMO in our database, we add languages from neighboring families to make an expanded list denoted by *FAMO*$^+$.

3.3 Iterative Pretraining

We have two stages of pretraining using multilingual order-preserving lexiconized transformer on the complete and the star configuration. We design iterative pretraining on symmetric data to address catastrophic forgetting that is common in training (French, 1999; Kirkpatrick et al., 2017).

3.3.1 Stage 1: Pretraining on Neighbors

Firstly, we pretrain on the complete graph configuration of translation paths using the top ten languages neighboring our target low resource language in FAMD, FAMP, and FAMO$^+$ respectively. Low resource data is excluded in training.

We use the multilingual order-preserving lexiconized transformer. Our vocabulary is the combination of the vocabulary for the top ten languages together with the low resource vocabulary built from the $\sim$1,000 lines. The final model can translate from any of the ten languages to each other.

3.3.2 Stage 2: Adding Low Resource Data

We include the low resource data in the second stage of training. Since the low resource data covers $\sim 3.5\%$ of the text while all the source languages cover the whole text, the data is highly asymmetric. To create symmetric data, we align the low resource data with the subset of data from all source languages. As a result, all source languages in the second stage of training have $\sim 3.5\%$ of the text that is aligned with the low resource data.

Source Sentence	IPML Translation	Reference
En terwyl Hy langs die see van Galiléa loop, sien Hy Simon en Andréas, sy broer, besig om 'n net in die see uit te gooi; want hulle was vissers.	And as He drew near to the lake of Galilee, He Simon saw Andrew, and his brother, lying in the lake, for they were fishermen.	And walking along beside the Sea of Galilee, He saw Simon and his brother Andrew casting a small net in the sea; for they were fishers.
En toe Hy daarvandaan 'n bietjie verder gaan, sien Hy Jakobus, die seun van Sebedéüs, en Johannes, sy broer, wat besig was om die nette in die skuit heel te maak.	And being in a distance, He saw James, the son of Zebedee, and John, his brother. who kept the nets in the boat.	And going forward from there a little, He saw James the son of Zebedee, and his brother John. And they were in the boat mending the nets.
En verder Jakobus, die seun van Sebedéüs, en Johannes, die broer van Jakobus- aan hulle het Hy die bynaam Boanérges gegee, dit is, seuns van die donder-	And James the son of Zebedee, and John the brother of James; and He gave to them the name, which is called Boanerges, being of the voice.	And on James the son of Zebedee, and John the brother of James, He put on them the names Boanerges, which is, Sons of Thunder.

Table 2: Examples of Iteratively Pretrained Multilingual Order-preserving Lexiconized Transformer (IPML) translation from Afrikaans to English as a hypothetical low resource language using *FAMP*. We train on only 1,093 lines of English data.

We therefore create a complete graph configuration of training paths using all the eleven languages.

Using the pretrained model from the previous stage, we train on the complete graph configuration of translation paths from all eleven languages including our low resource language. The vocabulary used is the same as before. We employ the multilingual order-preserving lexiconized transformer for pretraining. The final model can translate from any of the eleven languages to each other.

3.4 Final Training

Finally, we focus on translating into the low resource language. We use the symmetric data built from the second stage of pretraining. However, instead of using the complete configuration, we use the star configuration of translation paths from the all source languages to the low resource language. All languages have $\sim 3.5\%$ of the text.

Using the pretrained model from the second stage, we employ the multilingual order-preserving lexiconized transformer on the star graph configuration. We use the same vocabulary as before. The final trained model can translate from any of the ten source languages to the low resource language. Using the lexicon dictionaries, we decode the named entities and obtain our final translations.

3.5 Combination of Translations

We have multiple translations, one per each source language. Combining all translations is useful for both potential post-editting works and systematic comparison of different experiments especially when the sets of the source languages differ.

Our combination method assumes that we have the same text in all source languages. For each sentence, we form a cluster of translations from all source languages into the low resource language. Our goal is to find the translation that is closest to the center of the cluster. We rank all translations according to how centered this translation is with respect to other sentences by summing all its similarities to the rest. The top is closest to the center of the translation cluster. We take the most centered translation for every sentence to build the combined translation output. The expectated BLEU score of our combined translation is higher than translation from any of the individual source languages.

4 Data

We use the Bible dataset and the medical EMEA dataset (Mayer and Cysouw, 2014; Tiedemann, 2012). EMEA dataset is from the European Medicines Agency and contains a lot of medical information that may be beneficial to the low resource communities. Our method can be applied to other datasets like WASH guidelines.

For the Bible dataset, we use 124 source languages with 31,103 lines of data and a target low resource language with ~1,000 lines (~3.5%) of data. We have two setups for the target low resource language. One uses Eastern Pokomchi, a Mayan language; the other uses English as a hypothetical low resource language. We train on only ~1,000 lines of low resource data from the book of Luke and test on the 678 lines from the book of Mark. Mark is topically similar to Luke, but is written by a different author. For the first stage of pretraining, we use 80%, 10%, 10% split for training, validation and testing. For the second stage onwards, we use

95%, 5% split of Luke for training and validation, and 100% of Mark for testing.

Eastern Pokomchi is Mayan, and English is Germanic. Since our database does not have ten members of each family, we use FAMO$^+$, the expanded version of FAMO. For English, we include five Germanic languages and five Romance languages in FAMO$^+$; for Eastern Pokomchi, we include five Mayan languages and five Amerindian languages in FAMO$^+$. The Amerindian family is broadly believed to be close to the Mayan family by the linguistic community.

We construct FAMCs by comparing different ways of ranking linguistic distances empirically based on ~1,000 lines of training data. In Table 1, we list the top ten languages for Eastern Pokomchi and English in FAMD and FAMP respectively.

To imitate the real-life situation of having small seed target translation data, we choose to use ~1,000 lines (~3.5%) of low resource data. We also include Eastern Pokomchi in addition to using English as a hypothetical low resource language. Though data size can be constrained to mimic severely low resource scenarios, much implicit information is still used for the hypothetical low resource language that is actually rich resource. For example, implicit information like English is Germanic is often used. For real low resource scenarios, the family information may have yet to be determined; the neighboring languages may be unknown, and if they are known, they are highly likely to be low resource too. We thus use Eastern Pokomchi as our real-life severely low resouce language.

In addition to the Bible dataset, we work with the medical EMEA dataset (Tiedemann, 2012). Using English as a hypothetical language, we train on randomly sampled 1,093 lines of English data, and test on 678 lines of data. Since there are only 9 languages in Germanic and Romance families in EMEA dataset, we include a slavic language Polish in our FAMO$^+$ for experiments.

The EMEA dataset is less than ideal comparing with the Bible dataset. The Bible dataset contains the same text for all source languages; however, the EMEA dataset does not contain the same text. It is built from similar documents but has different parallel data for each language pair. Therefore, during test time, we do not combine the translations from various source languages in the EMEA dataset.

Experiments	IPML	MLc	MLs	PMLc	PMLs	AML
Pretrained	✓			✓	✓	
Iterative	✓					
Lexiconized	✓	✓	✓	✓	✓	✓
Symmetrical	✓	✓	✓	✓	✓	
Star	✓		✓		✓	
Complete	✓	✓		✓		✓
Combined	37.3	13.4	14.7	34.7	35.7	27.0
German	35.0	11.6	12.3	33.3	34.5	25.4
Danish	36.0	12.5	12.4	33.3	34.2	26.2
Dutch	35.6	11.5	11.1	32.3	33.7	25.0
Norwegian	35.7	12.3	12.0	33.2	34.1	25.8
Swedish	34.5	11.8	12.4	32.3	33.4	24.9
Spanish	36.4	11.7	11.8	34.1	35.0	26.2
French	35.3	10.8	10.8	33.1	34.0	25.8
Italian	35.9	11.7	11.7	34.3	34.5	26.1
Portuguese	31.5	9.6	10.1	30.0	30.4	23.1
Romanian	34.6	11.3	12.1	32.3	33.2	25.0

Table 3: Comparing our iteratively pretrained multilingual order-preserving lexiconized transformer (IPML) with the baselines training on 1,093 lines of English data in *FAMO*$^+$. We checkmark the key components used in each experiments and explain all the baselines in details in Section 5.

5 Results

We compare our iteratively pretrained multilingual order-preserving lexiconized transformer (IPML) with five baselines in Table 3. *MLc* is a baseline model of multilingual order-preserving lexiconized transformer training on complete configuration; in other words, we skip the first stage of pretraining and train on the second stage in Chapter 3.3.2 only. *MLs* is a baseline model of multilingual order-preserving lexiconized transformer training on star configuration; in other words, we skip both steps of pretraining and train on the final stage in Chapter 3.4 only. *PMLc* is a baseline model of pretrained multilingual order-preserving lexiconized transformer training on complete configuration; in other words, we skip the final stage of training after completing both stages of pretraining. *PMLs* is a baseline model of pretrained multilingual order-preserving lexiconized transformer training on star configuration; in other words, after the first stage of pretraining, we skip the second stage of pretraining and proceed to the final training directly. Finally, *AML* is a baseline model of multilingual order-preserving lexiconized transformer on asymmetric data. We replicate the ~1,000 lines of the low resource data till it matches the training size of other source languages; we train on the complete graph configuration using eleven languages. Though the number of low resource training lines is the same as others, information is highly asym-

Input Language Family					
By Linguistics		By Distortion		By Performance	
FAMO$^+$		*FAMD*		*FAMP*	
Source	BLEU	Source	BLEU	Source	BLEU
Combined	37.3	Combined	38.3	Combined	39.4
German	35.0	German	36.7	German	37.6
Danish	36.0	Danish	37.1	Danish	37.5
Dutch	35.6	Dutch	35.6	Dutch	36.7
Norwegian	35.7	Norwegian	36.9	Norwegian	37.1
Swedish	34.5	Afrikaans	38.3	Afrikaans	39.3
Spanish	36.4	Marshallese	34.7	Spanish	38.4
French	35.3	French	36.0	French	36.6
Italian	35.9	Italian	36.9	Italian	37.7
Portuguese	31.5	Portuguese	32.9	Portuguese	33.1
Romanian	34.6	Frisian	36.1	Frisian	36.9

Table 4: Performance of Iteratively Pretrained Multilingual Order-preserving Lexiconized Transformer (IPML) training for English on *FAMO*$^+$, *FAMD* and *FAMP*. We train on only 1,093 lines of English data.

Input Language Family					
By Linguistics		By Distortion		By Performance	
FAMO$^+$		*FAMD*		*FAMP*	
Source	BLEU	Source	BLEU	Source	BLEU
Combined	23.0	Combined	23.1	Combined	22.2
Chuj	21.8	Chuj	21.9	Chuj	21.6
Cakchiquel	22.2	Cakchiquel	22.1	Cakchiquel	21.3
Guajajara	19.7	Guajajara	19.1	Guajajara	18.8
Mam	22.2	Russian	22.2	Mam	21.7
Kanjobal	21.9	Toba	21.9	Kanjobal	21.4
Cuzco	22.3	Myanmar	19.1	Thai	21.8
Ayacucho	21.6	Slovenský	22.1	Dadibi	19.8
Bolivian	22.2	Latin	21.9	Gumatj	19.1
Huallaga	22.2	Ilokano	22.5	Navajo	21.3
Aymara	21.5	Norwegian	22.6	Kim	21.5

Table 5: Performance of Iteratively Pretrained Multilingual Order-preserving Lexiconized Transformer (IPML) training for Eastern Pokomchi on *FAMO*$^+$, *FAMD* and *FAMP*. We train on only 1,086 lines of Eastern Pokomchi data.

metric.

Pretraining is key as IPML beats the two baselines that skip pretraining in Table 3. Using English as a hypothetical low resource language training on FAMO$^+$, combined translation improves from 13.4 (MLc) and 14.7 (MLs) to 37.3 (IPML) with iterative pretraining. Training with the low resource language on both the source and the target sides boosts translation into the target side. Star configuration has a slight advantage over complete configuration as it gives priority to translation into the low resource language. Iterative pretraining with BLEU score 37.3 has an edge over one stage of pretraining with scores 34.7 (PMLc) and 35.7 (PMLs).

All three pretrained models on symmetric data, IPML, PMLc and PMLs, beat asymmetric baseline AML. In Table 3, IPML has a +10.3 BLEU increase over our asymmetric baseline on combined translation using English as a hypothetical low resource language training on FAMO$^+$. All four use the same amount of data, but differ in training strategies and data configuration. In severely low resource scenarios, effective training strategies on symmetric data improve translation greatly.

We compare IPML results training on different sets of source languages in FAMO$^+$, FAMD, and FAMP, for English and Eastern Pokomchi in Table 4 and 5. FAMP performs the best for translation into English while both FAMP and FAMD outperforms FAMO$^+$ as shown in Table 4. FAMD performs best for translation into Eastern Pokomchi as shown in Table 5. Afrikaans has the highest score for English's FAMD and FAMP, outperforming Dutch, German or French. A reason may be that Afrikaans is the youngest language in the Germanic family with many lexical and syntactic borrowings from English and multiple close neighbors of English (Gordon Jr, 2005). When language family information is limited, constructing FAMC to determine neighbors is very useful in translation.

Source	BLEU
Combined	N.A.
German	34.8
Danish	37.7
Dutch	39.7
Swedish	37.7
Spanish	42.8
French	41.6
Italian	39.2
Portuguese	42.8
Romanian	40.0
Polish	34.1

Table 6: IPML Performance on the EMEA dataset trained on only 1,093 lines of English data.

Source	BLEU
Combined	31.3
German	29.4
Danish	28.8
Dutch	29.9
Norwegian	29.7
Swedish	29.0
Spanish	30.3
French	28.9
Italian	29.7
Portuguese	24.4
Romanian	28.8

Table 7: IPML Performance on the entire Bible excluding ~1k lines of training and validation data.

Comparing Eastern Pokomchi results with English results, we see that translation into real-life severely low resource languages is more difficult than translation into hypothetical ones. The combined score is 38.3 for English in Table 4 and 23.1 for Eastern Pokomchi on FAMD in Table 5. Eastern Pokomchi has ejective consonants which makes tokenization process difficult. It is agglutinative, morphologically rich and ergative just like Basque (Aissen et al., 2017; Clemens et al., 2015). It is complex, unique and nontransparent to the out-

Source Sentence	IPML Translation	Reference
Caso detecte efeitos graves ou outros efeitos não mencionados neste folheto, informe o médico veterinário.	If you notice any side effects or other side effects not mentioned in this leaflet, please inform the vétérinaire.	If you notice any serious effects or other effects not mentioned in this leaflet, please inform your veterinarian.
No tratamento de Bovinos com mais de 250 Kg de peso vivo, dividir a dose de forma a não administrar mais de 10 ml por local de injecção.	In the treatment of infants with more than 250 kg in vivo body weight, a the dose to not exceed 10 ml per injection.	For treatment of cattle over 250 kg body weight, divide the dose so that no more than 10 ml are injected at one site.
No entanto, uma vez que é possível a ocorrência de efeitos secundários, qualquer tratamento que exceda as 1-2 semanas deve ser administrado sob supervisão veterinária regular.	However, because any of side effects is possible, any treatment that 1-5 weeks should be administered under regular supraveghere.	However, since side effects might occur, any treatment exceeding 1–2 weeks should be under regular veterinary supervision.

Table 8: Examples of IPML translation on medical EMEA dataset from Portuguese to English using *FAMO*$^+$.

sider (England, 2011). Indeed, translation into real severely low resource languages is difficult.

We are curious of how our model trained on ~1,000 lines of data performs on the rest of the Bible. In other words, we would like to know how IPML performs if we train on ~3.5% of the Bible and test on ~96.5% of the Bible. In Table 7, we achieve a BLEU score of 31.3 training IPML on randomly sampled 1,093 lines of data for English on FAMO$^+$. Note that the training data is randomly sampled in Table 7 comparing to training on Luke in Table 4 and Table 5. We use this experiment to show that we have good results not only with specific book, but also with randomly sampled data.

We show qualitative examples in Table 2 and 9. The source content is translated well overall and there are a few places for improvement in Table 2. The words "fishermen" and "fishers" are paraphrases of the same concept. IPML predicts the correct concept though it is penalized by BLEU.

Infusing the order-preserving lexiconized component to our training greatly improves qualitative evaluation. But it does not affect BLEU much as BLEU has its limitations in severely low resource scenarios. This is why all experiments include the lexiconized component in training. The BLEU comparison in our paper also applies to the comparison of all experiments without the order-preserving lexiconized component. This is important in real-life situations when a low resource lexicon list is not available, or has to be invented. For example, a person growing up in a local village in Papua New Guinea may have met many people named "Bosai" or "Kaura", but may have never met a person named "Matthew", and we may need to create a lexicon word in the low resource language for "Matthew" possibly through phonetics.

We also see good results with the medical EMEA dataset. Treating English as a hypothetical low resource language, we train on only 1,093 lines of English data. For Portuguese-English translation, we obtain a BLEU score of 42.8 while the rest of languages all obtain BLEU scores above 34 in Table 6 and Table 8. In Table 8, we see that our translation is very good, though a few words are carried from the source language including "vétérinaire". This is mainly because our ~1,000 lines contain very small vocabulary; however, by carrying the source word over, key information is preserved.

6 Conclusion

We use ~1,000 lines of low resource data to translate a closed text that is known in advance to a severely low resource language by leveraging massive source parallelism. We present two metrics to rank the 124 source languages and construct FAMCs. We build an iteratively pretrained multilingual order-preserving lexiconized transformer and combine translations from all source languages into one by using our centric measure. Moreover, we add a multilingual order-preserving lexiconized component to translate the named entities accurately. We build a massively parallel lexicon table for 2,939 Bible named entities in 124 source languages, covering more than 66 severely low resource languages. Our good result for the medical EMEA dataset shows that our method is useful for other datasets and applications.

Our final result can also serve as a ranking measure for linguistic distances though it is much more expensive in terms of time and resources. In the future, we would like to explore more metrics that are fast and efficient in ranking linguistic distances to the severely low resource language.

References

Oliver Adams, Adam Makarucha, Graham Neubig, Steven Bird, and Trevor Cohn. 2017. Cross-lingual word embeddings for low-resource language modeling. In *Proceedings of the 15th Conference of the European Chapter of the Association for Computational Linguistics*, pages 937–947.

Ife Adebara, El Moatez Billah Nagoudi, and Muhammad Abdul Mageed. 2020. Translating similar languages: Role of mutual intelligibility in multilingual transformers. *arXiv preprint arXiv:2011.05037*.

Judith Aissen, Nora C England, and Roberto Zavala Maldonado. 2017. *The Mayan languages*. Taylor & Francis.

Antonios Anastasopoulos, Sameer Bansal, David Chiang, Sharon Goldwater, and Adam Lopez. 2017. Spoken term discovery for language documentation using translations. In *Proceedings of the Workshop on Speech-Centric Natural Language Processing*, pages 53–58.

Sameer Bansal, Herman Kamper, Sharon Goldwater, and Adam Lopez. 2017. Weakly supervised spoken term discovery using cross-lingual side information. In *Acoustics, Speech and Signal Processing*, pages 5760–5764. IEEE.

Christos Baziotis, Barry Haddow, and Alexandra Birch. 2020. Language model prior for low-resource neural machine translation. *arXiv preprint arXiv:2004.14928*.

Alexandre Bérard, Zae Myung Kim, Vassilina Nikoulina, Eunjeong Lucy Park, and Matthias Gallé. 2020. A multilingual neural machine translation model for biomedical data. In *Proceedings of the 1st Workshop on NLP for COVID-19 (Part 2) at EMNLP 2020*.

Alexandra Birch, Miles Osborne, and Philipp Koehn. 2008. Predicting success in machine translation. In *Proceedings of the 2008 Conference on Empirical Methods in Natural Language Processing*, pages 745–754.

Steven Bird. 2020. Decolonising speech and language technology. In *Proceedings of the 28th International Conference on Computational Linguistics*, pages 3504–3519.

John S Brownstein, Clark C Freifeld, Ben Y Reis, and Kenneth D Mandl. 2008. Surveillance sans frontieres: Internet-based emerging infectious disease intelligence and the healthmap project. *PLoS medicine*, 5(7):e151.

Jasone Cenoz. 2001. The effect of linguistic distance, l2 status and age on cross-linguistic influence in third language acquisition. *Cross-linguistic influence in 2nd language acquisition: Psycholinguistic perspectives*, 111(45):8–20.

Koel Dutta Chowdhury, Cristina España-Bonet, and Josef van Genabith. 2020. Understanding translationese in multi-view embedding spaces. In *Proceedings of the 28th International Conference on Computational Linguistics*, pages 6056–6062.

Alexandra Chronopoulou, Dario Stojanovski, and Alexander Fraser. 2020. Reusing a pretrained language model on languages with limited corpora for unsupervised nmt. *arXiv preprint arXiv:2009.07610*.

Lauren Eby Clemens, Jessica Coon, Pedro Mateo Pedro, Adam Milton Morgan, Maria Polinsky, Gabrielle Tandet, and Matthew Wagers. 2015. Ergativity and the complexity of extraction: A view from mayan. *Natural Language & Linguistic Theory*, 33(2):417–467.

Bernard Comrie. 2005. *The world atlas of language structures*. Oxford University Press.

Boele De Raad, Marco Perugini, and Zsófia Szirmák. 1997. In pursuit of a cross-lingual reference structure of personality traits: Comparisons among five languages. *European Journal of Personality*, 11(3):167–185.

Zi-Yi Dou, Antonios Anastasopoulos, and Graham Neubig. 2020. Dynamic data selection and weighting for iterative back-translation. *arXiv preprint arXiv:2004.03672*.

Haim Dubossarsky, Ivan Vulić, Roi Reichart, and Anna Korhonen. 2020. The secret is in the spectra: Predicting cross-lingual task performance with spectral similarity measures. In *Proceedings of the 2020 Conference on Empirical Methods in Natural Language Processing (EMNLP)*, pages 2377–2390.

Chris Dyer, Victor Chahuneau, and Noah A Smith. 2013. A simple, fast, and effective reparameterization of ibm model 2. In *Proceedings of the 12th Conference of the North American Chapter of the Association for Computational Linguistics on Human Language Technologies*, pages 644–648.

Paul S Earle, Daniel C Bowden, and Michelle Guy. 2012. Twitter earthquake detection: earthquake monitoring in a social world. *Annals of Geophysics*, 54(6).

Nora C England. 2011. *A grammar of Mam, a Mayan language*. University of Texas Press.

Orhan Firat, Kyunghyun Cho, and Yoshua Bengio. 2016. Multi-way, multilingual neural machine translation with a shared attention mechanism. In *Proceedings of the 15th Conference of the North American Chapter of the Association for Computational Linguistics on Human Language Technologies*, pages 866–875.

Jerry A Fodor and Zenon W Pylyshyn. 1988. Connectionism and cognitive architecture: A critical analysis. *Cognition*, 28(1):3–71.

Markus Freitag and Orhan Firat. 2020. Complete multilingual neural machine translation. *arXiv preprint arXiv:2010.10239*.

Robert M French. 1999. Catastrophic forgetting in connectionist networks. *Trends in cognitive sciences*, 3(4):128–135.

Dan Gillick, Cliff Brunk, Oriol Vinyals, and Amarnag Subramanya. 2016. Multilingual language processing from bytes. In *Proceedings of the 15th Conference of the North American Chapter of the Association for Computational Linguistics on Human Language Technologies*, pages 1296–1306.

Raymond G Gordon Jr. 2005. Ethnologue, languages of the world. *http://www. ethnologue. com/*.

Alex Graves, Greg Wayne, and Ivo Danihelka. 2014. Neural turing machines. *arXiv preprint arXiv:1410.5401*.

Jiatao Gu, Hany Hassan, Jacob Devlin, and Victor OK Li. 2018. Universal neural machine translation for extremely low resource languages. *arXiv preprint arXiv:1802.05368*.

Thanh-Le Ha, Jan Niehues, and Alexander Waibel. 2016. Toward multilingual neural machine translation with universal encoder and decoder. *arXiv preprint arXiv:1611.04798*.

Jan Hajič. 2000. Machine translation of very close languages. In *Sixth Applied Natural Language Processing Conference*.

Lynne Hansen, Karri Lam, Livia Orikasa, Paul Rama, Geraldine Schwaller, and Ronald Mellado Miller. 2012. In the beginning was the word. *Second Language Acquisition Abroad: The LDS Missionary Experience*, 45:89.

Theo Hermans. 2003. Cross-cultural translation studies as thick translation. *Bulletin of the School of Oriental and African Studies*, 66(3):380–389.

Eric W Holman, Søren Wichmann, Cecil H Brown, Viveka Velupillai, André Müller, Dik Bakker, et al. 2008. Advances in automated language classification. *Quantitative investigations in theoretical linguistics*, pages 40–43.

Chu-Ren Huang, Laurent Prévot, I-Li Su, and Jia-Fei Hong. 2007. Towards a conceptual core for multicultural processing: A multilingual ontology based on the swadesh list. In *International Workshop on Intercultural Collaboration*, pages 17–30. Springer.

Melvin Johnson, Mike Schuster, Quoc V Le, Maxim Krikun, Yonghui Wu, Zhifeng Chen, Nikhil Thorat, Fernanda Viégas, Martin Wattenberg, Greg Corrado, et al. 2017. Google's multilingual neural machine translation system: Enabling zero-shot translation. *Transactions of the Association for Computational Linguistics*, 5:339–351.

Pratik Joshi, Sebastin Santy, Amar Budhiraja, Kalika Bali, and Monojit Choudhury. 2020. The state and fate of linguistic diversity and inclusion in the nlp world. *arXiv preprint arXiv:2004.09095*.

James Kirkpatrick, Razvan Pascanu, Neil Rabinowitz, Joel Veness, Guillaume Desjardins, Andrei A Rusu, Kieran Milan, John Quan, Tiago Ramalho, Agnieszka Grabska-Barwinska, et al. 2017. Overcoming catastrophic forgetting in neural networks. *Proceedings of the national academy of sciences*, 114(13):3521–3526.

Guillaume Klein, Yoon Kim, Yuntian Deng, Jean Senellart, and Alexander Rush. 2017. Opennmt: Open-source toolkit for neural machine translation. *Proceedings of the 55th annual meeting of the Association for Computational Linguistics, System Demonstrations*, pages 67–72.

Philipp Koehn. 2009. *Statistical machine translation*. Cambridge University Press.

Anne Lauscher, Vinit Ravishankar, Ivan Vulić, and Goran Glavaš. 2020. From zero to hero: On the limitations of zero-shot language transfer with multilingual transformers. In *Proceedings of the 2020 Conference on Empirical Methods in Natural Language Processing (EMNLP)*, pages 4483–4499.

Zheng Li, Mukul Kumar, William Headden, Bing Yin, Ying Wei, Yu Zhang, and Qiang Yang. 2020. Learn to cross-lingual transfer with meta graph learning across heterogeneous languages. In *Proceedings of the 2020 Conference on Empirical Methods in Natural Language Processing (EMNLP)*, pages 2290–2301.

Yu-Hsiang Lin, Chian-Yu Chen, Jean Lee, Zirui Li, Yuyan Zhang, Mengzhou Xia, Shruti Rijhwani, Junxian He, Zhisong Zhang, Xuezhe Ma, et al. 2019. Choosing transfer languages for cross-lingual learning. *arXiv preprint arXiv:1905.12688*.

Zehui Lin, Xiao Pan, Mingxuan Wang, Xipeng Qiu, Jiangtao Feng, Hao Zhou, and Lei Li. 2020. Pre-training multilingual neural machine translation by leveraging alignment information. *arXiv preprint arXiv:2010.03142*.

Minh-Thang Luong, Ilya Sutskever, Quoc V Le, Oriol Vinyals, and Wojciech Zaremba. 2014. Addressing the rare word problem in neural machine translation. *arXiv preprint arXiv:1410.8206*.

Thomas Mayer and Michael Cysouw. 2014. Creating a massively parallel bible corpus. *Oceania*, 135(273):40.

Farhad Nooralahzadeh, Giannis Bekoulis, Johannes Bjerva, and Isabelle Augenstein. 2020. Zero-shot cross-lingual transfer with meta learning. *arXiv preprint arXiv:2003.02739*.

Terence Odlin. 1989. *Language transfer: Cross-linguistic influence in language learning*. Cambridge University Press.

Arturo Oncevay, Barry Haddow, and Alexandra Birch. 2020. Bridging linguistic typology and multilingual machine translation with multi-view language representations. *arXiv preprint arXiv:2004.14923*.

Robert Östling and Jörg Tiedemann. 2017. Neural machine translation for low-resource languages. *arXiv preprint arXiv:1708.05729*.

Steve Parker. 2012. Sonority distance vs. sonority dispersion–a typological survey. *The sonority controversy*, 18:101–165.

Jonas Pfeiffer, Ivan Vulić, Iryna Gurevych, and Sebastian Ruder. 2020. Mad-x: An adapter-based framework for multi-task cross-lingual transfer. *arXiv preprint arXiv:2005.00052*.

Manfred Pienemann, Bruno Di Biase, Satomi Kawaguchi, and Gisela Håkansson. 2005. Processability, typological distance and l1 transfer. *Cross-linguistic aspects of Processability Theory*, pages 85–116.

Ye Qi, Devendra Singh Sachan, Matthieu Felix, Sarguna Janani Padmanabhan, and Graham Neubig. 2018. When and why are pre-trained word embeddings useful for neural machine translation? *arXiv preprint arXiv:1804.06323*.

Taraka Rama and Prasanth Kolachina. 2012. How good are typological distances for determining genealogical relationships among languages? In *Proceedings of COLING 2012: Posters*, pages 975–984.

Marc'Aurelio Ranzato, Sumit Chopra, Michael Auli, and Wojciech Zaremba. 2015. Sequence level training with recurrent neural networks. *arXiv preprint arXiv:1511.06732*.

Edward Sapir. 1921. How languages influence each other. *Language: an Introduction to the Study of Speech*.

Maurizio Serva and Filippo Petroni. 2008. Indo-european languages tree by levenshtein distance. *EPL (Europhysics Letters)*, 81(6):68005.

Philippa Shoemark, Sharon Goldwater, James Kirby, and Rik Sarkar. 2016. Towards robust cross-linguistic comparisons of phonological networks. In *Proceedings of the 14th Workshop on Computational Research in Phonetics, Phonology, and Morphology*, pages 110–120.

Gary F Simons and Charles D Fennig. 2017. *Ethnologue: languages of Asia*. sil International Dallas.

Lucia Specia, Stella Frank, Khalil Sima'an, and Desmond Elliott. 2016. A shared task on multimodal machine translation and crosslingual image description. In *Proceedings of the 1st Conference on Machine Translation*, volume 2, pages 543–553.

Agneta M-L Svalberg and Hjh Fatimah Bte Hj Awg Chuchu. 1998. Are english and malay worlds apart? typological distance and the learning of tense and aspect concepts. *International Journal of Applied Linguistics*, 8(1):27–60.

Brian Thompson, Huda Khayrallah, Antonios Anastasopoulos, Arya D McCarthy, Kevin Duh, Rebecca Marvin, Paul McNamee, Jeremy Gwinnup, Tim Anderson, and Philipp Koehn. 2018. Freezing subnetworks to analyze domain adaptation in neural machine translation. *arXiv preprint arXiv:1809.05218*.

Jörg Tiedemann. 2012. Parallel data, tools and interfaces in opus. In *Lrec*, volume 2012, pages 2214–2218.

Antonio Toral and Andy Way. 2018. What level of quality can neural machine translation attain on literary text? *arXiv preprint arXiv:1801.04962*.

USAID. 2009. How to Wash Hands. `https://www.pseau.org/outils/biblio/resume.php?d=3319&l=en`. [Online; accessed 23-Nov-2020].

Ashish Vaswani, Noam Shazeer, Niki Parmar, Jakob Uszkoreit, Llion Jones, Aidan N Gomez, Łukasz Kaiser, and Illia Polosukhin. 2017. Attention is all you need. In *Advances in neural information processing systems*, pages 5998–6008.

Alex Waibel and Christian Fugen. 2008. Spoken language translation. *IEEE Signal Processing Magazine*, 25(3):70–79.

Zirui Wang, Zachary C Lipton, and Yulia Tsvetkov. 2020. On negative interference in multilingual models: Findings and a meta-learning treatment. *arXiv preprint arXiv:2010.03017*.

Hao-Ran Wei, Zhirui Zhang, Boxing Chen, and Weihua Luo. 2020. Iterative domain-repaired back-translation. *arXiv preprint arXiv:2010.02473*.

Winston Wu, Nidhi Vyas, and David Yarowsky. 2018. Creating a translation matrix of the bible's names across 591 languages. In *Proceedings of the 11th International Conference on Language Resources and Evaluation*.

Zhong Zhou, Matthias Sperber, and Alex Waibel. 2018a. Massively parallel cross-lingual learning in low-resource target language translation. In *Proceedings of the 3rd conference on Machine Translation Worshop of the 23rd Conference on Empirical Methods in Natural Language Processing*. Association for Computational Linguistics.

Zhong Zhou, Matthias Sperber, and Alex Waibel. 2018b. Paraphrases as foreign languages in multilingual neural machine translation. *Proceedings of the Student Research Workshop at the 56th Annual Meeting of the Association for Computational Linguistics*.

Changfeng Zhu, Heng Yu, Shanbo Cheng, and Weihua Luo. 2020. Language-aware interlingua for multilingual neural machine translation. In *Proceedings of the 58th Annual Meeting of the Association for Computational Linguistics*, pages 1650–1655.

Barret Zoph, Deniz Yuret, Jonathan May, and Kevin Knight. 2016. Transfer learning for low-resource neural machine translation. In *Proceedings of the 21st Conference on Empirical Methods in Natural Language Processing*, pages 1568–1575.

7 Appendix

In Table 1 and Table 5, Kanjobal is Eastern Kanjobal, Mam is Northern Mam, Cuzco is Cuzco Quechua, Ayacucho is Ayacucho Quechua, Bolivian is South Bolivian Quechua, and Huallaga is Huallaga Quechua.

We show an illustration of WASH guidelines in Figure 2. We also show IPML translations into Eastern Pokomchi (Mayan) in Table 9.

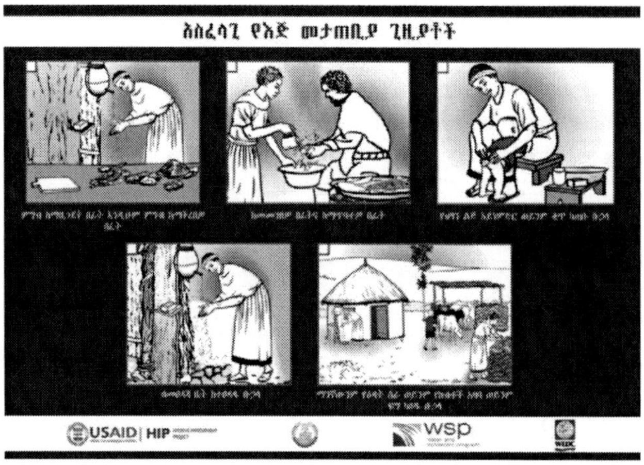

Figure 2: An Amharic illustration of translation of water, sanitation, and hygiene (WASH) guidelines in Ethiopia (USAID, 2009).

Source Sentence	IPML Translation	Reference
Ket idi limmabas iti dinna ti baybay ti Galilea, nakitana ni Simon ken ni Andres a cabsatna, nga iwaywayatda ti iket iti baybay; ta dumadaclisda idi.	Eh noq ojik i rub'an i Jesús juntar i k'isa palaw i Galilea, xrilow reje i Simón ruch'ihil i Andres, re' i rutuut i k'isa palaw, ruum jinaj i k'isa palaw barco.	Noq k'ahchi' rik'iik i Jesús chi chii' i k'isa palaw ar Galilea, xrilow reje wach i Simón ruch'ihil i ruchaaq', Andres rub'ihnaal. Re' keh aj karineel taqe, k'ahchi' kikutum qohoq i kiya'l pan palaw.
Ket idi nagna pay bassit nakitana ni Santiago nga anac ni Zebedeo ken ni Juan a cabsatna, nga addada idi iti barangayda, a tartarimaanenda dag-iti iketda.	Eh noq ojik i rub'an i Jesús, xrilow i Jacobo, re' i Jacobo rak'uun i Zebedeo, re' Juan rub'ihnaal, ruch'ihil taqe i raj tahqaneel. eh xkikoj wo' wach chinaah i k'isa palaw.	Eh junk'aam-oq chik i xb'ehik reje i Jesús, xrilow kiwach i ki'ib' chi winaq kichaaq' kiib', re' Jacobo, re' Juan, rak'uun taqe i Zebedeo. Eh wilkeeb' chupaam jinaj i barco, k'ahchi' kik'ojem wach i kiya'l b'amb'al kar.
Ket immasideg ni Jesus ket inigga-manna iti imana ket pinatacderna; ket pinanawan ti gorigor , ket nagservi cadacuada.	Eh re' Jesús xujil i koq riib', xutz'a'j i koq chinaah i q'ab'. eh re' i kaq tz'a' chi riij. eh jumehq'iil xwuktik johtoq, re' chik i reh xutoq'aa' cho yej-anik kiwa'.	Eh re' i Jesús xujil i koq riib' ruuk' i yowaab', xuchop chi q'ab', xruksaj johtoq, eh jumehq'iil xik'ik i tz'a' chi riij. Eh re' chik i reh xutoq'aa' cho yej-anik kiwa'.

Table 9: Examples of Iteratively Pretrained Multilingual Order-preserving Lexiconized Transformer (IPML) translation from Ilokano to Eastern Pokomchi using *FAMD*. We train on only 1,086 lines of Eastern Pokomchi data.

Measuring Prefixation and Suffixation in the Languages of the World

Harald Hammarström
Department of Linguistics and Philology
Uppsala University
Box 635
751 26 Uppsala
Sweden
harald.hammarstrom@lingfil.uu.se

Abstract

It has long been recognized that suffixing is more common than prefixing in the languages of the world. More detailed statistics on this tendency are needed to sharpen proposed explanations for this tendency. The classic approach to gathering data on the prefix/suffix preference is for a human to read grammatical descriptions (948 languages), which is time-consuming and involves discretization judgments. In this paper we explore two machine-driven approaches for prefix and suffix statistics which are crude approximations, but have advantages in terms of time and replicability. The first simply searches a large collection of grammatical descriptions for occurrences of the terms 'prefix' and 'suffix' (4 287 languages). The second counts substrings from raw text data in a way indirectly reflecting prefixation and suffixation (1 030 languages, using New Testament translations). The three approaches largely agree in their measurements but there are important theoretical and practical differences. In all measurements, there is an overall preference for suffixation, albeit only slightly, at ratios ranging between 0.51 and 0.68.

1 Introduction

It has long been recognized that suffixing is more common than prefixing in the languages of the world (see Himmelmann 2014, 927 and references therein). More detailed statistics on this tendency are needed to sharpen and evaluate proposed explanations for this tendency. In particular, dense data is needed to properly account for genealogical and areal effects (cf. Murawaki and Yamauchi 2018). With some 7 000 languages in the world, gathering these data is a gargantuan task. In this paper, we investigate three approaches that span the range from minimal to maximal curation.

Motivated by potential functional explanations (Himmelmann, 2014), the ideal measure for prefixing/suffixing would be to count the proportion of prefixes/suffixes per phonological word in a morphologically segmented corpus (cf. Greenberg 1954, 1957). It is believed that such ratios converge as the corpus grows towards infinite amounts of sampled data produced by the speakers of a language, and as such the ratios constitute properties of the language. The ideal measure would range from 0 to (potentially) infinity but, in practice, ratios beyond 5 are unheard of. An alternative equivalent characterization is to have an affixation score (AS) from 0 to (potentially) infinity comprising both prefixes and suffixes, along with a ratio — called the suffix ratio (SR) — from 0.0 to 1.0 of the division of labour between suffixes and prefixes ($\frac{S}{S+P}$). We use this characterization here, remembering that it is only defined for languages which have at least some affixation.

Since large morphologically segmented corpora are not available for a wide range of languages of the world, the ideal token count measure must be approximated. The classic approach, which we may call **Humans read grammars (HRG)**, is for a human to extract the relevant information from grammatical descriptions of the languages of the world. This approach is ideal in many ways, but requires a large amount of manual labour and requires a certain amount of judiciousness on behalf of the curator. While grammars are systematizations of raw text/spoken data, they rarely contain token counts, so this approach can only reflect any specific ratios indirectly. At the other end of the spectrum, a quick-and-dirty approach where **Machines read grammars (MRG)** is possible now that large collections of digitized grammatical descriptions are available and practical to use. We may obtain a crude approximation of the functional load of prefixes/suffixes by simply counting the occurrences of the terms `prefix` and `suffix` of the same grammatical descriptions that were written for a human audience. While there are obvious drawbacks to such a "naive" measure, it has obvi-

Proceedings of the Third Workshop on Computational Typology and Multilingual NLP, pages 81–89
June 10, 2021.

ous advantages in terms of speed, replicability and transparency. A similar crude measure may also be obtained by **Machines Read Raw Text (MRT)** given that a large collection of (not infinite-size, but comparable) raw text collection of New Testaments are available electronically (McCarthy et al., 2020). Correct automatic morphological segmentation and labeling of such a large array languages is not possible at present. Nevertheless, measures inspired by work in Unsupervised Learning of Morphology (Hammarström and Borin, 2011) may be enough to gauge the amount and ratio of affixation even if the tokens cannot be accurately segmented.

2 Related Work

Currently the largest available humanly curated database on prefixation/suffixation in the languages of the world is the WALS chapter 26A by Dryer (2005) featuring 948 languages. It continues a long tradition of growing databases of similar kinds (see, e.g., Himmelmann 2014, 927). We use the Dryer (2005) database here as it represents the culmination of these efforts and is available and methodologically explicit.

Information Extraction from grammatical descriptions has only recently become possible in practice, with the advent of a large collection of digitized grammars (Virk et al., 2020). Given its novelty, only a few embryonic approaches (Virk et al., 2019; Wichmann and Rama, 2019; Macklin-Cordes et al., 2017; Virk et al., 2017; Hammarström et al., 2021) have addressed the task so far. Arguably, the task in the present study is keyword-associated (of the simplest kind) wherefore we follow the method of Hammarström et al. (2021) which requires no tuning of parameters and estimates a noise-level for each source in addition to the simple counts.

While there are no comparable morphologically segmented corpora for a wide range of languages, it should be noted that there is a growing body of scattered resources in the NLP world (e.g., Mott et al. 2020), morphologically segmented texts in the DOBeS and ELAR archives (e.g., Paschen et al. 2020), and Interlinear Glossed Text extracted from miscellaneous publications (see references cited in Round et al. 2020 and Howell 2020). These resources do not yet have the breadth and comparability required for the present study, but the large raw text parallel Bible corpus of McCarthy et al. (2020) does — the culmination of a several decades long tradition of amassing Bible corpora for NLP. Combined with unsupervised morphological segmentation they could provide an excellent resource for direct measurements of affixation. A very large body of work in Unsupervised Learning of Morphology (see Hammarström and Borin 2011 for an overview up to 2010 and, e.g., Eskander et al. 2020 for an overview of more recent work) seeks to do segmentation of raw text. However, despite some progress to date, no off-the-shelf method exists that will segment a very broad range of languages accurately without a large amount of manual tuning of parameters, if even then. Fortunately, for the present task, we only need a score reflecting affixation, not necessarily an accurate segmentation itself. We have thus chosen one of the simplest counting techniques for overrepresentation of initial/terminal string segments (cf. Hammarström and Borin 2011, 322-326) explained in Section 3.3, thought to reflect actual segmentation proportionately. Many other choices would have been possible, with, we suspect, largely equivalent outcomes.

3 Methods

3.1 Humans Read Grammars

Dryer (2005)'s database, reflected in WALS Feature `26A Prefixing vs. Suffixing in Inflectional Morphology`[1], proceeds by calculating a prefix/suffix index for a given language by considering inflectional endings of ten different types, shown in Table 1 (top) along with four example languages. The relative proportion of suffixes versus prefixes ($\frac{S}{S+P}$), called the affixing index (AI), is discretized into five categories along with one category for languages with little or no affixation, as shown in Table 1 (bottom). We only have access to the languages labeled with the discretized labels, not the underlying counts, which would have been a richer rendering (cf. Gerdes et al. 2021). The scope of Dryer (2005) excludes non-inflectional, i.e., derivational prefixes/affixes, pre-/postclitics, intercalated fixes (also known as templatic morphology), tonal changes, preverbs, etc.

3.2 Machines Read Grammars

The data for the experiments in this paper consists of a collection of over 10 000 raw text grammatical descriptions digitally available for computational processing (Virk et al., 2020). A listing of the

[1]Available at online at `https://wals.info/feature/26A`.

		Swedish [swe]		Swahili [swh]		Nuaulu [nxl]	
		P	S	P	S	P	S
(i)	**case affixes on nouns**	-	-	-	-	-	-
(ii)	**pronominal subject affixes on verbs**	-	-	2	-	2	-
(iii)	**tense-aspect affixes on verbs**	-	2	2	-	-	-
(iv)	plural affixes on nouns	-	1	1	-	-	1
(v)	pronominal possessive affixes on nouns	-	-	-	-	0.5	0.5
(vi)	definite or indefinite affixes on nouns	-	1	-	-	-	-
(vii)	pronominal object affixes on verbs	-	-	1	-	-	-
(viii)	negative affixes on verbs	-	-	1	-	-	-
(ix)	interrogative affixes on verbs	-	-	-	-	-	-
(x)	adverbial subordinator affixes on verbs	-	-	-	-	-	-
		0	3	7	0	2.5	1.5
Affixing index (AI)		$\frac{3}{3+0} = 1.0$		$\frac{0}{0+7} = 0.0$		$\frac{1.5}{1.5+2.5} = 0.375$	

	Label	# lgs	Examples
$P + S \leq 2$	**Little or no inflectional morphology**	141	Thai [tha] (0+0), Vai [vai] (0+2), ...
$0.8 \leq AI$	**Strongly suffixing**	406	Swedish [swe] (3/3), Turkish [tur] (11/11), ...
$0.6 \leq AI < 0.8$	**Weakly suffixing**	123	Beja [bej] (10/13), Mokilese [mkj] (2/3), ...
$0.4 \leq AI < 0.6$	**Equal prefixing and suffixing**	147	Ubykh [uby] (5/10), Kiribati [gil] (2/4), ...
$0.2 \leq AI < 0.4$	**Weakly prefixing**	94	Mohawk [moh] (3/9), Au [avt](1/3), ...
$AI < 0.2$	**Strongly Prefixing**	58	Hunde [hke] (0.5/10), Sango [sag] (0/3), ...
		948	

Table 1: Top: Calculating the affixing index (AI) as per Dryer (2005) given the existence of different types of inflectional prefixes (P) and suffixes (S). The three boldfaced types are considered important enough to count double, hence the 2 points in the respective cells. Bottom: Labels used in Dryer (2005) for different types of prefix/suffix languages given the Affixing index (AI).

collection can be enumerated via the open-access bibliography Glottolog (`glottolog.org`, Hammarström et al. 2020). For each item, we know the (i) language it is written in (the meta-language, usually English, French, German, Spanish, Russian or Mandarin Chinese, see Table 2), (ii) the language(s) described in it (the vernacular, typically one of the thousands of minority languages throughout the world), and (iii) the type of description (comparative study, description of a specific features, phonological description, grammar sketch, full grammar etc). For the experiments in the present study, we used grammars and grammar sketches written in the ten most popular meta-languages. The subset counts 12 032 documents describing 4 287 languages of the world (Table 2). The collection has been OCRed using ABBYY Finereader 14 with using the meta-language as recognition language. The original digital documents are of quality varying from barely legible typescript copies to high-quality scans and even born-digital documents. We have no reason to believe that OCR quality plays any significant role in the experiments to follow. We have however taken care to read latin ligatures accurately as the `fi` ligature (U+FB01) affects the searches for prefix/suffix.

The search over the grammar was done using the Regexps in Table 3 tailored to each language, giving a number of suffix hits S and prefix hits P. In the result output, sources are grouped by language for easy browsing and inspection, as shown in Figure 1. Also included is the total number of tokens[2] of each grammar as well as the "purity level" α_i and associated threshold t automatically calculated using the technique of Hammarström et al. (2021). The suffix ratio for Machines Read Grammars is $SR_{MRG} = \frac{S}{S+P}$ if $S + P > 0$ and conventionally set to 0.5 otherwise.

[2]For Chinese, the Jieba `https://github.com/fxsjy/jieba` tokenizer was employed.

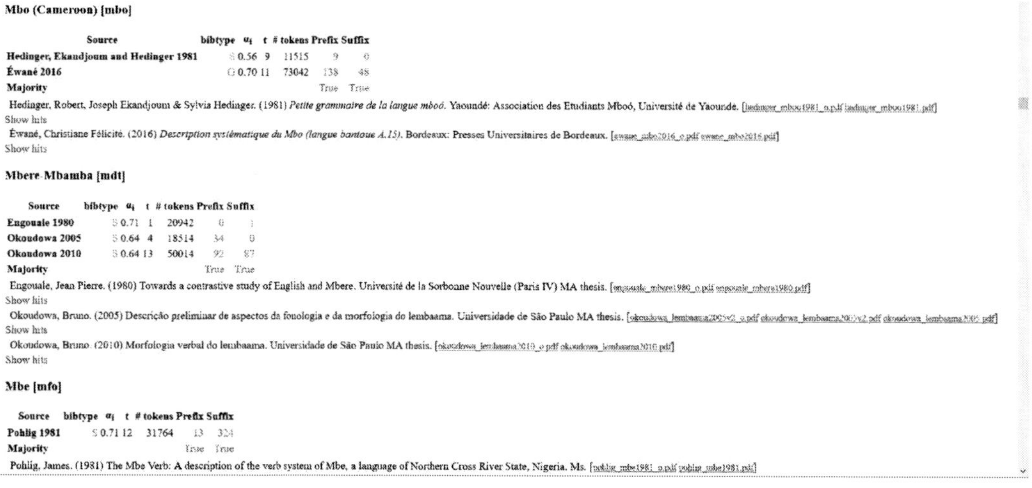

Figure 1: Example output of the Machines Read Grammars approach.

Meta-language		# lgs	# docs
English	eng	3 345	7 451
French	fra	792	1 323
German	deu	561	815
Spanish	spa	388	849
Russian	rus	288	537
Mandarin Chinese	cmn	166	249
Portuguese	por	136	285
Indonesian	ind	131	217
Dutch	nld	88	165
Italian	ita	81	139
			12 032

Table 2: Meta-languages of the grammatical descriptions for for the present study. The total number of distinct languages covered is 4 287.

3.3 Machines Read Raw Text

New Testament translations for over 1 000 languages are available in the Bible corpus collection of McCarthy et al. (2020). For the purpose of the present study, we assume that whitespace-indicated boundaries correspond to phonological words of the language in question. Languages written in a script that does not indicate word boundaries are excluded from computation. For comparability, we selected only the New Testament and excluded languages which had less than 7 000 verses thereof[3]. The longest text was selected when different versions were available for the same language. A total of 1 030 languages remained.

The type/token ratio is widely taken to be proportionate to the amount of affixation of a language. To measure the division between prefixing and suffixing, we adopt the RA measure of Hammarström (2009, 25-30). As noted above, the technique is one of many variations of the essentially the same theme (Hammarström and Borin, 2011, 322-326). Given any string x and a set W of word types of a corpus, we may calculate the probability of x as final occurrence and the probability of x as a non-final occurrence. $RA(-x)$ is simply the ratio between final and non-final probability, and $RA(x-)$, analogously, the ratio between initial and non-initial probability. For example, $RA(-ing) \approx 35.1$ and $RA(ing-) \approx 0.01$ in the English New Testament. Each segment x may thus be ranked according to prefixhood and suffixhood. From the entire set of attested segments, we keep only the set of suffixes S which are the best suffix-parse (= highest RA) for some word in W and only the set of prefixes P which are the best prefix-parse for some word in W. This makes the very long lists of potential affixes less unwieldy, and the length of the resulting list is believed to be proportionate to the actual number of affixes of each kind. However, it is known that resulting lists of this kind contain segments that are too long compared the actual segmentation, i.e., that contain the true affix plus one or more common characters of the stem or affix of an inner layer. Since we are only interested in the relative amount of prefixation/suffixation here — not the actual segmentation — we may hy-

[3]From inspection of the verse number distribution of the corpus at hand, this number emerges as a cut-off for what may be called a near-complete New Testament.

Heading	Chinese [cmn]	German [deu]	English [eng]	French [fra]
Prefix	字首|词头	\W[Pp]r[eä]fix	\W[Pp]refix	\W[Pp]r..?fix
Suffix	后缀|字尾|词尾	\W[Ss]uffix	\W[Ss]uffix	\W[Ss]uffix
Heading	**Italian [ita]**	**Portuguese [por]**	**Russian [rus]**	**Spanish [spa]**
Prefix	\W[Pp]refiss	\W[Pp]refix	\Wпрефикс	\W[Pp]refij
Suffix	\W[SS]ufiss	\W[Ss]ufix	\Wсуффикс	\W[Ss]ufij
Heading	**Indonesian [ind]**	**Dutch [nld]**		
Prefix	\W[Pp]refiks|	\W[Pp]refix|		
	\W[Aa]walan	\W[Vv]oorvoegsel		
Suffix	\W[Ss]ufiks|	\W[Ss]uffix|		
	\W[Aa]khiran	\W[Aa]chtervoegsel		

Table 3: Regular expressions for various meta-languages used in the Machines Read Grammar search.

	Swedish [swe]		English [eng]		Swahili [swh]	
	x	$RA(x)$	x	$RA(x)$	x	$RA(x)$
1	*-igt*	814.7	*-ned*	556.3	*nili-*	1655.0
2	*-ades*	362.8	*-teth*	475.9	*hawa-*	1365.8
3	*förb-*	343.7	*-ions*	407.9	*wame-*	1341.7
4	*upp-*	316.6	*-nts*	339.9	*-okea*	1261.3
5	*fram-*	248.2	*-ity*	321.4	*walio-*	1140.8
6	*-ligen*	222.7	*-ered*	290.5	*-ieni*	1124.8
7	*förh-*	216.4	*-ied*	284.3	*-zwa*	1108.7
8	*tills-*	203.6	*-neth*	259.6	*nina-*	1100.7
9	*förk-*	203.6	*-tly*	253.4	*wanao-*	1012.3
10	*förm-*	197.3	*-ias*	253.4	*nim-*	988.2
...	...		...		...	

Table 4: Examples of top RA scoring affixes in three languages.

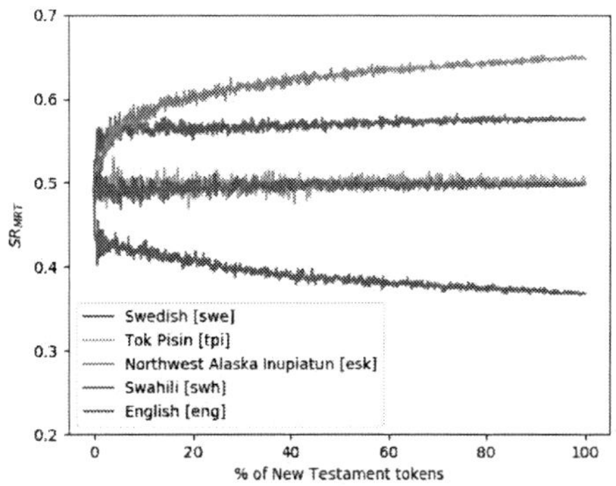

Figure 2: The convergence of SR_{MRT} given increasing percentages of (random) tokens of the New Testament for some example languages including the ones with the lowest (Tok Pisin) and highest (Northwest Alaska Inupiatun) type-token ratio.

pothesize that the erroneous "prolongation" affects prefix and suffix extraction uniformly. Examples of the top RA affixes are shown shown in Table 4 for three languages. The suffix ratio for Machines Read Raw Text is defined to be $SR_{MRT} = \frac{|S|}{|S|+|P|}$. For example $SR_{MRT}(Swedish) = \frac{3629}{3629+2679} \approx 0.58$, $SR_{MRT}(English) = \frac{2930}{2930+2965} \approx 0.5$, $SR_{MRT}(Swahili) = \frac{3109}{3109+5405} \approx 0.37$.

The amount of raw text data needed to reach a stable SR_{MRT} is shown in Figure 2 for some example languages including the most isolating Tok Pisin [tpi] and the record polysynthetic Northwest Alaska Inupiatun [esk]. As expected, all languages show diminishing variation with increased corpus size, but they differ as to how quickly the global value is approximated. Some languages with less morphology appear to reach it with only 10% (or less) of the New Testament, i.e., 700 verses, which corresponds to 15 691 tokens / 2095 types / 63 857 characters in English, 25 239 tokens / 767 types / 95 700 characters in Tok Pisin and 15 792 tokens / 2771 types / 67 745 characters in Swedish. But the more morphologically rich languages appear to require almost the entire text. For the purposes of the present paper, we will assume that the entire New Testament is enough to approximate the true SR_{MRT} of the languages involved.

4 Experiments

4.1 The Individual Measures

For the Humans Read Grammars (HRG) approach, there are no experiments to report, but we may note that the average suffix ratio is $SR_{HRG} = 0.67$ (using the midpoint of the range associated with each label, i.e., 0.1, 0.3, 0.5, 0.7, 0.9) or $SR_{HRG} = 0.65$ if the languages with little affixation are conven-

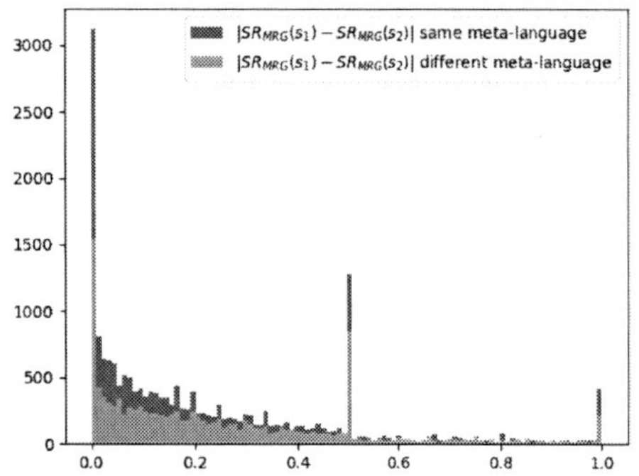

Figure 3: Differences in SR_{MRG} for pairs of different source documents s_1, s_2 describing the *same* language.

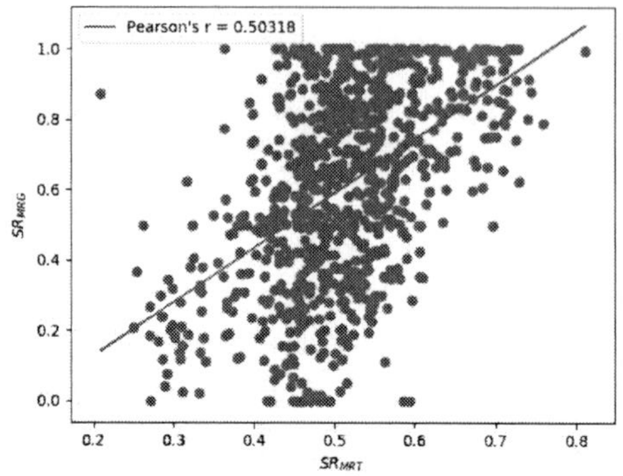

Figure 4: The correlation between MRG and MRT.

tionally said to have a ratio of 0.5.

For the Machines Read Grammars (MRG) approach, there is some latitude in how to treat different sources for the same language. More than half of the languages (2 516 of 4 287) have more than one source and the average number of sources per language is 2.81. Surprisingly, sources for the same language differ quite a lot in their suffix ratio, on average $|SR_{MRG}(s_1) - SR_{MRG}(s_2)| \approx 0.24$ (see Figure 3 for a histogram). This discrepancy is likely not driven by any effects related to different meta-languages as it is ≈ 0.24 when the sources have the same meta-language, only slightly lower than ≈ 0.26 when they do not. Different sources agree on whether $SR_{MRG} > 0.5$ only 68.6% of the time (70.2% if the same meta-language versus 66.3% if different). Manual inspection suggests that the discrepancies are mainly due to differences in scope and attention to functional load across descriptions of the same language, but also relate to differences in author style. For example, Lazard (1981)'s description frequently uses the term 'préfix' along with a hyphenated form *x*-, as expected, but does not use the term suffix when discussing suffixes (that the language does have) which are introduced as -*x* without any explicit accompanying term. The differences notwithstanding, if the suffix ratio of a language is understood as the average suffix ratio of its sources, the average suffix ratio across all 4 287 in MRG is 0.59. It is only a little different, 0.61, if instead we take the source with the most hits (suffix + prefix) per language.

For the Machines Read Raw Text (MRT) approach, the average $SR_{MRT} \approx 0.51$ — only a minimal suffix preference.

4.2 Comparison Between the Three Measures

Table 5 shows a comparison between the three dataset in terms of number of languages in common, average SR for the languages in common, Pearson's r and agreement on whether $SR > 0.5$. HRG and MRG agree on a SR of over 0.6 while MRT exhibits only a small suffix preference. All three measures are correlated with an $r > 0.5$. A scatter plot for $MRG \cap MRT$ — the two continuous measures — is shown in Figure 4. The agreement between all three measures increases to around 0.7 if we only consider the polarity of SR.

We should not expect these measures to fully agree given the significant theoretical differences. HRG has been forcibly discretized, considers only inflectional morphology and has an opaque link to the token ratio. MRG is quite sensitive to the descriptive aims (and whims) of particular authors and is unable to discern the type and context of affixes. Some authors discuss more comparative aspects, some include detailed discussions of morphophonology, some describe subordinate clauses in more detail than others and so on. It is telling that MRG agrees with the other measures roughly as much as MRG for different sources of the same language. It thus seems that this accuracy is a natural limit to what naive keyword counting can achieve on this (and similar) tasks. Similarly, MRT can not differentiate between derivational, inflectional or fossilized/productive affixation and it is not known how close the HRT measure is to the ideal token count and/or if there is a simple improvement.

To exemplify these differences, consider the comparison of SR-measurements for ten randomly

Dataset	# lgs	Avg SR	Pearson's r	SR polarity agreement
MRT ∩ HRG	306	MRT: 0.53, HRG: 0.68	0.54	0.73
MRT ∩ MRG	880	MRT: 0.51, HRG: 0.61	0.50	0.67
HRG ∩ MRG	917	HRG: 0.65, MRG: 0.65	0.67	0.75
∩ All three	301	MRT: 0.53, HRG: 0.66, MRG: 0.64	-	-

Table 5: Overlap and comparison of the three approaches for measuring the suffix ratio.

Language		$\|S\|$	$\|P\|$	Tokens	Types	SR_{MRT}	SR_{HRG}	SR_{MRG}
Adamawa Fulfulde	fub	2639	1773	138713	8394	0.60	0.70	0.91
Alekano	gah	2524	3879	206212	14206	0.39	0.90	0.85
Amharic	amh	7158	6259	99866	24751	0.53	0.70	0.67
Burarra	bvr	811	674	120804	1544	0.55	0.30	0.25
Nogai	nog	5876	2509	127036	18787	0.70	0.90	0.75
Nyankole	nyn	3007	6780	109603	19855	0.31	0.10	0.14
Páez	pbb	2588	1646	97749	8043	0.61	0.90	0.67
Uighur	uig	5908	1869	140666	20655	0.76	0.90	0.79
Woun Meu	noa	3262	1562	217057	10167	0.68	0.90	0.91
Wubuy	nuy	814	775	69363	2172	0.51	0.50	0.38

Table 6: New Testament data size and SR-measurements for ten randomly chosen languages featured for all three methods.

chosen languages in Table 6. We have not been able to investigate in depth the judgment of MRT of Alekano as a prefix-dominant language. A possibility informally observed in some other cases is that frequent stems are judged as prefixes. Indeed the MRT method lacks any information needed to distinguish stems from affixes if not for their frequency distributions. Amharic is written in an abugida script which should theoretically make the MRT estimate more coarse grained, and this is possibly reflected in its comparatively lower SR_{MRT}. Burarra is judged by MRT as a suffixing language, but here the explanation may be related to the orthography. The Burarra words as rendered in the Bible corpus contain a lot of dashes, likely indicating (some? all?) affix boundaries, possibly interfering with the MRT method (but this has not been investigated in depth). The two grammars used in MRG for Wubuy (one of which, Heath 1984, also underlies the HRG value) do discuss the prefixes much more than the suffixes since the prefix system indicating noun classes in this language is quite complicated.

Judging from the three-way comparison, the MRT measure is more often deviant from the other two. A closer look is needed to determine the source(s) of discrepancy more systematically. More research is needed into the robustness of the MRT-measure and related techniques, especially as it concerns the influence of orthography/writing system.

While the above discusion concerns the division of labour between suffixes and prefixes, we should also note how well the amount of affixation can be measured. In HRG, 141 of 948 languages are said to have "Little Affixation". Simple logistic regression gives an accuracy of 86% in predicting this class from the type/token ratio of MRT and 85% in predicting the class from the suffix, prefix, purity level and token count of the grammar with the most hits for each language. But these numbers do not improve on the baseline, and so add no actual information as to this class. Furthermore, there is only a weak correlation ($r \approx 0.15$) between the type-token ratio of MRT and the ratio of affixation hits to tokens times purity level. Clearly, predicting the amount of affixation is not as simple as it appears at first glance (cf. Bentz et al. 2016).

5 Conclusion

We have compared three ways to obtain data on the amount of prefixes/suffixes in the languages of the world. The three measures, correlate to a high degree but none can be said to reflect an ideal measure. At the same time, there are considerable differences in the measurements of individual languages. These differences reflect differences in aim and scope as well as sketchy measurements. The

Humans Read Grammars method only focusses on inflectional morphology with only weak integration of functional load. The Machines Read Grammars approach is vulnerable to differences in scope of description and individual styles, of which there is plenty of variation for the same language. More research is needed in to see to what extent these dimensions of variation can somehow be normalized automatically. The Machines Read Raw Text method reads a very noisy reflection of prefixation/suffixing from the raw data and cannot differentiate between derivational, inflectional or fossilized/productive affixation. The simple measure used here should be abandoned in favour of a more complicated, but less noisy measure. The resulting database, in total spanning the tremendous 4 437 languages, is freely available for future research at Zenodo `http://doi.org/10.5281/zenodo.4731249` on a Creative Commons Attribution 4.0 International license.

Acknowledgements

This research was made possible thanks to the financial support of the From Dust to Dawn: Multilingual Grammar Extraction from Grammars project funded by Stiftelsen Marcus och Amalia Wallenbergs Minnesfond 2017.0105 awarded to Harald Hammarström (Uppsala University) and the Dictionary/Grammar Reading Machine: Computational Tools for Accessing the World's Linguistic Heritage (DReaM) Project awarded 2018-2020 by the Joint Programming Initiative in Cultural Heritage and Global Change, Digital Heritage and Riksantikvarieämbetet, Sweden.

References

Christian Bentz, D. Alikaniotis, T. Samardžić, and P. Buttery. 2016. Variation in word frequency distributions: Definitions, measures and implications for a corpus-based language typology. *Journal of Quantitative Linguistics*, 23(2):1–41.

Matthew S. Dryer. 2005. Prefixing versus suffixing in inflectional morphology. In Bernard Comrie, Matthew S. Dryer, David Gil, and Martin Haspelmath, editors, *World Atlas of Language Structures*, pages 110–113. Oxford: Oxford University Press.

Ramy Eskander, Francesca Callejas, Elizabeth Nichols, Judith Klavans, and Smaranda Muresan. 2020. Morphagram, evaluation and framework for unsupervised morphological segmentation. In *Proceedings of The 12th Language Resources and Evaluation Conference*, pages 7114–7124, Marseille, France. European Language Resources Association.

Kim Gerdes, Sylvain Kahane, and Xinying Chen. 2021. Typometrics: From implicational to quantitative universals in word order typology. *Glossa: a journal of general linguistics*, 6(1):1–31.

Joseph H. Greenberg. 1954. A quantitative approach to the morphological typology of language. In Robert F. Spencer, editor, *Method and Perspective in Anthropology: Papers in Honor of Wilson D. Wallis*, pages 192–220. Minneapolis: University of Minnesota Press.

Joseph H. Greenberg. 1957. Order of affixing: A study in general linguistics. In Joseph H. Greenberg, editor, *Essays in linguistics*, pages 86–97. Chicago: University of Chicago Press.

Harald Hammarström, Robert Forkel, Martin Haspelmath, and Sebastian Bank. 2020. Glottolog 4.3. Jena: Max Planck Institute for the Science of Human History. Available at `http://glottolog.org`. Accessed on 2020-11-02.

Harald Hammarström. 2009. *Unsupervised Learning of Morphology and the Languages of the World*. Ph.D. thesis, Chalmers University of Technology and University of Gothenburg.

Harald Hammarström and Lars Borin. 2011. Unsupervised learning of morphology. *Computational Linguistics*, 37(2):309–350.

Harald Hammarström, One-Soon Her, and Marc Tang. 2021. Keyword spotting: A quick-and-dirty method for extracting typological features of language from grammatical descriptions. In *Proceedings of SLTC 2020*, page submitted, Gothenburg, Sweden. Nordic Journal of Language Technology.

Jeffrey Heath. 1984. *Functional Grammar of Nunggubuyu*. Canberra: Australian Institute of Aboriginal Studies.

Nikolaus Himmelmann. 2014. Asymmetries in the prosodic phrasing of function words: Another look at the suffixing preference. *Language*, 90(4):927–960.

Kristen Howell. 2020. *Inferring Grammars from Interlinear Glossed Text: Extracting Typological and Lexical Properties for the Automatic Generation of HPSG Grammars*. Ph.D. thesis, University of Washington.

Gilbert Lazard. 1981. Le dialecte des juifs de kerman. In *Monumentum Georg Morgenstierne 1*, volume 21 of *Acta Iranica*, pages 333–346. Paris: Brill.

Jayden L. Macklin-Cordes, Nathaniel L. Blackbourne, Thomas J. Bott, Jacqueline Cook, T. Mark Ellison, Jordan Hollis, Edith E. Kirlew, Genevieve C. Richards, Sanle Zhao, and Erich R. Round. 2017.

Robots who read grammars. Poster presented at CoEDL Fest 2017, Alexandra Park Conference Centre, Alexandra Headlands, QLD.

Arya D. McCarthy, Rachel Wicks, Dylan Lewis, Aaron Mueller, Winston Wu, Oliver Adams, Garrett Nicolai, Matt Post, and David Yarowsky. 2020. The johns hopkins university bible corpus: 1600+ tongues for typological exploration. In *Proceedings of The 12th Language Resources and Evaluation Conference*, pages 2877–2885, Marseille, France. European Language Resources Association.

Justin Mott, Ann Bies, Stephanie Strassel, Jordan Kodner, Caitlin Richter, Hongzhi Xu, and Mitchell Marcus. 2020. Morphological segmentation for low resource languages. In *Proceedings of The 12th Language Resources and Evaluation Conference*, pages 3989–3995, Marseille, France. European Language Resources Association.

Yugo Murawaki and Kenji Yamauchi. 2018. A statistical model for the joint inference of vertical stability and horizontal diffusibility of typological features. *Journal of Language Evolution*, 3(1):13–25.

Ludger Paschen, François Delafontaine, Christoph Draxler, Susanne Fuchs, Matthew Stave, and Frank Seifart. 2020. Building a time-aligned cross-linguistic reference corpus from language documentation data (doreco). In *Proceedings of The 12th Language Resources and Evaluation Conference*, pages 2650–2659, Marseille, France. European Language Resources Association.

Erich Round, Mark Ellison, Jayden Macklin-Cordes, and Sacha Beniamine. 2020. Automated parsing of interlinear glossed text from page images of grammatical descriptions. In *Proceedings of The 12th Language Resources and Evaluation Conference*, pages 2871–2876, Marseille, France. European Language Resources Association.

Shafqat Mumtaz Virk, Lars Borin, Anju Saxena, and Harald Hammarström. 2017. Automatic extraction of typological linguistic features from descriptive grammars. In Kamil Ekštein and Václav Matoušek, editors, *Text, Speech, and Dialogue: 20th International Conference, TSD 2017, Prague, Czech Republic, August 27-31, 2017, Proceedings*, volume 10415 of *Lecture Notes in Computer Science*, pages 111–119. Berlin: Springer.

Shafqat Mumtaz Virk, Harald Hammarström, Markus Forsberg, and Søren Wichmann. 2020. The dream corpus: A multilingual annotated corpus of grammars for the world's languages. In *Proceedings of The 12th Language Resources and Evaluation Conference*, pages 871–877. Marseille, France: European Language Resources Association, Marseille, France.

Shafqat Mumtaz Virk, Azam Sheikh Muhammad, Lars Borin, Muhammad Irfan Aslam, Saania Iqbal, and Nazia Khurram. 2019. Exploiting frame-semantics and frame-semantic parsing for automatic extraction of typological information from descriptive grammars of natural languages. In *Proceedings of the International Conference on Recent Advances in Natural Language Processing (RANLP 2019)*, page 1247–1256. Varna, Bulagaria: NCOMA Ltd.

Søren Wichmann and Taraka Rama. 2019. Towards unsupervised extraction of linguistic typological features from language descriptions. First Workshop on Typology for Polyglot NLP, Florence, Aug. 1, 2019 (Co-located with ACL, July 28-Aug. 2, 2019).

Predicting and Explaining French Grammatical Gender

Saumya Yashmohini Sahai*
The Ohio State University, USA
sahai.17@osu.edu

Dravyansh Sharma*
Carnegie Mellon University, USA
dravyans@cs.cmu.edu

Abstract

Grammatical gender may be determined by semantics, orthography, phonology, or could even be arbitrary. Identifying patterns in the factors that govern noun genders can be useful for language learners, and for understanding innate linguistic sources of gender bias. Traditional manual rule-based approaches may be substituted by more accurate and scalable but harder-to-interpret computational approaches for predicting gender from typological information. In this work, we propose interpretable gender classification models for French, which obtain the best of both worlds. We present high accuracy neural approaches which are augmented by a novel global surrogate based approach for explaining predictions. We introduce *auxiliary attributes* to provide tunable explanation complexity.

1 Introduction

Grammatical gender is a categorization of nouns in certain languages which forms a basis for agreement with related words in sentences, and plays an important role in disambiguation and correct usage (Ibrahim, 2014). An estimated third of the current world population are native speakers of gendered languages, and over one-sixth are L2 speakers. Having a gender assigned to nouns can potentially affect how the speakers think about the world (Samuel et al., 2019). A systematic study of rules governing these assignments can point to the origin of and potentially help mitigate gender biases, and improve gender-based inclusivity (Sexton, 2020).

Grammatical gender (hereon referred to by gender) need not coincide with "natural gender", which can make language acquisition more challenging. For example, Irish *cailín* (meaning "girl") is assigned a masculine gender. Works investigating the role of gender in acquiring a new language (Sabourin et al., 2006; Ellis et al., 2012) have found that the speakers of a language with grammatical gender have an advantage when acquiring a new gendered language. Automated generation of simple rules for assigning gender can be helpful for L2 learners, especially when L1 is genderless.

Tools for understanding predictions of statistical models, for example variable importance analysis of Friedman (2001), have been used even before the widespread use of black-box neural models. Recently the interest in such tools, reformulated as *explainability* in the neural context (Guidotti et al., 2018), has surged, with a corresponding development of a suite of solutions (Bach et al., 2015; Sundararajan et al., 2017; Shrikumar et al., 2017; Lundberg and Lee, 2017). These approaches typically *explain* the model prediction by attributing it to relevant bits in the input encoding. While faithful to the black box model's "decision making", the explanations obtained may not be readily intuited by human users. Surrogate models, which globally approximate the model predictions by a more interpretable model, or obtain prediction-specific explanations by perturbing the input in domain-specific ways, have been introduced to remedy this problem (Ribeiro et al., 2016; Molnar, 2019).

We consider a novel surrogate approach to explainability, where we map the feature embedding learned by the black box models to an *auxiliary* space of explanations. We contend that the best way to arrive at a decision (prediction) may not necessarily be the best way to explain it. While prior work is largely limited to the input encodings, by designing a set of auxiliary attributes we can provide explanations at desired levels of complexity, which could (for example) be made to suit the language learner's ability in our motivating setting. Our techniques overcome issues in prior art in our setting and are completely language-independent, with potential for use in broader natural language processing and other deep learning explanations.

* Equal contribution

Proceedings of the Third Workshop on Computational Typology and Multilingual NLP, pages 90–96
June 10, 2021.

For illustration, we examine French in detail where the explanations require both meaning and form.

2 Related Work

We consider the problem of obtaining rules for assigning grammatical gender, which has been extensively studied in the linguistic context (Brugmann, 1897; Konishi, 1993; Starreveld and La Heij, 2004; Nelson, 2005; Nastase and Popescu, 2009; Varlokosta, 2011), but these studies are often limited to identifying semantic or morpho-phonological rules specific to languages and language families. In computational linguistics, prediction models have been discussed in contextual settings (Cucerzan and Yarowsky, 2003) and the role of semantics has been discussed (Williams et al., 2019). Williams et al. (2020) use information-theoretic tools to quantify the strength of the relationships between declension class, grammatical gender, distributional semantics, and orthography for Czech and German nouns. Classification of gender using data mining approaches has been studied for Konkani (Desai, 2017). In this work we look at explainable prediction using neural models.

The noun gender can be predicted better by considering the word form (Nastase and Popescu, 2009). Rule-based gender assignment in French has been extensively studied based on both morphonological endings (Lyster, 2006) and semantic patterns (Nelson, 2005). These studies carefully form rules that govern the gender, argue merits and demerits that often involve factors beyond what rules concisely explain the patterns. Further they are organized as tedious lists of dozens of rules, and evaluated only manually on smaller corpora (less than 8% the size of our dataset). Cucerzan and Yarowsky (2003) show that it is possible to learn the gender by using a small set of annotated words, with their proposed algorithm combining both contextual and morphological models. The encoding of grammatical gender in contextual word embeddings has been explored for some languages in Veeman and Basirat (2020). They find that adding more context to the contextualized word embeddings of a word is detrimental to the gender classifier's performance. Moreover these embeddings often learn gender from contextual agreement, like associated articles, which are not suitable for explanation (Lyster, 2006). In contrast, here we will study the role of semantics in gender determination by learning an encoding of the lexical definition of the word, along with the role of form.

In modern applications of machine learning, it is often desirable to augment the model predictions with *faithful* (accurately capturing the model) and *interpretable* (easily understood by humans) *explanations* of "why" an algorithm is making a certain prediction (Samek et al., 2019). This is typically formulated as an *attribution problem*, that is one of identifying properties of the input used in a given prediction, and has been studied in the context of deep neural feedforward and recurrent networks (Fong and Vedaldi, 2019; Arras et al., 2019). The *attributes* are usually just input features (encoding) used in training. By studying how these features, or perturbations thereof, propagate through a network, one obtains faithful explanations which may not necessarily be easy to interpret. In this work, we consider explanations obtained using *auxiliary attributes* which are not used in training, but correspond to a simpler and more intuitive space of interpretations. We learn a mapping of feature embedding (learned by the black-box neural model) to this space, to approximate faithfulness, at the profit of better explanations. A similar local surrogate based approach is considered by (Ribeiro et al., 2016), but it involves domain-specific input perturbations (e.g. deleting words in text, or pixels in image inputs) for explanation.

3 Dataset

We extract French words, their definitions and phonetic representations from Dbnary (Sérasset, 2015), a Wiktionary-based multilingual lexical database. The words are filtered so that only nouns tagged with a unique gender are retained (for example *voile* which has senses with both genders is removed). For words with multiple definitions but the same gender, we retain the one that appears first as the semantic feature. We retrieve 124803 words, which are split 90-10-10 into train, validation and test sets respectively. The class distribution of the resulting dataset is not skewed, with 58% masculine and 42% feminine words.

4 Methods

4.1 Models

Baselines. We consider two baselines. The *majority* baseline always predicts the masculine gender, while the *textbook* orthographic baseline is based on the following simple rules — predict masculine unless the word ends in `-tion`, `-sion`, `-té`,

-son, or -e, excepting -age, -me or -ège endings.

Semantic models (SEM). The definition of words is used to generate its semantic representation. These are tokenized on whitespace, and are then passed through a trainable embedding layer. These representations are passed through 2 layer bidirectional LSTM of size 25 each, with additive attention. The hidden representation is passed through fully connected layers, of sizes 1500, 1000 and 1. The last layer output is used to calculate cross entropy loss. The representations generated by the penultimate layer (size 1000) is the LSTM semantic embedding.

XLM-R semantic embedding is also generated for the defintion using XLM-R (Conneau et al., 2020). The [CLS] token is fine-tuned to predict the gender. The sequence of hidden states at the last layer represents the embedding.

Phonological model (PHON). To represent the phonology of a word, we use n-grams features, which are constructed by taking last n characters of the syllabized phoneme sequence (derived from Wiktionary IPA transcriptions) where n is in $\{1, 2, \ldots, k\}$ for an empirically set k. A logistic classifier is trained using these features to predict the gender.

Orthographic model (ORTH). To encode the orthography of a word, we use two models. As with phonology, we consider n-grams features, which are constructed here by taking last n characters of the word spelling where n is in $\{1, 2, \ldots, k\}$ for an empirically set k. A logistic classifier to predict the gender is trained using these features.

To generate dense representations for these features, the words are tokenized at character level. The tokens are passed through a 32 unit LSTM and then 2 fully connected layers of sizes 30 and 1. The output from the last layer is used to calculate cross entropy loss by comparing with the true gender labels. Once trained, the representation of penultimate layer (of size 30) is used as the orthographic embedding.

Combined models. A logistic classifier is trained on the concatenated orthographic and semantic features embeddings to discriminate between genders. This is done for both types of semantic embeddings, from LSTM and XLM-R models. We also add phonemic n-gram sequences (n is a hyperparameter set to a jointly optimal value here) as an additional model. All models and their test and validation accuracies are summarized in Table 1.

4.2 Explainability

For each word, we calculate a set of easy-to-interpret *auxiliary features*, with semantic or orthographic connotations. Orthographic features are the top 1000 n-grams in a logistic regression fit. For semantic features, we calculate the scores of the meanings of the words by using word vectors implemented in SEANCE (Crossley et al., 2017). The assignment of words to psychologically meaningful space can lead to increased interpretability. SEANCE package reports many lexical categories for words based on pre-existing sentiment and cognition dictionaries and has been shown by Crossley et al. (2017) to outperform LIWC (Tausczik and Pennebaker, 2010). As SEANCE is only available for the English language, we use translation[1] of the French definitions to English.

Global explanations. The global explanations are evaluated for *i)* masculine and feminine class predictions and for *ii)* classes generated by clustering the best performing combined model embeddings (Table 1). The embeddings are clustered using BIRCH (Zhang et al., 1996) into 10 clusters. The number of clusters are chosen to minimize the overall misclassification rate (calculated by assigning the majority predicted class to a cluster). Decision tree classifiers are fit using the interpretable features[2] of about 25k samples (including those for which an explanation is to be generated) to predict the black box model's gender prediction and the cluster of a word.

Local explanations. We extend the LIME approach of (Ribeiro et al., 2016) to our setting. A local decision tree classifier is trained on the k nearest neighbors of a given test point, to approximate the black box model on the neighborhood.

The size of the decision tree is a hyperparameter which may be reduced to improve interpretability (i.e. smaller, more easily understood explanations) at the cost of model faithfulness (Figure 3).

[1] azure.microsoft.com/en-us/services/cognitive-services/translator/. The authors manually verified the accuracy of translations, the word error rate was less than 2% on a sample of 250 words.

[2] Not to be confused with 'interpretable' and 'uninterpretable' features from formal linguistics (Svenonius, 2006).

5 Results and discussion

The best orthographic model achieves an accuracy of 92.5%, whereas the semantic model alone achieves only 77.23%. Combining the features from the two models leads to a gain in the accuracy of the classifier, to 94.01%. We can conclude that for French, the gender can be predicted robustly by the word orthography, but adding semantic information can further improve prediction. Adding phonology to the mix does not seem to help much. This may be attributed to the fact that phonological forms contain less information than the orthographical forms in French, e.g. *lit* /li/ (bed, m.) and *lie* /li/ (dregs, f.). Not only are the written forms phonetic here (i.e. pronunciation is typically unambiguous given spelling) but they often contain additional (e.g. etymological) information which may be missing in the spoken forms. A more detailed error analysis and comparison of model pairs is presented in Appendix A.

Model	Test	Val
Majority baseline	57.76	57.98
"Textbook" ORTH rules	83.69	84.10
LSTM (SEM)	76.30	77.13
XLM-R-base (SEM)	77.29	78.71
[N-grams(PHON)]logistic	81.67	81.24
[N-grams(ORTH)]logistic	86.30	86.28
[N-grams(ORTH+pos)]logistic	92.50	92.12
[LSTM(ORTH)]logistic	92.21	92.22
[LSTM(ORTH)+N-grams(PHON)]logistic	92.69	92.40
[LSTM(ORTH)+XLM-R(SEM)]logistic	93.84	93.82
[LSTM(ORTH)+LSTM(SEM)]logistic	94.01	94.00
[LSTM(ORTH)+N-grams(PHON)+LSTM(SEM)]logistic	94.09	93.73

Table 1: Accuracy results of various models on test and validation sets.

We define a 'good explanation' to be one with high model fidelity (measured by F1) and if it involves fewer rules (more easily interpretable). This can be quantified in the case of decision trees as the length of path from root to leaf node, when making a prediction. A class with higher average decision tree path length for its sample is less interpretable.

We observe the trade-off between achieving interpretability and model accuracy for masculine and feminine classes (Figure 1) and for clusters generated via embeddings (Figure 2). The clusters are generated so that within a gender class, a distinction could be made for nouns that could have different rules, so that easier explanations per class could be generated. Both Figures 1 and 2 show that increasing size of the tree, always increases F1 score, but that comes at the cost of interpretability due to higher number of decision rules. Some ex-

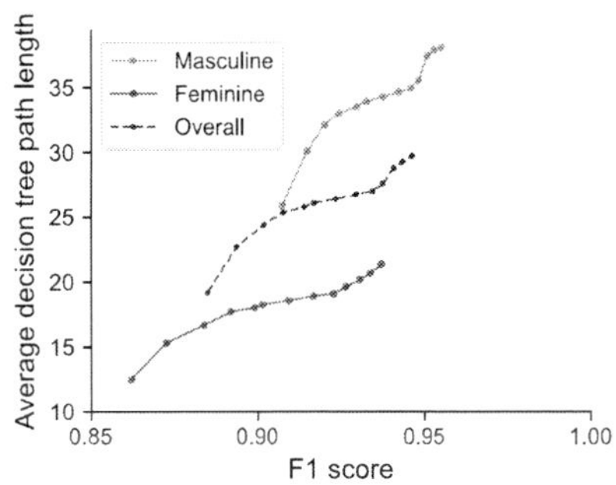

Figure 1: Class-specific/overall explainability (interpretability vs. fidelity) trade-off.

ample features that distinguish the different clusters are noted in Appendix B.

We see in Figure 1 that the explainability is higher for feminine nouns than masculine. This is consistent with the fact that there are many rules to indicate the feminine gender (such as words ending in *-ine, -elle, -esse*), whereas masculine gender is a default category leading to more complex, and harder to explain rules.

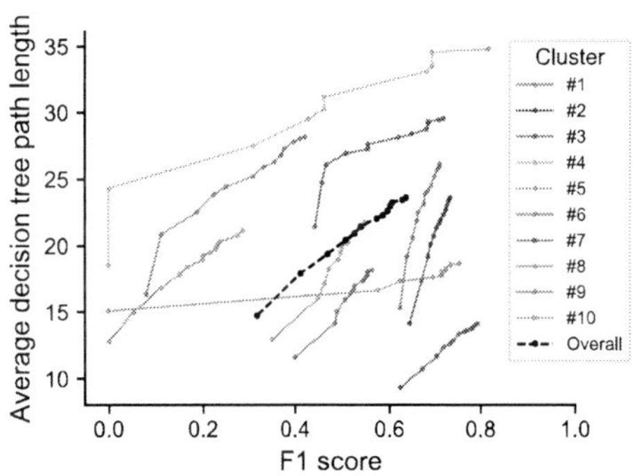

Figure 2: Cluster-specific explainability trade-off.

For the clusters, the misclassification rate for validation and testing set are 4.07% and 4.11% respectively, indicating that clusters mostly have one kind of gender. Figure 2 shows that some clusters (such as #2, #6, #7) are more explainable than the others (such as #1, #4), as latter show a poor F1 performance and low interpretability. Cluster #1 is majority feminine and #4 is majority masculine, indicating existence of exceptions in either gender. Identifying these clusters in the feature embedding can help in figuring out cases where the grammatical gender is assigned for formal reasons, in exception to semantic or morphonological rules. Moreover, these may be useful in designing a system with human-in-the-loop curation, for example by identifying relevant new auxiliary attributes.

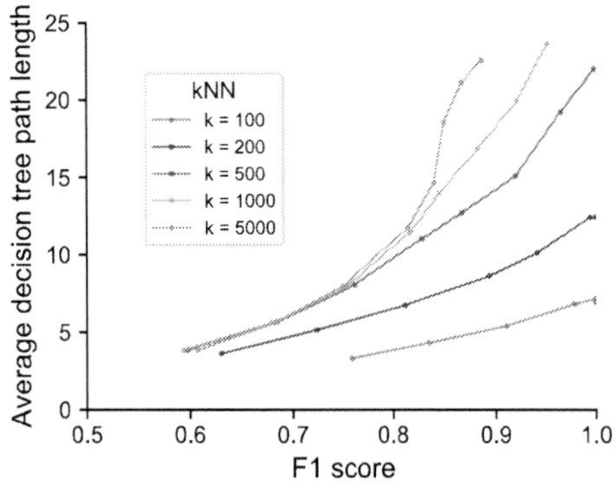

Figure 3: Explainability trade-off for local explanations for various neighborhood sizes.

The local explanations seem to outperform global ones, and the performance improves as we reduce the size of the local neighborhood considered. However, we note that this comes at some cost to consistency of explanations. For example, two local explanations for test points distant in the feature embedding may contain some contradictory rules. This is usually not an issue in typical applications of LIME which simply highlight part of the input as an explanation to provide some model justification. However, inconsistent rules can be of consequence in some applications considered here, for instance language learning where these contradictions are undesirable. Also, while per example explanations are larger on average for the global approach, we have the same rule for entire clusters, giving fewer rules overall.

6 Conclusion

Orthography predicts the grammatical gender in French with high accuracy, and adding semantic features can improve this prediction. The blackbox embedding can be explained by simpler decision tree models over a given auxiliary explanation space, both locally and globally. Global explanations lead to fewer rules across examples but are more complex on individual instances. Explainable gender prediction can be useful to language learners and gender bias researchers. A cross-linguistic extension of our study is deferred to future work.

Acknowledgements

We thank the reviewers for their useful feedback.

References

Leila Arras, José Arjona-Medina, Michael Widrich, Grégoire Montavon, Michael Gillhofer, Klaus-Robert Müller, Sepp Hochreiter, and Wojciech Samek. 2019. Explaining and interpreting lstms. In *Explainable ai: Interpreting, explaining and visualizing deep learning*, pages 211–238. Springer.

Sebastian Bach, Alexander Binder, Grégoire Montavon, Frederick Klauschen, Klaus-Robert Müller, and Wojciech Samek. 2015. On pixel-wise explanations for non-linear classifier decisions by layer-wise relevance propagation. *PloS one*, 10(7):e0130140.

Karl Brugmann. 1897. *The nature and origin of the noun genders in the Indo-European languages: A lecture delivered on the occasion of the sesquicentennial celebration of Princeton University*. C. Scribner's sons.

Alexis Conneau, Kartikay Khandelwal, Naman Goyal, Vishrav Chaudhary, Guillaume Wenzek, Francisco Guzmán, Edouard Grave, Myle Ott, Luke Zettlemoyer, and Veselin Stoyanov. 2020. Unsupervised cross-lingual representation learning at scale. In *Proceedings of the 58th Annual Meeting of the Association for Computational Linguistics, ACL 2020, Online, July 5-10, 2020*, pages 8440–8451. Association for Computational Linguistics.

Scott A Crossley, Kristopher Kyle, and Danielle S McNamara. 2017. Sentiment analysis and social cognition engine (seance): An automatic tool for sentiment, social cognition, and social-order analysis. *Behavior research methods*, 49(3):803–821.

Silviu Cucerzan and David Yarowsky. 2003. Minimally supervised induction of grammatical gender. In *Proceedings of the 2003 Human Language Technology Conference of the North American Chapter of the Association for Computational Linguistics*.

Ms Shilpa Desai. 2017. Data mining techniques for konkani grammatical gender identification. *Fr. Agnel College of Arts & Commerce Re-accredited by NAAC with "A" Grade Pilar-Goa*, page 38.

Carla Ellis, Simone Conradie, and Kate Huddlestone. 2012. The acquisition of grammatical gender in l2 german by learners with afrikaans, english or italian as their l1. *Stellenbosch Papers in Linguistics*, 41:17–27.

Ruth Fong and Andrea Vedaldi. 2019. Explanations for attributing deep neural network predictions. In *Explainable AI: Interpreting, Explaining and Visualizing Deep Learning*, pages 149–167. Springer.

Jerome H Friedman. 2001. Greedy function approximation: a gradient boosting machine. *Annals of statistics*, pages 1189–1232.

Riccardo Guidotti, Anna Monreale, Salvatore Ruggieri, Franco Turini, Fosca Giannotti, and Dino Pedreschi. 2018. A survey of methods for explaining black box models. *ACM computing surveys (CSUR)*, 51(5):1–42.

Muhammad Hasan Ibrahim. 2014. *Grammatical gender: its origin and development*, volume 166. Walter de Gruyter.

Toshi Konishi. 1993. The semantics of grammatical gender: A cross-cultural study. *Journal of psycholinguistic research*, 22(5):519–534.

Scott M Lundberg and Su-In Lee. 2017. A unified approach to interpreting model predictions. *Advances in Neural Information Processing Systems*, 30:4765–4774.

Roy Lyster. 2006. Predictability in french gender attribution: A corpus analysis. *Journal of French Language Studies*, 16(1):69.

Christoph Molnar. 2019. Interpretable machine learning.

Vivi Nastase and Marius Popescu. 2009. What's in a name? In some languages, grammatical gender. In *Proceedings of the 2009 Conference on Empirical Methods in Natural Language Processing*, pages 1368–1377.

Don Nelson. 2005. French gender assignment revisited. *Word*, 56(1):19–38.

Marco Tulio Ribeiro, Sameer Singh, and Carlos Guestrin. 2016. " why should i trust you?" explaining the predictions of any classifier. In *Proceedings of the 22nd ACM SIGKDD international conference on knowledge discovery and data mining*, pages 1135–1144.

Laura Sabourin, Laurie A Stowe, and Ger J De Haan. 2006. Transfer effects in learning a second language grammatical gender system. *Second Language Research*, 22(1):1–29.

Wojciech Samek, Grégoire Montavon, Andrea Vedaldi, Lars Kai Hansen, and Klaus-Robert Müller. 2019. *Explainable AI: interpreting, explaining and visualizing deep learning*, volume 11700. Springer Nature.

Steven Samuel, Geoff Cole, and Madeline J Eacott. 2019. Grammatical gender and linguistic relativity: A systematic review. *Psychonomic bulletin & review*, 26(6):1767–1786.

Gilles Sérasset. 2015. Dbnary: Wiktionary as a lemon-based multilingual lexical resource in rdf. *Semantic Web*, 6(4):355–361.

Samantha R. Sexton. 2020. Cross linguistic analysis of grammatical gender: Implications for critical language pedagogy. *Thesis, Linguistics and Education departments of the University of Massachusetts Amherst.*

Avanti Shrikumar, Peyton Greenside, and Anshul Kundaje. 2017. Learning important features through propagating activation differences. In *International Conference on Machine Learning*, pages 3145–3153. PMLR.

Peter Starreveld and Wido La Heij. 2004. Phonological facilitation of grammatical gender retrieval. *Language and Cognitive Processes*, 19(6):677–711.

Mukund Sundararajan, Ankur Taly, and Qiqi Yan. 2017. Axiomatic attribution for deep networks. In *International Conference on Machine Learning*, pages 3319–3328. PMLR.

Peter Svenonius. 2006. Interpreting uninterpretable features. *Linguistic Analysis*.

Yla R Tausczik and James W Pennebaker. 2010. The psychological meaning of words: Liwc and computerized text analysis methods. *Journal of language and social psychology*, 29(1):24–54.

Spyridoula Varlokosta. 2011. The role of morphology in grammatical gender assignment. *Morphology and its interfaces*, 178.

Hartger Veeman and Ali Basirat. 2020. An exploration of the encoding of grammatical gender in word embeddings. *arXiv preprint arXiv:2008.01946*.

Adina Williams, Damian Blasi, Lawrence Wolf-Sonkin, Hanna Wallach, and Ryan Cotterell. 2019. Quantifying the semantic core of gender systems. In *Proceedings of the 2019 Conference on Empirical Methods in Natural Language Processing and the 9th International Joint Conference on Natural Language Processing (EMNLP-IJCNLP)*, pages 5738–5743.

Adina Williams, Tiago Pimentel, Hagen Blix, Arya D McCarthy, Eleanor Chodroff, and Ryan Cotterell. 2020. Predicting declension class from form and meaning. In *Proceedings of the 58th Annual Meeting of the Association for Computational Linguistics*, pages 6682–6695.

Tian Zhang, Raghu Ramakrishnan, and Miron Livny. 1996. Birch: an efficient data clustering method for very large databases. *ACM sigmod record*, 25(2):103–114.

Appendix

A Error analysis

We examine in detail the errors of all our models. Some salient observations are noted below. The errors of our baselines indicate their insufficiency but are easier to understand in isolation. For our models, it is perhaps best to look at interesting pairs of models and compare their errors.

ORTH+SEM vs. ORTH: Adding phonology did not seem to help much in predicting gender beyond

Cluster	Majority gender	Error	Top-10 features
#1	Masculine	0.05	Role_GI, *sme*, *ien*, *n*, *sion*, *ade*, *che*, *nce*, *ue*, *ière*
#2	Feminine	0.08	*ien*, *sion*, *n*, *ade*, *r*, *che*, *ière*, *nce*, Role_GI, *ue*
#3	Masculine	0.00	*rice*, *sme*, *n*, *ien*, *age*, Ptlw_Lasswell, *tte*, *lle*, *té*, *ite*
#4	Masculine	0.00	Polit_2_GI, negative_adjectives_component, *age*, *ois*, *ne*, *se*, *ie*, *tion*, *ée*, *ite*
#5	Masculine	0.00	*sme*, *ien*, *n*, Social_GI, *sion*, *ade*, *che*, *ue*, *té*, *ite*
#6	Masculine	0.03	*l*, *sme*, *ien*, *n*, *sion*, *ade*, *che*, *ue*, *ite*, *té*
#7	Feminine	0.01	*ière*, Quan_GI, Fear_GALC, Role_GI, *ure*, *n*, Rctot_Lasswell, polarity_nouns_component, *ée*, *r*
#8	Feminine	0.00	*sme*, *ade*, *sion*, *ien*, *n*, *ière*, *che* , *nce*, *r*, *tte*
#9	Masculine	0.00	*ade*, *sion*, *che*, *nce*, *ue*, *ure*, *ée*, *ité*, *té*, *ite*
#10	Feminine	0.00	*ologie*, *n*, *r*, Fear_GALC, Anticipation_EmoLex, *ière*, *che*, Role_GI, *nce*, *ue*

Table 2: Top-10 features from decision tree with at most 500 leaf nodes for the clusters defined in Section 4.2.

orthography itself. Even though phonology alone (PHON) is more accurate than the best semantics (SEM) model in predicting gender (81% vs. 77%), semantics provide more useful additions over what orthography already encodes. For example, *poix* (meaning "pitch" or "tar"), *polio* ("polio") and *ardeur* ("ardor") are recognized as feminine with help from semantics (ORTH+SEM) but are classified incorrectly by the ORTH model. Similarly the meaning helps identify that *brais* ("crushed barley"), *polyane* ("plastic film") and *jurisconsulte* ("law expert") should be classified as masculine.

ORTH vs. PHON: Some examples which are correctly classified by the ORTH model but misclassified by the PHON model include *meringue* ("meringue", f.), *boulaie* ("birch grove", f.), *coccyx* ("coccyx", m.) and *explicit* ("end of a chapter or book", m.).

ORTH+SEM: Finally we look at errors of our best model (we consider ORTH+SEM as better than ORTH+SEM+PHON as it gets the same accuracy with fewer features). The list seems to include relatively rarer words, where it often seems hard to explain the gender assignment. Some examples are — *myrsite* ("Old medical wine", m.), *fomite* ("inanimate disease vector", m.) *cholestrophane* ("a chemical derived from caffeine", f.), *interpolateur* ("interpolator", f.).

B Auxiliary features for global explanations

For the 10 clusters described for global explainability in section 4.2, we show the top-10 important features in Table 2. These features are generated by training a decision tree classifier that could have at most 500 leaf nodes. The importance of a feature in each cluster was defined by the number of times it appeared on the decision path of the samples. The features are a mix of orthographic features (generated from word endings) and semantic features (generated from SEANCE) [3]. We emphasize that the features noted here are determined as the most common features for examples in the cluster, and are therefore more likely to appear in explanations of examples from that cluster — the exact explanation for an example is determined by the appropriate decision tree path.

The Table 2 also shows the error rates per clusters, which are fraction of misclassified labels per cluster with respect of predictions from the combined black-box model.

[3]Feature descriptions may be found at the following link: `https://drive.google.com/file/d/1SUfSYNyuaWT2i4tQkiyr2rxVeqnh3cQe/view`

Morph Call: Probing Morphosyntactic Content of Multilingual Transformers

Vladislav Mikhailov[1,2], **Oleg Serikov**[2,3], **Ekaterina Artemova**[2,4]
[1] SberDevices, Sberbank, Moscow, Russia
[2] HSE University, Moscow, Russia
[3] Neural Networks and Deep Learning Lab
Moscow Institute of Physics and Technology, Dolgoprudny, Russia
[4] Huawei Noah's Ark lab, Moscow, Russia
Mikhaylov.V.Nikola@sberbank.ru {oserikov,elartemova}@hse.ru

Abstract

The outstanding performance of transformer-based language models on a great variety of NLP and NLU tasks has stimulated interest in exploring their inner workings. Recent research has focused primarily on higher-level and complex linguistic phenomena such as syntax, semantics, world knowledge, and common sense. The majority of the studies are anglocentric, and little remains known regarding other languages, precisely their morphosyntactic properties. To this end, our work presents **Morph Call**, a suite of 46 probing tasks for four Indo-European languages of different morphology: English, French, German and Russian. We propose a new type of probing task based on the detection of guided sentence perturbations. We use a combination of neuron-, layer- and representation-level introspection techniques to analyze the morphosyntactic content of four multilingual transformers, including their less explored distilled versions. Besides, we examine how fine-tuning for POS-tagging affects the model knowledge. The results show that fine-tuning can improve and decrease the probing performance and change how morphosyntactic knowledge is distributed across the model. The code and data are publicly available, and we hope to fill the gaps in the less studied aspect of transformers.

1 Introduction

In the last few years, transformer language models (Vaswani et al., 2017) have accelerated the growth in the field of NLP. The models have established new state-of-the-art results in multiple languages and even demonstrated superiority in NLU benchmarks compared to human solvers (Raffel et al., 2020; Xue et al., 2020; He et al., 2020). Their distilled versions, or so-called student models, have shown competitive performance on many NLP tasks while having fewer parameters (Tsai et al., 2019). However, many questions remain on how these models work and what they know about language. The previous research focuses on what knowledge has been learned during and after pre-training phases (Chiang et al., 2020; Rogers et al., 2020a), and how it is affected by fine-tuning (Gauthier and Levy, 2019; Peters et al., 2019; Miaschi et al., 2020; Merchant et al., 2020). Besides, a wide variety of language phenomena has been investigated including syntax (Hewitt and Manning, 2019a; Liu et al., 2019a), world knowledge (Petroni et al., 2019; Jiang et al., 2020), reasoning (van Aken et al., 2019), common sense understanding (Zhou et al., 2020; Klein and Nabi, 2019), and semantics (Ettinger, 2020).

Most of these studies involve *probing* which measures how well linguistic knowledge can be inferred from the intermediate representations of the model. The methods range from individual neuron analysis (Dalvi et al., 2020; Durrani et al., 2020a), examination of attention mechanisms (Kovaleva et al., 2019; Vig and Belinkov, 2019), correlation-based similarity measures (Wu et al., 2020), to probing tasks accompanied by linguistic supervision (Adi et al., 2016; Conneau et al., 2018).

Despite growing interest in interpreting the models, morphology has remained understudied, specifically for languages other than English. The majority of prior works on this subject are devoted to the introspection of machine translation models, word-level embedding models, or transformers, fine-tuned for POS-tagging (see Section 2).

To this end, we introduce **Morph Call**, a probing suite for the exploration of morphosyntactic content in transformer language models. The contributions of this paper are summarized as follows. First, we propose 46 probing tasks in four Indo-European languages of different morphology: Russian, French, English, and German. Inspired by techniques for model acceptability judgments

Proceedings of the Third Workshop on Computational Typology and Multilingual NLP, pages 97–121
June 10, 2021.

(Warstadt et al., 2019a) and adversarial training (Alzantot et al., 2018; Tan et al., 2020b,c), we present a new type of probing tasks based on the detection of guided sentence perturbations. Since the latter is automatically generated, the tasks can be adapted to other languages. Second, we use complementary probing methods to analyze four multilingual transformer encoders, including their distilled versions. We examine how fine-tuning for POS-tagging affects the probing performance and establish count-based and non-contextualized baselines for the tasks. Finally, we publicly release the tasks and code[1], hoping to fill the gaps in the less studied aspect of transformers.

2 Related Work

A large body of recent research is devoted to analyzing and interpreting the linguistic capacities of pre-trained contextualized encoders. The most common approach is to train a simple classifier for solving a probing task over the word- or sentence-level features produced by the models (Conneau et al., 2018; Liu et al., 2019a). The classifier's performance is used as a proxy to assess the model knowledge about a particular linguistic property. However, lately, the method has been critiqued: is the property truly learned by the model, or does the model encode the property for the classifier to easily extract it given the supervision? Besides, a new set of additional classifier parameters can make it challenging to interpret the results (Hewitt and Liang, 2019; Hewitt and Manning, 2019b; Saphra and Lopez, 2019; Voita and Titov, 2020).

Nevertheless, the probing classifiers are widely applied in the field of model interpretation, including morphology. One of the first works on morphological content is carried out on machine translation models where the classifier is learned to predict POS-tags in multiple languages (Belinkov et al., 2017, 2018). The latest studies involving POS properties in transformers show that they are predominantly captured at the lower layers (Tenney et al., 2019b; Liu et al., 2019b; Rogers et al., 2020a), and can be evenly distributed across all layers (Durrani et al., 2020b). *Amnesic* probing explores how removing information at a particular layer affects the probe performance at the final layer (Elazar et al., 2020). This allows measuring the layer importance with respect to a linguistic property. The results claim that removing POS information may affect the performance more at the higher layers as compared to the lower ones.

Another line of research is devoted to various linguistic phenomena at the juxtaposition of morphology, syntax, and semantics. LSTM-based models and transformers are probed to capture subject-verb agreement in different languages (Linzen et al., 2016; Giulianelli et al., 2018; Ravfogel et al., 2018; Goldberg, 2019). Recently, the agreement has been at the core of inflectional perturbations for adversarial training (Tan et al., 2020a), and linguistic acceptability judgments along with morphological, syntactic, and semantic violations (Warstadt et al., 2019b).

Our work is closely related to (Edmiston, 2020) who explore morphological properties and subject-verb agreement in the hidden representations and self-attention heads of transformer models. However, there are several differences. First, we investigate the knowledge in multilingual transformers and their distilled versions instead of monolingual ones. Second, we carry out the experiments on an extended set of tasks, such as detecting syntactic and inflectional perturbations (see Section 3.2). Third, we apply several probing methods to analyze from different perspectives. Finally, we study the impact of fine-tuning for POS-tagging on the probe performance. Despite the similarities and differences, we find the studies complementary.

Finally, such benchmarks as LINSPECTOR (Şahin et al., 2020) and XTREME (Hu et al., 2020) provide means for evaluation of multilingual embedding models and cross-lingual transferring methods with regards to multiple linguistic properties, specifically morphology.

3 Method

3.1 Morphosyntactic Inventories

This paper investigates four Indo-European languages that fall under different morphological types: Russian, French, English, and German. Russian and French have fusional morphology, while English is an analytic language, and German exhibits peculiarities of fusional and agglutinative types. We consider the nominal morphosyntactic features of Number, Case, Person, and Gender. Even though the feature inventory is mostly shared across the languages, the latter differ significantly in their richness of morphology (Baerman, 2007).

[1] https://github.com/morphology-probing/morph-call

The morphosyntactic inventories of the analyzed languages are outlined in Table 1.

3.2 Probing Tasks

Data We use sentences from the Universal Dependencies (UD) (Nivre et al., 2016) for all our probing tasks, keeping in mind possible inconsistency between the Treebanks (de Marneffe et al., 2017; Alzetta et al., 2017; Droganova et al., 2018), and consequent inconsistency in dataset sizes across languages. All sentences are filtered by a 5-to-25 token range, and each task is split into 80/10/10 train/val/test partitions with no sentence overlap. The partitions are balanced by the number of instances per target class. Notably, the availability of the UD Treebanks in different languages allows for an adaptation of the method to the other ones. The used Treebanks are listed in Appendix A, and a brief statistics of the tasks is presented in Appendix B.

Task Description We construct four groups of probing tasks framed as binary or multi-class classification tasks: **Morphosyntactic Features**, **Masked Token**, **Morphosyntactic Values** and **Perturbations**.

Morphosyntactic Features probe the encoder for the occurrence of the morphosyntactic properties. The goal is to detect if a word exhibits a particular property based on its contextualized representation. Consider an example for the Russian sentence *'The clock stopped in a month.'*:

Chasy $\underbrace{\textbf{ostanovilis'}}_{\text{to stop+3PL+PST (1)}}$ $\underbrace{\textbf{cherez}}_{\text{in (0)}}$ mesyats .

Here, the target words are indicated by bold, and the labels denote if they have the category of Number.

Masked Token tasks are analogous to **Morphosyntactic Features** with the exception that the target word is replaced with a tokenizer-specific mask token. The tasks test if it is possible to recover the properties of the masked token purely from the context. Below is an example where the sentence mentioned above *'The clock stopped in a month.'* contains masked target words, and labels denote the occurrence of the Number feature at the position of the token:

Chasy $\underset{1}{\textbf{[MASK]}}$ cherez mesyats .

Chasy ostanovilis' $\underset{0}{\textbf{[MASK]}}$ mesyats .

Morphosyntactic Values is a group of k-way classification tasks for each feature where k is the number of values that the feature can take (see Table 1). For instance, the goal is to identify whether the word *girl* is in the singular or plural form: 'The **girl** has either pink or brown.'

Perturbations tasks test the encoder sensitivity to various sentence perturbations. Removing words from a text has recently been used to obtain adversarial attacks (Liang et al., 2017; Li et al., 2018), whereas inflectional perturbations have been applied for adversarial training of transformers (Tan et al., 2020b,c). In contrast, we extend the perturbations to probe the encoders for linguistic knowledge. To this end, we construct eight tasks that involve syntactic perturbations and inflectional perturbations in the subject-predicate agreement and deictic words. Note that we apply a set of language-specific rules to control the quality of the error generation procedure. To obtain the inflectional candidates, we make use of pymorphy2 for Russian (Korobov, 2015), lemminflect[2] for English, and word paradigm tables from Wiktionary for French[3] and German[4].

Stop-words Removal involves corruption of a syntax tree by removing stop-words. We use lists of stop-words provided by NLTK library (Loper and Bird, 2002). Consider an example of the French sentence *'**Les** Irakiens **ont** tout détruit **à le** Koweit'*, where the bolded words correspond to the removed stop-words.

Article Removal is a special case of the previous task, revealing whether the encoders are sensitive to discarded articles. This task is only constructed for French, English, and German. Note that such perturbation may also strain the semantics of the sentence: *'It's on loan, by **the** way'*.

Subject Number includes inflectional perturbations of the subject in the main clause with respect to the Number: *'The **girls** has either pink or brown.'*

[2]https://github.com/bjascob/LemmInflect

[3]https://dumps.wikimedia.org/frwiktionary/latest/

[4]https://dumps.wikimedia.org/dewiktionary/latest/

Feature \ Language	English	French	German	Russian
Number	$\{Sing, Plur\}$	$\{Sing, Plur\}$	$\{Sing, Plur\}$	$\{Sing, Plur\}$
Case	–	–	$\{Nom, Acc, Dat, Gen\}$	$\{Nom, Acc, Dat, Gen, Loc, Ins\}$
Person	$\{1, 2, 3\}$	$\{1, 2, 3\}$	$\{1, 2, 3\}$	$\{1, 2, 3\}$
Gender	–	$\{Masc, Fem\}$	$\{Masc, Fem, Neut\}$	$\{Masc, Fem, Neut\}$

Table 1: Analyzed languages and their morphosyntactic feature inventories.

Subject Case comprises errors in the subject form of Case for Russian. Consider an example of the perturbed sentence *Kak* ***vy*** *vidite situatsiyu v Rossii?* 'How do you find the situation in Russia?', where the nominative form of the subject *vy* 'you' is changed to the accusative:

Kak $\underbrace{\textbf{vas}}_{\text{you+2PL+ACC}}$ vidite situatsiyu v Rossii ?

Predicate Number incorporates perturbations of the predicate in the main clause regarding the Number feature: *'It* ***make*** *a huge difference.'*

Predicate Gender contains errors in the Gender form of the predicate in the main clause. For example, the masculine form of the predicate *byl* 'was' in the Russian sentence *Dosug* ***byl*** *ves'ma odnoobrazen* 'The leisure was pretty monotonous' is changed to the feminine:

Dosug $\underbrace{\textbf{byla}}_{\text{to be+3SG+FEM}}$ ves'ma odnoobrazen .

Predicate Person comprises perturbations in the Person form of the predicate in the main clause. For instance, the Russian sentence *Ya* ***poedu*** *v Moskvu* 'I will go to Moscow' contains the perturbed predicate in the form of the second Person instead of the first one:

Ya $\underbrace{\textbf{poedesh'}}_{\text{to go+2SG}}$ v Mosckvu .

Deictic Word Number involves perturbations generated by the inflection of demonstrative pronouns (only in English and German). For example, the singular form of the pronoun *dieser* 'this' is changed to the plural form *diesen* 'these' in the sentence *Siehe zu* ***dieser*** *Technik auch* 'See also this technique':

Siehe zu $\underbrace{\textbf{diesen}}_{\text{this+PL+DAT}}$ Technik auch .

4 Experimental Setup

4.1 Models

The experiments are run on the following multilingual transformer models released as a part of HuggingFace library (Wolf et al., 2019):

M-BERT (Devlin et al., 2019) was pre-trained over concatenated monolingual Wikipedia corpora in 104 languages.

D-BERT (Sanh et al., 2019) or DistilBERT is a 6-layer distilled version of **M-BERT** model.

XLM-R (Conneau et al., 2019) was pre-trained over filtered CommonCrawl data in 100 languages (Wenzek et al., 2019).

MiniLM (Wang et al., 2020) is a distilled **M-BERT** model that uses **XLM-R** tokenizer.

Each model under investigation has two instances for each language:

1. *Fine-tuned model* is a transformer model fine-tuned for POS-tagging. We use the UD Treebanks and HuggingFace library for fine-tuning. The data is randomly split into 80/10/10 train/val/test sets.
2. *Pre-trained model* is a non-tuned transformer model with frozen weights.

4.2 Probing Methods

Probing Classifiers We use Logistic Regression from scikit-learn library (Pedregosa et al., 2011) as a probing classifier. The classifier is trained over hidden representations[5] produced by the encoders with the regularization parameter $L^2 \in [0.25, 0.5, 1, 2, 4]$ tuned on the validation set. The performance is evaluated by the ROC-AUC score.

[5]Morphosyntactic Features and Values: we take mean-pooled representations of the sub-word embeddings that correspond to a target word. Masked Token: we use embedding of a tokenizer-specific masked token. Perturbations: we use mean-pooled sentence representations.

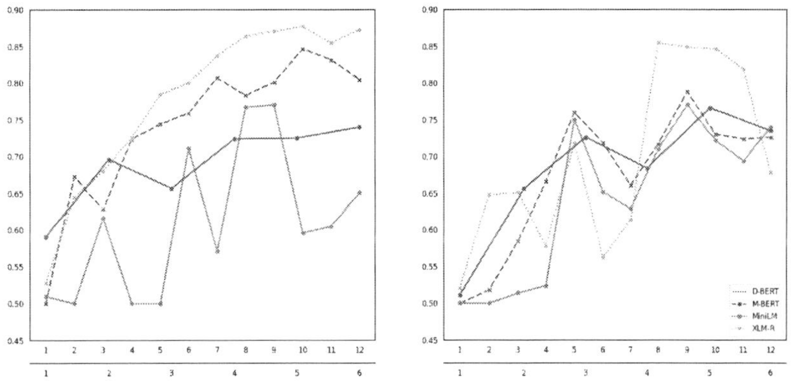

Figure 1: The performance of the probing classifier on **Case** masked token task for Russian. X-axis=Layer index score. Y-axis=Accuracy score. Left: pre-trained models. Right: fine-tuned models.

Neuron Analysis The neuron-level analysis allows retrieving a group of individual neurons that are most relevant to predict a linguistic property (Durrani et al., 2020a). Similarly, a linear classifier is trained over concatenated mean-pooled word/sentence representations using Elastic-net regularization (Zou and Hastie, 2005), and with L^1 and L^2 λ's $\in [0.1, \dots, 1e^{-5}]$ tuned on the validation set. The weights of the classifier are used to measure the relevance of each neuron.

Correlation Analysis Canonical correlation analysis (`ckasim`) is a representation-level similarity measure that allows identifying pairs of layers of similar behavior (Wu et al., 2020). We use `[CLS]`-pooled intermediate representations to analyze the encoders. The measure is computed with the help of the publicly available code[6].

4.3 Baselines

We train Logistic Regression over the following count-based and distributive baseline features (see Section 4.2). We use N-gram range $\in [1, 4]$ for each count-based baseline. Count-based features include **Char Number** (length of a word/sentence in characters), **TF-IDF over character N-grams**, **TF-IDF over BPE tokens** (BertTokenizer), and **TF-IDF over SentencePiece tokens** (XLMRobertaTokenizer). We use multilingual tokenizers by HuggingFace library to split words/sentences into the sub-word tokens. The distributive baseline is mean-pooled monolingual **fastText**[7] word/sentence embeddings (Bojanowski et al., 2017).

5 Results

5.1 Morphosyntactic Features

Probing Classifiers We learn the probing classifiers to estimate the model awareness of the morphosyntactic properties (see Section 4.2). The results demonstrate that pre-trained models perform slightly worse than their fine-tuned versions (2-4%). We find that the awareness is distributed in a very similar manner despite the language differences, for the models of both instances (see Tables 6–7, Appendix D). Specifically, the performance on **Number** and **Gender** is reaching its plateau at the middle layers $[5-8]$ of 12-layer models, and at layer $[3]$ of **D-BERT**. The probing curves[8] on **Case** are achieving their peak at the lower-to-middle layers $[4-5]$ and staying at the plateau towards the output layer. The only difference is observed on **Person** where the property is best inferred either across all layers (English, Russian) or at the lower-to-higher layers $[4-11]$ (French, German). The baseline features receive a strong performance, meaning that the occurrence of certain property may be inferred using the sub-word information (see Table 4, Appendix C).

[6]`https://github.com/johnmwu/contextual-corr-analysis`

[7]`https://fasttext.cc/docs/en/crawl-vectors.html`

[8]We refer to a *probing curve* as to a graphical representation of the probing classifier performance.

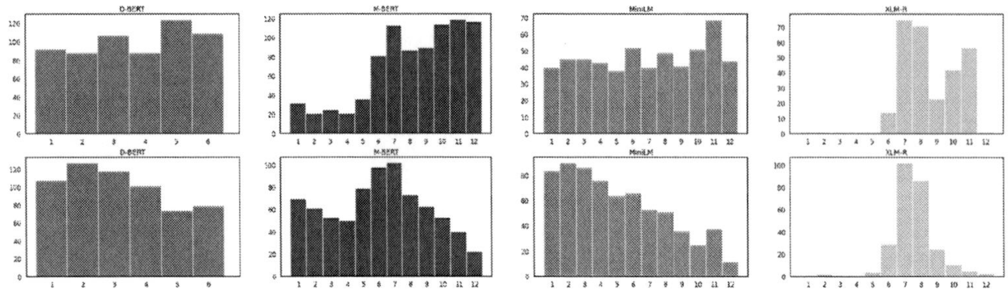

Figure 2: The distribution of top neurons over **Predicate Gender** perturbation task for each model. X-axis=Layer index number. Y-axis=Number of neurons. Top: pre-trained models. Bottom: fine-tuned models.

5.2 Masked Token

Probing Classifiers The results of the probing classifier performance on **Masked Token** tasks are presented in Tables 8 (pre-trained models) and 9 (fine-tuned models) (see Appendix D). The task has appeared to be more challenging as opposed to **Morphosyntactic Features** (see Section 5.1). An interesting observation in this setting is that the performance of the models predominantly drops or becomes unstable after fine-tuning. For instance, **BERT** may lose almost 10% in the tasks for Russian, and **D-BERT** may drop 5% in the tasks for French. The probing curves tend to show rapid increases and decreases across the layers. An exception to this pattern is **XLM-R** which is less affected by fine-tuning and exhibits a more stable probing behavior. Nevertheless, the models demonstrate their capability to infer the properties from the context. **XLM-R** makes correct predictions in almost 70% of cases, while the performance of **M-BERT** and **D-BERT** is slightly worse, and **MiniLM** may struggle the most. Figure 1 outlines the results on **Case** task for Russian, best solved among the others. The middle-to-higher layers account for more correct predictions in the models of both instances. However, the higher layers $[10 - 12]$ of 12-layer models and layer [6] of **D-BERT** may pertain to lower performance. A possible explanation is that the layers are affected by the objectives, i.e., Masked Language Modeling (pre-trained) or POS-tagging (fine-tuned). We find that the contextualized representations of a masked token produced by the final layers of pre-trained models may store the morphosyntactic properties. The probing curves demonstrate that the distribution of the properties may get affected by fine-tuning, or the knowledge can be partially lost, which is shown by the performance drops.

5.3 Morphosyntactic Values

Property-wise Neuron Analysis We apply property-wise neuron analysis to investigate the top-neurons per each morphosyntactic property (see Section 4.2). We find that some models require a larger group of neurons to learn a morphosyntactic property, and the number of these neurons may get changed after fine-tuning. We provide the results for each language in Appendix E. Figure 4 illustrates the distributions for pre-trained and fine-tuned models for French. While after fine-tuning the number of neurons on **Person** (**M-BERT**, **D-BERT**) and **Number** (**XLM-R**) has increased, **Number** and **Gender** are now handled by fewer neurons of the distilled models (**D-BERT**, **MiniLM**). A similar behavior is observed for Russian and English. **Case** (Russian), **Gender** (Russian) and **Person** (English) require more neurons (**M-BERT**), or fewer neurons over **Person** (Russian) and **Number** (Russian, English) (**MiniLM**, **D-BERT**). Notably, the fine-tuning phase does not affect the neuron distributions for German.

5.4 Perturbations

Probing Classifiers The results of the probing classifier performance on **Perturbations** tasks are presented in Table 10 (pre-trained models), and Table 11 (fine-tuned models) (see Appendix D). We find that the models perform on par with one another in the majority of the tasks. Notably, **XLM-R** is generally the most sensitive to the perturbations in each language compared to the other models. We find that the syntactic perturbations (**Article Removal**, **Stopwords Removal**) are better solved than the inflectional ones. Similarly, the count-based baselines receive the best performance on the syntactic perturbations since the latter are obtained over a limited set of words (see Table 5,

Appendix C). On the other hand, their performance is typically higher or close to random on the inflectional perturbations (see Table 5, Appendix C). We briefly describe the results in Appendix D for the sake of space.

Layer-wise Neuron Analysis Individual neuron analysis helps to observe how top-neurons are spread across the entire model, and identify the relevance of each layer by the number of its top-neurons[9] (see Section 4.2). Figure 2 demonstrates the results for **Predicate Gender** task in Russian. The sensitivity to the perturbation tends to be distributed across all layers of both pre-trained and fine-tuned models (**D-BERT**, **M-BERT**, **MiniLM**). The exception is provided by **XLM-R** which localizes the knowledge at the middle-to-higher layers $[6-11]$ (pre-trained), or in fewer layers but with larger groups of neurons $[6-9]$ (fine-tuned). The models of both instances store the sensitivity to the incorrect subject case form (**Subject Case**, Appendix E) at the middle-to-higher layers (**D-BERT**: $[3-5]$, **M-BERT**: $[6-11]$, **MiniLM**: $[4-8]$, **XLM-R**: $[5-12]$). Notably, the number of top-neurons in all models has decreased after the fine-tuning, and the information has been now more localized in two of them (**MiniLM**, **XLM-R**). A similar behavior of the models by language is observed on **Subject Number** (see Appendix E). The property is generally captured at the middle-to-higher layers of each pre-trained model for Russian, German and French (**D-BERT**: $[2, 3-6]$, **M-BERT**: $[6-12]$, **MiniLM**: $[5-12]$). The results are different for their fine-tuned versions, where the property gets more localized for Russian and German (**D-BERT**: $[3-5]$, **MiniLM**: $[5-7]$, **XLM-R**: $[6-9]$, **M-BERT**: $[6-11]$), or captured by fewer neurons at the same layers for French. In contrast, the property is predominantly distributed across all layers of both pre-trained and fine-tuned models for English.

Correlation Analysis To analyze the encoders with `ckasim`, we take `[CLS]`-pooled representations of the original sentence (without the perturbation) and its perturbed version. The similarity measure is computed on the resulted pairs of representations. For each model **M** we explore three settings by combining different model instances (see Section 4.1): (i) (*pre-trained* **M**, *pre-trained* **M**), (ii) (*pre-trained* **M**, *fine-tuned* **M**), (iii) (*fine-tuned* **M**, *fine-tuned* **M**). Figure 3 shows the most typical pattern achieved in the tasks. The biggest difference is observed over the combination (ii), where the perturbations are best captured at the lower-to-middle layers $[1-6]$ (**XLM-R**, **MiniLM**), or across all the layers (**M-BERT**, **DistilBERT**). The middle-to-higher layers $[7-12]$ tend to become more similar over combinations (i, iii) which may mean that they are able to restore the semantics of the perturbed sentences, being more robust to the perturbations as opposed to the lower ones.

[9]We selected top-20% neurons using the neuron ranking algorithm (Durrani et al., 2020b).

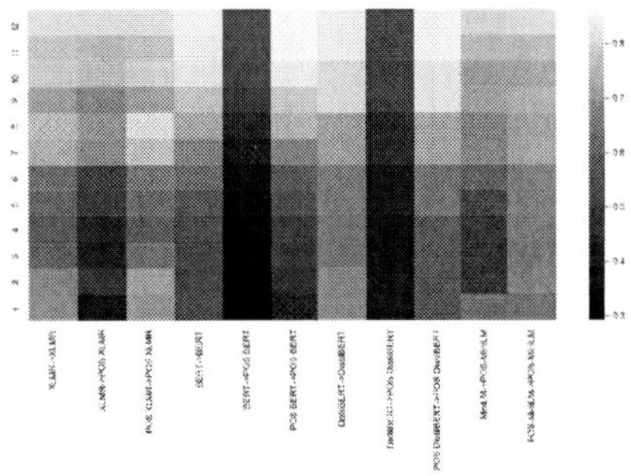

Figure 3: `ckasim` results on **Stopwords Removal** task in German. X-axis=Model instance combinations. Y-axis=Layer index number (left), `ckasim` score (right).

6 Discussion

Morphosyntactic content across languages The probing curves under layer-wise probing demonstrate that the multilingual transformers learn the morphosyntactic content in a greatly similar manner despite the language differences (see Section 5.1). The properties are predominantly distributed across the middle-to-higher layers $[5-12]$ for each language. In contrast, **Masked Token** tasks represent a challenge for the models causing rapid increases and decreases in the performance across the layers (see Section 5.2). The overall pattern for each language is that a masked token's properties are best inferred at the middle-to-higher layers. A possible reason for this is that the task requires incorporating syntactic and semantic information from the context since the target word remains unseen. The models demonstrate their sensitivity to **Perturbations** (see Section 5.4). While the syntactic perturbations are predominantly captured at the lower-to-middle layers $[3-8]$, the inflectional ones are stored at the middle-to-higher layers [5 − 12]. In contrast to other languages, the perturbation properties for English may be distributed across all layers of the models. The results are supported by the individual neuron analysis, an example of which is provided in Appendix E.

Same properties require different number of neurons Property-wise neuron analysis shows that **Person** and **Case** are learned using more neurons as compared to **Number** and **Gender** across the languages. Notably, the number of neurons required to learn a property may depend on the language. For example, **D-BERT** requires about 1000 neurons to learn **Case** in German and less than 1500 neurons to learn the property in Russian.

Are students good learners? A common method to compare pre-trained models and their distilled versions is based upon their performance on downstream tasks (Tsai et al., 2019), or NLU benchmarks (Wang et al., 2018, 2019). Still, little is investigated on what language properties are preserved after the knowledge distillation. We find that **D-BERT** and **MiniLM** mimic the behavior of their teachers under layer-wise probing (see Section 5.1), or display a similar perturbation sensitivity under `ckasim` (see Section 5.4). However, **MiniLM** tends to exhibit an uncertain behavior as opposed to their teacher (see Sections 5.2, 5.4).

Effect of fine-tuning The results show that the effect of fine-tuning for POS-tagging varies within a certain group of tasks. First, fine-tuned models may receive a better probing performance by 2-4% on **Morphosyntactic Features** tasks (see Section 5.1). Second, fine-tuning affects the way the properties are distributed or causes significant performance drops on **Masked Token** tasks, specifically at the higher layers (see Section 5.2). The impact on the property distribution is also demonstrated on **Perturbations** tasks under neuron-level probe (see Section 5.4). Besides, the analysis of top-neurons allows concluding that fine-tuning may affect localization (**MiniLM**, **XLM-R**) which is in line with (Wu et al., 2020). Finally, a number of neurons required to predict a property may increase (e.g., Russian: **Case**; French: **Person**), decrease (e.g., English: **Number**) or remain unchanged (German). We suggest that an interesting line for future work is to analyze the correlation between the number of neurons and the probe performance after fine-tuning. For instance, the results on **Perturbation** tasks indicate that some models may receive a better probing performance with fewer (**XLM-R**) or more neurons (**D-BERT**, **M-BERT**) (see Section 5.4). An exploration of fine-tuning for morphosyntactic analysis, specifically over UniMorph (Kirov et al., 2018) may be a fruitful avenue for future work.

Distribution of knowledge may depend on language morphology The analysis of the models under layer-wise and neuron-wise probing suggests that the behavior may depend on how morphologically rich a language is (see Sections 5.1, 5.4). The knowledge for English tends to be distributed across all layers of the models in contrast to the more morphologically rich languages that capture the properties at the middle-to-higher layers. The finding is in line with a few recent studies (Edmiston, 2020; Durrani et al., 2020b; Elazar et al., 2020) which contradict the common understanding that morphology is stored at the lower layers (Tenney et al., 2019a; Rogers et al., 2020b). We also find that the distribution of the properties varies based on the complexity of a probing task (see Sections 5.1, 5.2). An exciting direction for future work is to test this hypothesis on a more diverse set of morphologically contrasting languages. Besides, perturbing one aspect of a sentence can cause ambiguity elsewhere which is an interesting line for future exploration of the interdependence of the perturbations.

7 Conclusion

This paper proposes **Morph Call**, a suite of 46 probing tasks in four Indo-European languages that differ significantly in their richness of morphology: Russian, French, English, and German. The suite includes a new type of probing task based on the detection of syntactic and inflectional sentence perturbations. We apply a combination of three introspection methods based on neuron-, layer- and representation-level analysis to probe five multilingual transformer models, including their less explored distilled versions. The analysis of transformers' understudied aspect contradicts the common findings on how morphology is represented in the models. We find that the knowledge for English is predominantly distributed across all layers of the models in contrast to more morphologically rich languages (German, Russian, French), which house the properties at the middle-to-higher layers. The models demonstrate their sensitivity to the perturbations, and **XLM-R** tends to be the most robust among the others. We observe that distilled models inherit their teachers' knowledge, showing a comparative performance and exhibiting similar property distribution on several probing tasks. Another finding is that fine-tuning for POS-tagging can affect the model knowledge in various manners, ranging from improving and decreasing the probing classifier performance to changing the information's localization. We believe there is still room for exploring the models' morphosyntactic content and the effect of fine-tuning, specifically across a more diverse set of languages and types of model architectures.

Acknowledgements

We thank our reviewers for their insightful comments and suggestions. Ekaterina Artemova is supported by the framework of the HSE University Basic Research Program.

References

Yossi Adi, Einat Kermany, Yonatan Belinkov, Ofer Lavi, and Yoav Goldberg. 2016. Fine-grained Analysis of Sentence Embeddings Using Auxiliary Prediction Tasks. *arXiv preprint arXiv:1608.04207*.

Moustafa Alzantot, Yash Sharma, Ahmed Elgohary, Bo-Jhang Ho, Mani Srivastava, and Kai-Wei Chang. 2018. Generating natural language adversarial examples. *arXiv preprint arXiv:1804.07998*.

Chiara Alzetta, Felice Dell'Orletta, Simonetta Montemagni, and Giulia Venturi. 2017. Dangerous relations in dependency treebanks. In *Proceedings of the 16th International Workshop on Treebanks and Linguistic Theories*, pages 201–210.

Matthew Baerman. 2007. Syncretism. *Language and Linguistics Compass*, 1(5):539–551.

Yonatan Belinkov, Nadir Durrani, Fahim Dalvi, Hassan Sajjad, and James Glass. 2017. What do Neural Machine Translation Models Learn about Morphology? *arXiv preprint arXiv:1704.03471*.

Yonatan Belinkov, Lluís Màrquez, Hassan Sajjad, Nadir Durrani, Fahim Dalvi, and James Glass. 2018. Evaluating layers of representation in neural machine translation on part-of-speech and semantic tagging tasks. *arXiv preprint arXiv:1801.07772*.

Piotr Bojanowski, Edouard Grave, Armand Joulin, and Tomas Mikolov. 2017. Enriching word vectors with subword information. *Transactions of the Association for Computational Linguistics*, 5:135–146.

Cheng-Han Chiang, Sung-Feng Huang, and Hung-yi Lee. 2020. Pretrained Language Model Embryology: The Birth of ALBERT. pages 6813–6828.

Alexis Conneau, Kartikay Khandelwal, Naman Goyal, Vishrav Chaudhary, Guillaume Wenzek, Francisco Guzmán, Edouard Grave, Myle Ott, Luke Zettlemoyer, and Veselin Stoyanov. 2019. Unsupervised cross-lingual representation learning at scale. *arXiv preprint arXiv:1911.02116*.

Alexis Conneau, Germán Kruszewski, Guillaume Lample, Loïc Barrault, and Marco Baroni. 2018. What you can cram into a single vector: Probing sentence embeddings for linguistic properties. *arXiv preprint arXiv:1805.01070*.

Fahim Dalvi, Hassan Sajjad, Nadir Durrani, and Yonatan Belinkov. 2020. Analyzing Redundancy in Pretrained Transformer Models. pages 4908–4926.

Marie-Catherine de Marneffe, Matias Grioni, Jenna Kanerva, and Filip Ginter. 2017. Assessing the annotation consistency of the universal dependencies corpora. In *Proceedings of the Fourth International Conference on Dependency Linguistics (Depling 2017)*, pages 108–115.

Jacob Devlin, Ming-Wei Chang, Kenton Lee, and Kristina Toutanova. 2019. BERT: Pre-training of deep bidirectional transformers for language understanding. In *Proceedings of the 2019 Conference of the North American Chapter of the Association for Computational Linguistics: Human Language Technologies, Volume 1 (Long and Short Papers)*, pages 4171–4186, Minneapolis, Minnesota. Association for Computational Linguistics.

Kira Droganova, Olga Lyashevskaya, and Daniel Zeman. 2018. Data conversion and consistency of monolingual corpora: Russian ud treebanks. In *Proceedings of the 17th international workshop on treebanks and linguistic theories (tlt 2018)*, pages 52–65.

Nadir Durrani, Hassan Sajjad, Fahim Dalvi, and Yonatan Belinkov. 2020a. Analyzing Individual Neurons in Pre-trained Language Models. pages 4865–4880.

Nadir Durrani, Hassan Sajjad, Fahim Dalvi, and Yonatan Belinkov. 2020b. Analyzing individual neurons in pre-trained language models. In *Proceedings of the 2020 Conference on Empirical Methods in Natural Language Processing (EMNLP)*, pages 4865–4880, Online. Association for Computational Linguistics.

Daniel Edmiston. 2020. A systematic analysis of morphological content in bert models for multiple languages. *arXiv preprint arXiv:2004.03032*.

Yanai Elazar, Shauli Ravfogel, Alon Jacovi, and Yoav Goldberg. 2020. When bert forgets how to pos: Amnesic probing of linguistic properties and mlm predictions. *arXiv preprint arXiv:2006.00995*.

Allyson Ettinger. 2020. What bert is not: Lessons from a new suite of psycholinguistic diagnostics for language models. *Transactions of the Association for Computational Linguistics*, 8:34–48.

Jon Gauthier and Roger Levy. 2019. Linking artificial and human neural representations of language. In *Proceedings of the 2019 Conference on Empirical Methods in Natural Language Processing and the 9th International Joint Conference on Natural Language Processing (EMNLP-IJCNLP)*, pages 529–539.

Mario Giulianelli, Jack Harding, Florian Mohnert, Dieuwke Hupkes, and Willem Zuidema. 2018. Under the hood: Using diagnostic classifiers to investigate and improve how language models track agreement information. *arXiv preprint arXiv:1808.08079*.

Yoav Goldberg. 2019. Assessing bert's syntactic abilities. *arXiv preprint arXiv:1901.05287*.

Pengcheng He, Xiaodong Liu, Jianfeng Gao, and Weizhu Chen. 2020. Deberta: Decoding-enhanced bert with disentangled attention. *arXiv preprint arXiv:2006.03654*.

John Hewitt and Percy Liang. 2019. Designing and interpreting probes with control tasks. In *Proceedings of the 2019 Conference on Empirical Methods in Natural Language Processing and the 9th International Joint Conference on Natural Language Processing (EMNLP-IJCNLP)*, pages 2733–2743.

John Hewitt and Christopher D. Manning. 2019a. A structural probe for finding syntax in word representations. In *Proceedings of the 2019 Conference of the North American Chapter of the Association for Computational Linguistics: Human Language Technologies, Volume 1 (Long and Short Papers)*, pages 4129–4138, Minneapolis, Minnesota. Association for Computational Linguistics.

John Hewitt and Christopher D Manning. 2019b. A Structural Probe for Finding Syntax in Word Representations. pages 4129–4138.

Junjie Hu, Sebastian Ruder, Aditya Siddhant, Graham Neubig, Orhan Firat, and Melvin Johnson. 2020. Xtreme: A massively multilingual multi-task benchmark for evaluating cross-lingual generalization. *arXiv preprint arXiv:2003.11080*.

Zhengbao Jiang, Frank F Xu, Jun Araki, and Graham Neubig. 2020. How can we know what language models know? *Transactions of the Association for Computational Linguistics*, 8:423–438.

Christo Kirov, Ryan Cotterell, John Sylak-Glassman, Géraldine Walther, Ekaterina Vylomova, Patrick Xia, Manaal Faruqui, Sabrina J Mielke, Arya D McCarthy, Sandra Kübler, et al. 2018. UniMorph 2.0: Universal Morphology.

Tassilo Klein and Moin Nabi. 2019. Attention is (not) all you need for commonsense reasoning. In *Proceedings of the 57th Annual Meeting of the Association for Computational Linguistics*, pages 4831–4836.

Mikhail Korobov. 2015. Morphological analyzer and generator for russian and ukrainian languages. In *International Conference on Analysis of Images, Social Networks and Texts*, pages 320–332. Springer.

Olga Kovaleva, Alexey Romanov, Anna Rogers, and Anna Rumshisky. 2019. Revealing the dark secrets of BERT. In *Proceedings of the 2019 Conference on Empirical Methods in Natural Language Processing and the 9th International Joint Conference on Natural Language Processing (EMNLP-IJCNLP)*, pages 4365–4374, Hong Kong, China. Association for Computational Linguistics.

Jinfeng Li, Shouling Ji, Tianyu Du, Bo Li, and Ting Wang. 2018. Textbugger: Generating adversarial text against real-world applications. *arXiv preprint arXiv:1812.05271*.

Bin Liang, Hongcheng Li, Miaoqiang Su, Pan Bian, Xirong Li, and Wenchang Shi. 2017. Deep text classification can be fooled. *arXiv preprint arXiv:1704.08006*.

Tal Linzen, Emmanuel Dupoux, and Yoav Goldberg. 2016. Assessing the ability of lstms to learn syntax-sensitive dependencies. *Transactions of the Association for Computational Linguistics*, 4:521–535.

Nelson F Liu, Matt Gardner, Yonatan Belinkov, Matthew E Peters, and Noah A Smith. 2019a. Linguistic knowledge and transferability of contextual representations. In *Proceedings of the 2019 Conference of the North American Chapter of the Association for Computational Linguistics: Human Language Technologies, Volume 1 (Long and Short Papers)*, pages 1073–1094.

Nelson F. Liu, Matt Gardner, Yonatan Belinkov, Matthew E. Peters, and Noah A. Smith. 2019b. Linguistic knowledge and transferability of contextual representations. In *Proceedings of the 2019 Conference of the North American Chapter of the Association for Computational Linguistics: Human Language Technologies, Volume 1 (Long and Short Papers)*, pages 1073–1094, Minneapolis, Minnesota. Association for Computational Linguistics.

Edward Loper and Steven Bird. 2002. Nltk: the natural language toolkit. *arXiv preprint cs/0205028*.

Amil Merchant, Elahe Rahimtoroghi, Ellie Pavlick, and Ian Tenney. 2020. What happens to bert embeddings during fine-tuning? *arXiv preprint arXiv:2004.14448*.

Alessio Miaschi, Dominique Brunato, Felice Dell'Orletta, and Giulia Venturi. 2020. Linguistic profiling of a neural language model. *arXiv preprint arXiv:2010.01869*.

Joakim Nivre, Marie-Catherine De Marneffe, Filip Ginter, Yoav Goldberg, Jan Hajic, Christopher D Manning, Ryan McDonald, Slav Petrov, Sampo Pyysalo, Natalia Silveira, et al. 2016. Universal dependencies v1: A multilingual treebank collection. In *Proceedings of the Tenth International Conference on Language Resources and Evaluation (LREC'16)*, pages 1659–1666.

Fabian Pedregosa, Gaël Varoquaux, Alexandre Gramfort, Vincent Michel, Bertrand Thirion, Olivier Grisel, Mathieu Blondel, Peter Prettenhofer, Ron Weiss, Vincent Dubourg, et al. 2011. Scikit-learn: Machine learning in python. *the Journal of machine Learning research*, 12:2825–2830.

Matthew E Peters, Sebastian Ruder, and Noah A Smith. 2019. To tune or not to tune? adapting pretrained representations to diverse tasks. In *Proceedings of the 4th Workshop on Representation Learning for NLP (RepL4NLP-2019)*, pages 7–14.

Fabio Petroni, Tim Rocktäschel, Sebastian Riedel, Patrick Lewis, Anton Bakhtin, Yuxiang Wu, and Alexander Miller. 2019. Language models as knowledge bases? In *Proceedings of the 2019 Conference on Empirical Methods in Natural Language Processing and the 9th International Joint Conference on Natural Language Processing (EMNLP-IJCNLP)*, pages 2463–2473.

Colin Raffel, Noam Shazeer, Adam Roberts, Katherine Lee, Sharan Narang, Michael Matena, Yanqi Zhou, Wei Li, and Peter J Liu. 2020. Exploring the limits of transfer learning with a unified text-to-text transformer. *Journal of Machine Learning Research*, 21:1–67.

Shauli Ravfogel, Francis M Tyers, and Yoav Goldberg. 2018. Can lstm learn to capture agreement? the case of basque. *arXiv preprint arXiv:1809.04022*.

Anna Rogers, Olga Kovaleva, and Anna Rumshisky. 2020a. A primer in bertology: What we know about how bert works. *arXiv preprint arXiv:2002.12327*.

Anna Rogers, Olga Kovaleva, and Anna Rumshisky. 2020b. A primer in BERTology: What we know about how BERT works. *Transactions of the Association for Computational Linguistics*, 8:842–866.

Gözde Gül Şahin, Clara Vania, Ilia Kuznetsov, and Iryna Gurevych. 2020. LINSPECTOR: Multilingual probing tasks for word representations. *Computational Linguistics*, 46(2):335–385.

Victor Sanh, Lysandre Debut, Julien Chaumond, and Thomas Wolf. 2019. Distilbert, a distilled version of bert: smaller, faster, cheaper and lighter. *arXiv preprint arXiv:1910.01108*.

Naomi Saphra and Adam Lopez. 2019. Understanding learning dynamics of language models with SVCCA. In *Proceedings of the 2019 Conference of the North American Chapter of the Association for Computational Linguistics: Human Language Technologies, Volume 1 (Long and Short Papers)*, pages 3257–3267, Minneapolis, Minnesota. Association for Computational Linguistics.

Samson Tan, Shafiq Joty, Min-Yen Kan, and Richard Socher. 2020a. It's morphin' time! Combating linguistic discrimination with inflectional perturbations. In *Proceedings of the 58th Annual Meeting of the Association for Computational Linguistics*, pages 2920–2935, Online. Association for Computational Linguistics.

Samson Tan, Shafiq Joty, Min-Yen Kan, and Richard Socher. 2020b. It's morphin'time! combating linguistic discrimination with inflectional perturbations. *arXiv preprint arXiv:2005.04364*.

Samson Tan, Shafiq Joty, Lav Varshney, and Min-Yen Kan. 2020c. Mind Your Inflections! Improving NLP for Non-Standard Englishes with Base-Inflection Encoding. pages 5647–5663.

Ian Tenney, Dipanjan Das, and Ellie Pavlick. 2019a. BERT rediscovers the classical NLP pipeline. In *Proceedings of the 57th Annual Meeting of the Association for Computational Linguistics*, pages 4593–4601, Florence, Italy. Association for Computational Linguistics.

Ian Tenney, Patrick Xia, Berlin Chen, Alex Wang, Adam Poliak, R Thomas McCoy, Najoung Kim, Benjamin Van Durme, Sam Bowman, Dipanjan Das, and Ellie Pavlick. 2019b. What do you learn from context? probing for sentence structure in contextualized word representations. In *International Conference on Learning Representations*.

Henry Tsai, Jason Riesa, Melvin Johnson, Naveen Arivazhagan, Xin Li, and Amelia Archer. 2019. Small and Practical BERT Models for Sequence Labeling. pages 3623–3627.

Betty van Aken, Benjamin Winter, Alexander Löser, and Felix A Gers. 2019. How does bert answer questions? layer-wise analysis of transformer representations. In *Proceedings of the 28th ACM International Conference on Information and Knowledge Management*, pages 1823–1832.

Ashish Vaswani, Noam Shazeer, Niki Parmar, Jakob Uszkoreit, Llion Jones, Aidan N Gomez, Łukasz Kaiser, and Illia Polosukhin. 2017. Attention is All You Need. pages 5998–6008.

Jesse Vig and Yonatan Belinkov. 2019. Analyzing the structure of attention in a transformer language model. In *Proceedings of the 2019 ACL Workshop BlackboxNLP: Analyzing and Interpreting Neural Networks for NLP*, pages 63–76, Florence, Italy. Association for Computational Linguistics.

Elena Voita and Ivan Titov. 2020. Information-Theoretic Probing with Minimum Description Length. *arXiv preprint arXiv:2003.12298*.

Alex Wang, Yada Pruksachatkun, Nikita Nangia, Amanpreet Singh, Julian Michael, Felix Hill, Omer Levy, and Samuel Bowman. 2019. SuperGLUE: A Stickier Benchmark for General-purpose Language Understanding Systems. pages 3266–3280.

Alex Wang, Amanpreet Singh, Julian Michael, Felix Hill, Omer Levy, and Samuel R Bowman. 2018. Glue: A multi-task benchmark and analysis platform for natural language understanding. *arXiv preprint arXiv:1804.07461*.

Wenhui Wang, Furu Wei, Li Dong, Hangbo Bao, Nan Yang, and Ming Zhou. 2020. Minilm: Deep self-attention distillation for task-agnostic compression of pre-trained transformers. *arXiv preprint arXiv:2002.10957*.

Alex Warstadt, Amanpreet Singh, and Samuel R. Bowman. 2019a. Neural network acceptability judgments. *Transactions of the Association for Computational Linguistics*, 7:625–641.

Alex Warstadt, Amanpreet Singh, and Samuel R Bowman. 2019b. Neural network acceptability judgments. *Transactions of the Association for Computational Linguistics*, 7:625–641.

Guillaume Wenzek, Marie-Anne Lachaux, Alexis Conneau, Vishrav Chaudhary, Francisco Guzmán, Armand Joulin, and Edouard Grave. 2019. Ccnet: Extracting high quality monolingual datasets from web crawl data. *arXiv preprint arXiv:1911.00359*.

Thomas Wolf, Lysandre Debut, Victor Sanh, Julien Chaumond, Clement Delangue, Anthony Moi, Pierric Cistac, Tim Rault, Rémi Louf, Morgan Funtowicz, et al. 2019. Huggingface's transformers: State-of-the-art natural language processing. *ArXiv*, pages arXiv–1910.

John M Wu, Yonatan Belinkov, Hassan Sajjad, Nadir Durrani, Fahim Dalvi, and James Glass. 2020. Similarity analysis of contextual word representation models. *arXiv preprint arXiv:2005.01172*.

Linting Xue, Noah Constant, Adam Roberts, Mihir Kale, Rami Al-Rfou, Aditya Siddhant, Aditya Barua, and Colin Raffel. 2020. mt5: A massively multilingual pre-trained text-to-text transformer. *arXiv preprint arXiv:2010.11934*.

Xuhui Zhou, Yue Zhang, Leyang Cui, and Dandan Huang. 2020. Evaluating commonsense in pre-trained language models. In *AAAI*, pages 9733–9740.

Hui Zou and Trevor Hastie. 2005. Regularization and variable selection via the elastic net. *Journal of the royal statistical society: series B (statistical methodology)*, 67(2):301–320.

Appendix

A Description of Treebanks

Below is a list of the UD Treebanks used in the experiments:

- **Russian**: GramEval2020 Treebanks, GSD Russian Treebank, Russian-PUD, and SynTagRus Treebank.
- **English**: EWT Treebank, GUM Treebank, the English portion of ParTUT, English-PUD, and English-Pronouns Treebank.
- **French**: French Question Bank, GSD French Treebank, the French portion of ParTUT, French-PUD, Sequoia and French Spoken Treebank, adapted from the Rhapsoide prosodic-syntactic Treebank.
- **German**: GSD German Treebank, HDT-UD Treebank, German-PUD and LIT German Treebank.

B Dataset Statistics

Tables 1 – 3 provide a brief statistics on the partition sizes for each probing task.

Probing Task	Language	Train	Dev	Test	Overall
Number	Ru	174 720	21 937	21 379	218 036
	En	51 465	6492	6374	64 331
	De	533 898	66 984	66 984	668 271
	Fr	74 450	9385	9191	93 026
Case	Ru	174 884	21 768	21 974	218 626
	De	436 303	54 692	53 932	544 927
Person	Ru	162 345	20 313	20 319	202 977
	En	47 001	5945	5735	58 681
	De	471 132	58 847	58 438	588 417
	Fr	71 394	8853	8992	89 239
Gender	Ru	165 934	20 462	20 982	207 378
	De	500 628	62 163	62 612	625 403
	Fr	69 901	8840	8559	87 300

Table 1: Number of samples for each **Morphosyntactic Features** and **Masked Token** task. Languages: **Ru**=Russian, **En**=English, **De**=German, **Fr**=French.

Probing Task	Language	Train	Dev	Test	Overall
Number	Ru	100 738	12 592	12 593	125 923
	En	21 568	2696	2696	26 960
	De	339 744	42 468	42 468	424 680
	Fr	33 339	4167	4168	41 674
Case	Ru	92 320	11 540	11 540	115 400
	De	252 182	31 523	31 523	315 228
Person	Ru	15 748	11 540	11 540	19 685
	En	7255	907	907	9069
	De	184 788	23 099	23 099	230 986
	Fr	6364	796	796	7956
Gender	Ru	76 158	9520	9520	95 198
	De	252 182	31 523	31 523	315 228
	Fr	23 660	2957	2958	29 575

Table 2: Number of samples for each **Morphosyntactic Values** task. Languages: **Ru**=Russian, **En**=English, **De**=German, **Fr**=French.

Probing Task	Language	Train	Dev	Test	Overall
Stop-words Removal	**Ru**	38 838	4855	4855	48 548
	En	12 627	1578	1578	15 784
	De	121 272	15 159	15 159	151 590
	Fr	13 959	1745	1745	17 449
Article Removal	**En**	7770	971	972	15 784
	De	99 669	12459	12459	124 587
	Fr	10 083	1253	1276	12 612
Subject Number	**Ru**	9293	1164	1165	11 622
	En	471	58	60	589
	De	5 709	1007	1009	6005
	Fr	1219	151	153	1523
Subject Case	**Ru**	18 897	2344	2346	23 587
Predicate Number	**Ru**	7160	897	897	8 954
	En	1115	140	142	1397
	De	26 415	4374	4375	35 164
	Fr	2822	353	356	3531
Predicate Person	**Ru**	5240	644	646	6530
Predicate Gender	**Ru**	4414	550	553	5517
Deixis Word Number	**En**	1130	141	142	1413
	De	4804	600	601	6005

Table 3: Number of samples for each **Perturbation** task. Languages: **Ru**=Russian, **En**=English, **De**=German, **Fr**=French.

C Baseline Performance

Table 4 summarizes the results of the baseline models for **Morphosyntactic Features** tasks. Table 5 presents the performance of the baseline models for **Perturbations** tasks.

Probing Task	Lang	Char Num	TF-IDF Char	TF-IDF BPE	TF-IDF SP	fT
Number	**Ru**	0.78	**0.97**	0.96	0.96	0.94
	En	0.63	**0.95**	0.94	**0.95**	0.93
	De	0.57	**0.95**	**0.95**	0.95	0.89
	Fr	0.52	**0.91**	**0.91**	**0.91**	0.87
Case	**Ru**	0.69	**0.97**	0.96	0.96	0.90
	De	0.64	0.92	**0.93**	0.92	0.88
Person	**Ru**	0.60	**0.98**	**0.98**	**0.98**	0.93
	En	0.62	0.97	0.97	0.97	**0.98**
	De	0.66	**0.93**	**0.93**	**0.93**	0.91
	Fr	0.54	**0.93**	0.92	0.92	0.88
Gender	**Ru**	0.73	**0.96**	0.95	**0.96**	0.89
	De	0.47	**0.86**	**0.86**	**0.86**	0.81
	Fr	0.54	**0.88**	**0.88**	0.87	0.84

Table 4: Baseline results on **Morphosyntactic Features** tasks. **SP** refers to SentencePiece, and **fT** corresponds to fastText. Languages: **Ru**=Russian, **En**=English, **De**=German, **Fr**=French.

Probing Task	Lang	Char Num	TF-IDF Char	TF-IDF BPE	TF-IDF SP	fT
Stop-words Removal	**Ru**	0.57	**0.96**	0.92	0.92	0.93
	En	0.64	0.97	**0.98**	0.97	0.96
	De	0.63	**0.99**	**0.99**	**0.99**	0.97
	Fr	0.60	**0.98**	**0.98**	**0.98**	0.96
Article Removal	**En**	0.52	0.98	**0.99**	0.98	0.84
	De	0.55	**0.97**	**0.97**	**0.97**	0.87
	Fr	0.56	0.95	**0.97**	0.96	0.87
Subject Number	**Ru**	0.50	0.54	**0.55**	0.54	0.53
	En	**0.43**	0.35	0.37	**0.43**	0.40
	De	0.5	0.48	0.46	0.48	**0.57**
	Fr	0.44	**0.60**	0.50	0.55	0.55
Subject Case	**Ru**	0.51	**0.67**	0.62	0.62	0.60
Predicate Number	**Ru**	0.49	**0.64**	0.48	0.50	0.52
	En	**0.52**	0.49	0.45	0.47	0.48
	De	0.50	0.60	0.39	0.38	**0.68**
	Fr	0.49	0.64	0.47	0.49	**0.68**
Predicate Person	**Ru**	0.50	**0.81**	0.78	0.74	0.62
Predicate Gender	**Ru**	0.50	**0.62**	0.57	0.58	0.51
Deixis Word Number	**En**	0.48	0.71	**0.77**	0.75	0.70
	De	0.49	0.68	0.71	**0.72**	0.62

Table 5: Baseline results on **Perturbation** tasks. **SP** refers to SentencePiece, and **fT** corresponds to fastText. Languages: **Ru**=Russian, **En**=English, **De**=German, **Fr**=French.

D Probing Classifiers

Morphosyntactic Features Tables 6 – 7 summarize the results of the probing classifier on **Morphosyntactic Features** tasks for pre-trained and fine-tuned models. Figure 1 shows a few examples of the model behavior on the tasks. While **Gender** in German appears to be the most challenging property among the others for both pre-trained and fine-tuned models, **Case** in Russian is inferred by the models with great confidence.

Masked Token Tables 8 – 9 outline the performance of the probing classifier on **Masked Token** tasks.

Perturbations Tables 10 – 11 present the results of the probing classifier on **Perturbations** tasks for pre-trained and fine-tuned models. Figures 2 – 3 are the graphical representations of the probing classifier performance on **Article Removal** task for German, and **Predicate Number** task for French.

The overall pattern for the syntactic perturbations is that the sensitivity is captured at the lower-to-middle layers $[3-8]$ of pre-trained models. In its turn, the inflectional properties are predominantly distributed at the middle-to-higher layers $[5-12]$ of both pre-trained and fine-tuned models. However, fine-tuned versions may exhibit unpredictable behavior, an example of which we describe below. Figure 2 demonstrates the results on **Article Removal** task for German. While the probing curves of pre-trained models tend to be decaying after reaching their peak at the middle layers, they are confidently increasing towards the output layer after the fine-tuning phase. In contrast, a different behavior is observed on **Predicate Number** task for French (see Figure 3). The layers of many fine-tuned models lose their knowledge (**MiniLM**: $[5-12]$, **D-BERT**: $[5]$, **M-BERT**: $[6-11]$, **XLM-R**: $[7; 11-12]$).

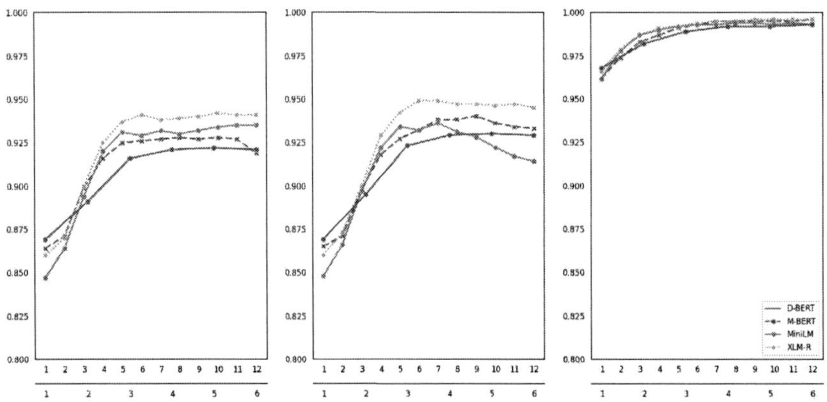

Figure 1: The performance of the probing classifier on **Morphosyntactic Features** tasks. Left: **Gender** in German (pre-trained). Middle: **Gender** in German (fine-tuned). Right: **Case** in Russian (fine-tuned).

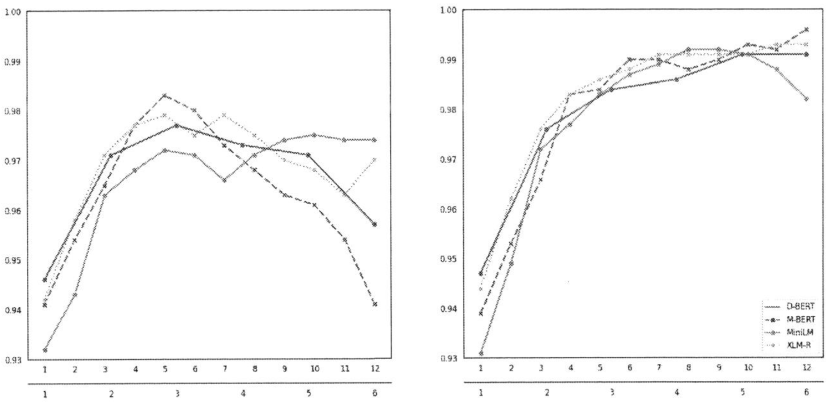

Figure 2: The performance of the probing classifier on **Article Removal** perturbation task for German. X-axis=Layer index number. Y-axis=Accuracy score. Left: pre-trained models. Right: fine-tuned models.

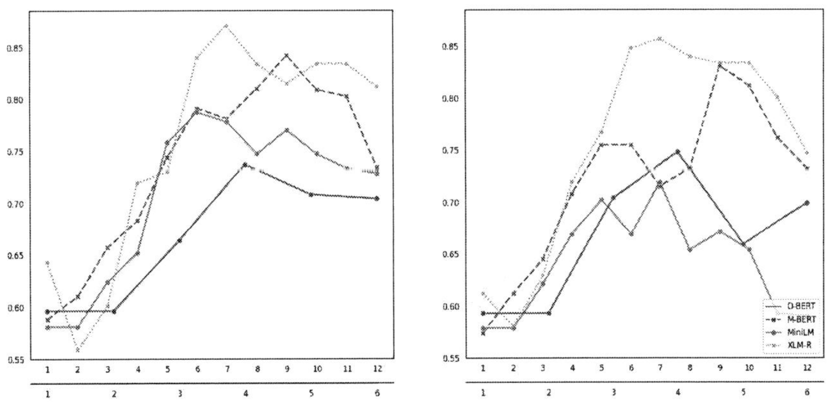

Figure 3: The performance of the probing classifier on **Predicate Number** perturbation task for French. X-axis=Layer index number. Y-axis=Accuracy score. Left: pre-trained models. Right: fine-tuned models.

Lang	Probing Task	D-BERT	MiniLM	BERT	XLM-R
De	Case	0.89	**0.91**	0.89	—
	Gender	0.91	**0.92**	0.91	**0.92**
	Number	0.93	**0.94**	0.93	**0.94**
	Person	0.95	**0.96**	0.95	—
En	Number	0.95	**0.96**	**0.96**	**0.96**
	Person	0.98	**0.99**	0.98	**0.99**
Fr	Gender	0.92	0.92	0.92	**0.93**
	Number	**0.94**	0.93	**0.94**	**0.94**
	Person	0.96	**0.97**	0.96	**0.97**
Ru	Case	0.98	**0.99**	0.98	**0.99**
	Gender	0.96	0.97	0.96	**0.98**
	Number	0.98	0.98	0.98	**0.99**
	Person	0.98	**0.99**	0.98	**0.99**

Table 6: The results of the probing classifier on **Morphosyntactic Features** tasks for pre-trained models. The scores are averaged across all layers. Languages: **Ru**=Russian, **En**=English, **De**=German, **Fr**=French.

Lang	Probing Task	D-BERT	MiniLM	BERT	XLM-R
De	Case	0.91	0.92	0.91	**0.93**
	Gender	0.91	0.91	0.92	**0.93**
	Number	0.94	0.94	0.94	**0.95**
	Person	0.95	0.96	0.96	**0.97**
En	Number	0.96	0.96	0.96	**0.97**
	Person	0.98	**0.99**	0.98	**0.99**
Fr	Gender	**0.93**	0.92	**0.93**	**0.93**
	Number	0.94	0.93	**0.95**	0.94
	Person	0.96	**0.97**	0.96	**0.97**
Ru	Case	**0.99**	**0.99**	**0.99**	**0.99**
	Gender	0.97	0.97	0.97	**0.98**
	Number	**0.99**	**0.99**	**0.99**	**0.99**
	Person	**0.99**	**0.99**	**0.99**	**0.99**

Table 7: The results of the probing classifier on **Morphosyntactic Features** tasks for fine-tuned models. The scores are averaged across all layers. Languages: **Ru**=Russian, **En**=English, **De**=German, **Fr**=French.

Lang	Probing Task	D-BERT	MiniLM	BERT	XLM-R
De	**Gender**	—	—	—	—
	Number	—	—	—	—
En	**Gender**	0.52	0.50	**0.53**	0.51
	Number	0.66	0.59	**0.68**	0.67
Fr	**Gender**	**0.72**	0.68	0.66	0.69
	Number	0.70	0.65	0.71	**0.73**
Ru	**Case**	0.67	0.61	0.74	**0.78**
	Gender	0.68	0.67	0.67	**0.73**
	Number	0.67	0.63	0.71	**0.75**
	Person	0.62	0.51	0.59	**0.69**

Table 8: The results of the probing classifier on **Masked Tokens** tasks for pre-trained models. The scores are averaged across all layers. Languages: **Ru**=Russian, **En**=English, **De**=German, **Fr**=French.

Lang	Probing Task	D-BERT	MiniLM	BERT	XLM-R
De	**Gender**	—	—	—	—
	Number	—	—	—	—
En	**Gender**	0.51	0.51	0.51	**0.52**
	Number	0.64	0.61	0.64	**0.66**
Fr	**Gender**	0.67	0.60	**0.69**	0.62
	Number	0.63	0.65	**0.69**	0.59
Ru	**Case**	0.67	0.62	0.67	**0.70**
	Gender	0.67	0.62	0.50	**0.68**
	Number	**0.66**	0.60	0.5	0.63
	Person	0.52	0.52	0.53	**0.55**

Table 9: The results of the probing classifier on **Masked Tokens** tasks for fine-tuned models. The scores are averaged across all layers. Languages: **Ru**=Russian, **En**=English, **De**=German, **Fr**=French.

Lang	Probing Task	D-BERT	MiniLM	BERT	XLM-R
De	Article Removal	**0.97**	0.96	0.96	**0.97**
	Deixis Word Number	0.65	0.63	0.66	**0.73**
	Subject Number	0.6	0.66	0.68	**0.72**
	Predicate Number	0.67	0.67	0.72	**0.77**
En	Article Removal	**0.98**	0.97	0.97	0.97
	Stop-words Removal	**0.99**	**0.99**	0.98	**0.99**
	Subject Number	**0.53**	**0.53**	0.51	0.51
	Predicate Number	0.51	0.53	0.52	**0.59**
Fr	Article Removal	0.96	0.96	0.95	**0.97**
	Subject Number	0.63	0.65	**0.71**	**0.71**
	Predicate number	0.67	0.71	0.74	**0.76**
Ru	Stop-words Removal	0.95	**0.96**	0.94	**0.96**
	Subject Case	0.72	0.75	0.77	**0.82**
	Subject Number	0.63	0.68	0.7	**0.76**
	Predicate Gender	0.63	0.64	0.67	**0.71**
	Predicate Number	0.64	0.67	0.71	**0.75**
	Predicate Person	0.77	0.8	0.81	**0.86**

Table 10: The results of the probing classifier on **Perturbations** tasks for pre-trained models. The scores are averaged across all layers. Languages: **Ru**=Russian, **En**=English, **De**=German, **Fr**=French.

Lang	Probing Task	D-BERT	MiniLM	BERT	XLM-R
De	Article Removal	**0.98**	**0.98**	**0.98**	**0.98**
	Deixis Word Number	0.63	0.63	0.69	**0.72**
	Subject Number	0.62	0.62	0.68	**0.71**
	Predicate Number	0.67	0.64	0.7	**0.75**
En	Article Removal	**0.99**	0.98	**0.99**	**0.99**
	Stop-words Removal	**0.99**	**0.99**	**0.99**	**0.99**
	Subject Number	0.54	0.52	**0.57**	0.55
	Predicate Number	0.51	0.52	0.54	**0.6**
Fr	Article	0.97	0.96	0.96	**0.98**
	Subject Number	0.65	0.67	0.73	**0.76**
	Predicate Number	0.67	0.64	0.72	**0.76**
Ru	Stop-words Removal	0.96	0.95	0.96	**0.97**
	Subject Case	0.75	0.75	0.79	**0.84**
	Subject Number	0.65	0.65	0.72	**0.77**
	Predicate Gender	0.63	0.62	0.67	**0.71**
	Predicate Number	0.62	0.62	0.7	**0.75**
	Predicate Person	0.79	0.8	0.8	**0.85**

Table 11: The results of the probing classifier on **Perturbations** tasks for fine-tuned models. The scores are averaged across all layers. Languages: **Ru**=Russian, **En**=English, **De**=German, **Fr**=French.

E Individual Neuron Analysis

Property-wise analysis Figures 4 – 7 depict property-wise neuron distribution for French, Russian, German and English.

Layer-wise analysis Figures 8 – 10 demonstrate the results of the individual neuron analysis on **Subject Number** perturbation task for Russian, English and French.

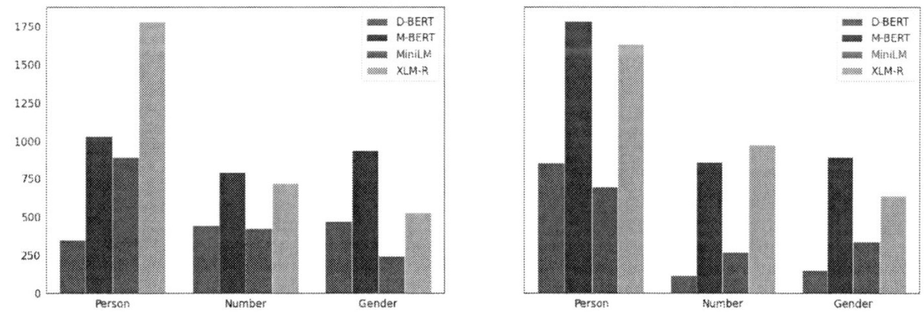

Figure 4: Number of neurons per each property for French. Y-axis=Number of neurons. Left: pre-trained models. Right: fine-tuned models.

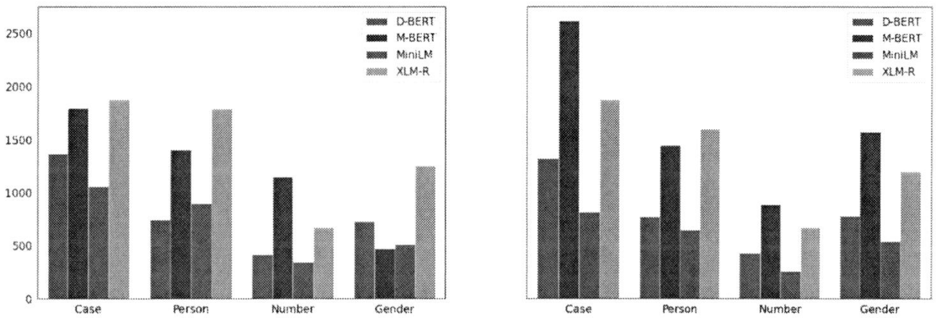

Figure 5: Number of neurons per each property for Russian. Y-axis=Number of neurons. Left: pre-trained models. Right: fine-tuned models.

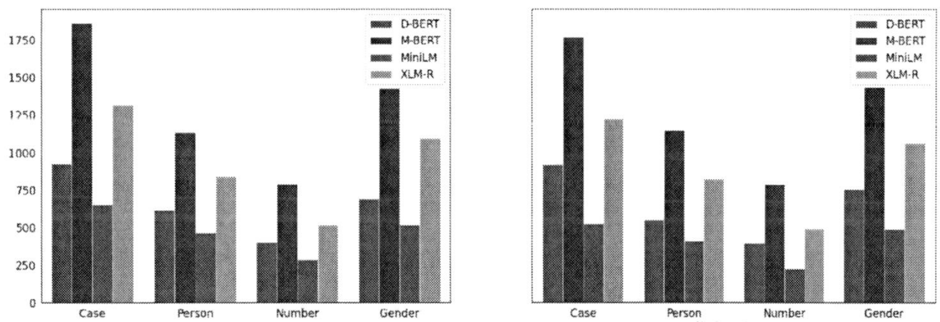

Figure 6: Number of neurons per each property for German. Y-axis=Number of neurons. Left: pre-trained models. Right: fine-tuned models.

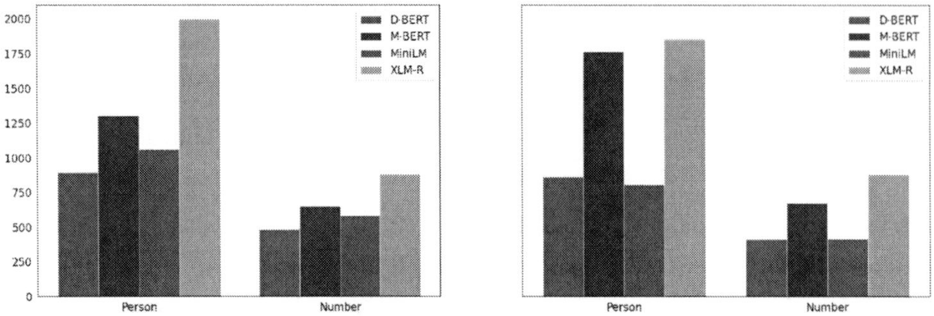

Figure 7: Number of neurons per each property for English. Y-axis=Number of neurons. Left: pre-trained models. Right: fine-tuned models.

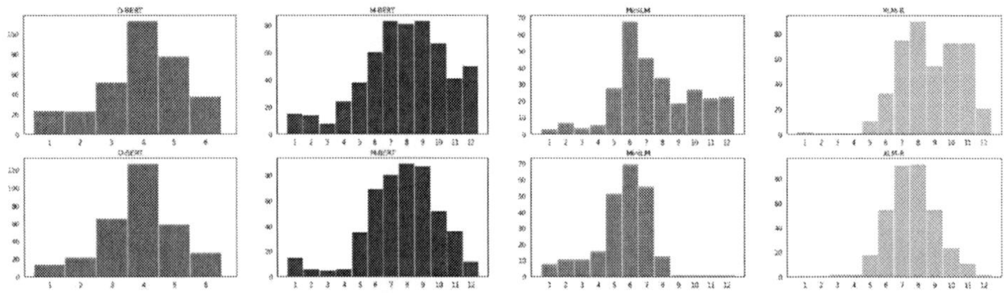

Figure 8: The distribution of top neurons over **Subject Number** perturbation task for each model (**Russian**). X-axis=Layer index number. Y-axis=Number of neurons. Top: pre-trained models. Bottom: fine-tuned models.

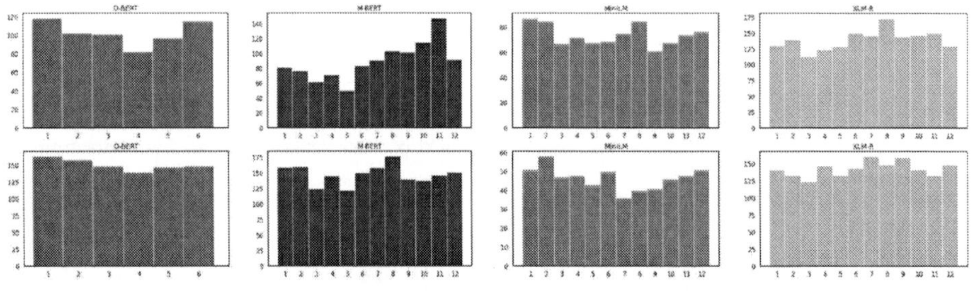

Figure 9: The distribution of top neurons over **Subject Number** perturbation task for each model (**English**). X-axis=Layer index number. Y-axis=Number of neurons. Top: pre-trained models. Bottom: fine-tuned models.

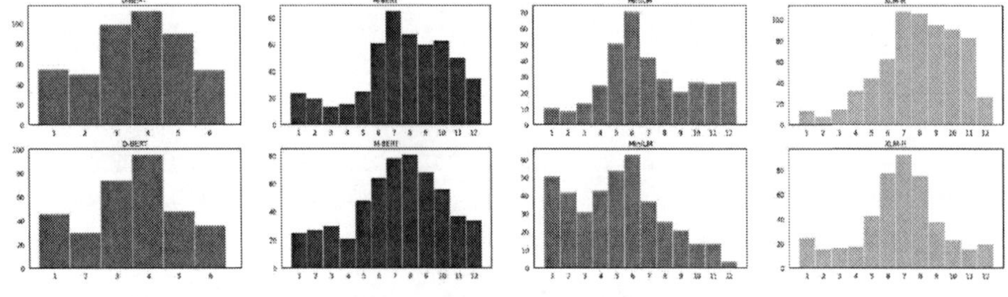

Figure 10: The distribution of top neurons over **Subject Number** perturbation task for each model (**French**). X-axis=Layer index number. Y-axis=Number of neurons. Top: pre-trained models. Bottom: fine-tuned models.

F POS-Tagging Performance

Tables 12 – 15 describe the results of the fine-tuning on POS-tagging task for each language.

Model / Metric	Accuracy	F1	Precision	Recall
M-BERT	**0.98**	**0.98**	**0.98**	**0.98**
DistilBERT	**0.98**	**0.98**	**0.98**	**0.98**
MiniLM	**0.98**	**0.98**	**0.98**	**0.98**
XLM-R	**0.98**	**0.98**	**0.98**	**0.98**

Table 12: Metrics of the models fine-tuned for POS-tagging task for German.

Model / Metric	Accuracy	F1	Precision	Recall
M-BERT	**0.96**	0.95	0.95	0.95
DistilBERT	**0.95**	0.94	0.94	0.94
MiniLM	**0.95**	0.94	0.94	0.94
XLM-R	**0.96**	**0.96**	**0.96**	**0.96**

Table 13: Metrics of the models fine-tuned for POS-tagging task for English.

Model / Metric	Accuracy	F1	Precision	Recall
M-BERT	**0.98**	0.97	0.97	0.97
DistilBERT	**0.97**	**0.97**	**0.97**	**0.97**
MiniLM	**0.97**	0.96	0.96	0.96
XLM-R	**0.98**	**0.98**	**0.98**	**0.98**

Table 14: Metrics of the models fine-tuned for POS-tagging task for French.

Model / Metric	Accuracy	F1	Precision	Recall
M-BERT	**0.99**	**0.99**	**0.99**	**0.99**
DistilBERT	**0.99**	**0.99**	**0.99**	**0.99**
MiniLM	**0.99**	0.98	0.98	0.98
XLM-R	**0.99**	**0.99**	**0.99**	**0.99**

Table 15: Metrics of the models fine-tuned for POS-tagging task for Russian.

SIGTYP 2021 Shared Task: Robust Spoken Language Identification

Elizabeth Salesky[◇*] **Badr M. Abdullah**[‡*] **Sabrina J. Mielke**[◇*]
Elena Klyachko[◁,▷] **Oleg Serikov**[◁] **Edoardo Ponti**[□]
Ritesh Kumar[•] **Ryan Cotterell**[☉] **Ekaterina Vylomova**[♯]
[◇]Johns Hopkins University [‡]Saarland University [◁]Higher School of Economics
[▷]The Institute of Linguistics RAS [□]Mila/McGill University Montreal
[•]Bhim Rao Ambedkar University [☉]ETH Zürich [♯]University of Melbourne

Abstract

While language identification is a fundamental speech and language processing task, for many languages and language families it remains a challenging task. For many low-resource and endangered languages this is in part due to resource availability: where larger datasets exist, they may be single-speaker or have different domains than desired application scenarios, demanding a need for domain and speaker-invariant language identification systems. This year's shared task on robust spoken language identification sought to investigate just this scenario: systems were to be trained on largely single-speaker speech from one domain, but evaluated on data in other domains recorded from speakers under different recording circumstances, mimicking realistic low-resource scenarios. We see that domain and speaker mismatch proves very challenging for current methods which can perform above 95% accuracy in-domain, which domain adaptation can address to some degree, but that these conditions merit further investigation to make spoken language identification accessible in many scenarios.

1 Introduction

Depending on how we count, there are roughly 7000 languages spoken around the world today. The field of linguistic typology is concerned with the study and categorization of the world's languages based on their linguistic structural properties (Comrie, 1988; Croft, 2002). While two languages may share structural properties across some typological dimensions, they may vary across others. For example, two languages could have identical speech sounds in their phonetic inventory, yet be perceived as dissimilar because each has its own unique set of phonological rules governing possible sound combinations. This leads to tremendous variation and diversity in speech patterns across the world languages (Tucker and Wright, 2020), the effects of which are understudied across many downstream applications due in part to lack of available resources. Building robust speech technologies which are applicable to any language is crucial to equal access as well as the preservation, documentation, and categorization of the world's languages, especially for endangered languages with a declining speaker community.

Unfortunately, robust (spoken) language technologies are only available for a small number of languages, mainly for speaker communities with strong economic power. The main hurdle for the development of speech technologies for under-represented languages is the lack of high-quality transcribed speech resources (see Joshi et al. (2020) for a detailed discussion on linguistic diversity in language technology research). The largest multilingual speech resource in terms of language coverage is the CMU Wilderness dataset (Black, 2019), which consists of read speech segments from the Bible in ~700 languages. Although this wide-coverage resource provides an opportunity to study many endangered and under-represented languages, it has a narrow domain and lacks speaker diversity as the vast majority of segments are recorded by low-pitch male speakers. It remains unclear whether such resources can be exploited to build generalizable speech technologies for under-resourced languages.

Spoken language identification (SLID) is an enabling technology for multilingual speech communication with a wide range of applications. Earlier SLID systems addressed the problem using the phonotactic approach whereby generative models are trained on sequences of phones transduced from the speech signal using an acoustic model (Lamel and Gauvain, 1994; Li and Ma, 2005). Most current state-of-the-art SLID systems are based on deep neural networks which are trained end-to-end from a spectral representation of the acoustic sig-

*Equal contribution

Proceedings of the Third Workshop on Computational Typology and Multilingual NLP, pages 122–129
June 10, 2021. ©2021 Association for Computational Linguistics

nal (e.g., MFCC feature vectors) without any intermediate symbolic representations (Lopez-Moreno et al., 2014; Gonzalez-Dominguez et al., 2014). In addition to their ability to effectively learn to discriminate between closely related language varieties (Gelly et al., 2016; Shon et al., 2018), it has been shown that neural networks can capture the degree of relatedness and similarity between languages in their emergent representations (Abdullah et al., 2020).

Several SLID evaluation campaigns have been organized in the past, including the NIST Language Recognition Evaluation (Lee et al., 2016; Sadjadi et al., 2018), focusing on different aspects of this task including closely related languages, and typically used conversational telephone speech. However, the languages were not sampled according to typologically-aware criteria but rather were geographic or resource-driven choices. Therefore, while the NIST task languages may represent a diverse subset of the world's languages, there are many languages and language families which have not been observed in past tasks. In this shared task, we aim to address this limitation by broadening the language coverage to a set of typologically diverse languages across seven languages families. We also aim to assess the degree to which single-speaker speech resources from a narrow domain can be utilized to build robust speech language technologies.

2 Task Description

While language identification is a fundamental speech and language processing task, it remains a challenging task, especially when going beyond the small set of languages past evaluation has focused on. Further, for many low-resource and endangered languages, only single-speaker recordings may be available, demanding a need for domain and speaker-invariant language identification systems.

We selected 16 typologically diverse languages, some of which share phonological features, and others where these have been lost or gained due to language contact, to perform what we call robust language identification: systems were to be trained on largely single-speaker speech from one domain, but evaluated on data in other domains recorded from speakers under different recording circumstances, mimicking more realistic low-resource scenarios.

2.1 Provided Data

To train models, we provided participants with speech data from the CMU Wilderness dataset (Black, 2019), which contains utterance-aligned read speech from the Bible in 699 languages,[1] but predominantly recorded from a single speaker per language, typically male. Evaluation was conducted on data from other sources—in particular, multi-speaker datasets recorded in a variety of conditions, testing systems' capacity to generalize to new domains, new speakers, and new recording settings. Languages were chosen from the CMU Wilderness dataset given availability of additional data in a different setting, and include several language families as well as more closely-related challenge pairs such as Javanese and Sundanese. These included data from the Common Voice project (CV; Ardila et al., 2020) which is read speech typically recorded using built-in laptop microphones; radio news data (SLR24; Juan et al., 2014, 2015); crowd-sourced recordings using portable electronics (SLR35, SLR36; Kjartansson et al., 2018); cleanly recorded microphone data (SLR64, SLR65, SLR66, SLR79; He et al., 2020); and a collection of recordings from varied sources (SS; Shukla, 2020). Table 1 shows the task languages and their data sources for evaluation splits for the robust language identification task.

We strove to provide balanced data to ensure signal comes from salient information about the language rather than spurious correlations about e.g. utterance length. We selected and/or trimmed utterances from the CMU Wilderness dataset to between 3 to 7 seconds in length. Training data for all languages comprised 4,000 samples each. We selected evaluation sources for validation and blind test sets to ensure no possible overlap with CMU Wilderness speakers. We held out speakers between validation and test splits, and balanced speaker gender within splits to the degree possible where annotations were available. We note that the Marathi dataset is female-only. Validation and blind test sets each comprised 500 samples per language. We release the data as derivative MFCC features.

3 Evaluation

The robust language identification shared task allowed two kinds of submissions: first, *constrained* submissions, for which only the provided training

[1]Data source: `bible.is`

ISO	Wilderness ID	Language name	Family	Genus	Macroarea	Train	Eval
kab	KABCEB	Kabyle	Afro-Asiatic	Berber	Africa	Wilderness	CV
iba	IBATIV	Iban	Austronesian	Malayo-Sumbawan	Papunesia	Wilderness	SLR24
ind	INZTSI	Indonesian	Austronesian	Malayo-Sumbawan	Papunesia	Wilderness	CV
sun	SUNIBS	Sundanese	Austronesian	Malayo-Sumbawan	Papunesia	Wilderness	SLR36
jav	JAVNRF	Javanese	Austronesian	Javanese	Papunesia	Wilderness	SLR35
eus	EUSEAB	Euskara	Basque	Basque	Eurasia	Wilderness	CV
tam	TCVWTC	Tamil	Dravidian	Southern Dravidian	Eurasia	Wilderness	SLR65
kan	ERVWTC	Kannada	Dravidian	Southern Dravidian	Eurasia	Wilderness	SLR79
tel	TCWWTC	Telugu	Dravidian	South-Central Dravidian	Eurasia	Wilderness	SLR66
hin	HNDSKV	Hindi	Indo-European	Indic	Eurasia	Wilderness	SS
por	PORARA	Portuguese	Indo-European	Romance	Eurasia	Wilderness	CV
rus	RUSS76	Russian	Indo-European	Slavic	Eurasia	Wilderness	CV
eng	EN1NIV	English	Indo-European	Germanic	Eurasia	Wilderness	CV
mar	MARWTC	Marathi	Indo-European	Indic	Eurasia	Wilderness	SLR64
cnh	CNHBSM	Chin, Hakha	Niger-Congo	Gur	Africa	Wilderness	CV
tha	THATSV	Thai	Tai-Kadai	Kam-Tai	Eurasia	Wilderness	CV

Table 1: Provided data with language family and macroarea information. **ISO** shows ISO 639-3 codes. Training data (**Train**) for all languages is taken from CMU Wilderness dataset; validation and evaluation data (**Eval**) is derived from multiple data sources.

data was used; and second, *unconstrained* submissions, in which the training data may be extended with any external source of information (e.g. pretrained models, additional data, etc.).

3.1 Evaluation Metrics

We evaluate task performance using precision, recall, and F_1. For each metric we report both micro-averages, meaning that the metric average is computed equally-weighted across all samples for all languages, and macro-averages, meaning that we first computed the metric for each language and then averaged these aggregates to see whether submissions behave differently on different languages. Participant submissions were ranked according to macro-averaged F_1.

3.2 Baseline

For our baseline SLID system, we use a deep convolutional neural network (CNN) as sequence classification model. The model can be viewed as two components trained end-to-end: a segment-level feature extractor (f) and a language classifier (g). Given as input a speech segment parametrized as sequence of MFCC frames $\mathbf{x}_{1:T} = (\mathbf{x}_1, \ldots, \mathbf{x}_T) \in \mathbb{R}^{k \times T}$, where T is the number of frames and k is the number of the spectral coefficients, the segment-level feature extractor first transforms $\mathbf{x}_{1:T}$ into a segment-level representation as $\mathbf{u} = f(\mathbf{x}_{1:T}; \boldsymbol{\theta}_f) \in \mathbb{R}^d$. Then, the language classifier transforms $\mathbf{u}$ into a logit vector $\hat{\mathbf{y}} \in \mathbb{R}^{|\mathcal{Y}|}$, where $\mathcal{Y}$ is the set of languages, through a series of non-linear transformations as $\hat{\mathbf{y}} = g(\mathbf{u}; \boldsymbol{\theta}_g)$. The logit vector $\hat{\mathbf{y}}$ is then fed to a softmax function to get a probability distribution over the languages.

The segment-level feature extractor consists of three 1-dimensional, temporal convolution layers with 64, 128, 256 filters of widths 16, 32, 48 for each layer and a fixed stride of 1 step. Following each convolutional operation, we apply batch normalization, ReLU non-linearity, and unit dropout with probability which was tuned over $\{0.0, 0.4, 0.6\}$. We apply average pooling to downsample the representation only at the end of the convolution block, which yields a segment representation $\mathbf{u} \in \mathbb{R}^{256}$. The language classifier consists of 3 fully-connected layers ($256 \rightarrow 256 \rightarrow 256 \rightarrow 16$), with a unit dropout with probability 0.4 between the layers, before the softmax layer. The model is trained with the ADAM optimizer with a batch size of 256 for 50 epochs. We report the results of the best epoch on the validation set as our baseline results.

3.3 Submissions

We received three constrained submissions from three teams, as described below.

Anlirika (Shcherbakov et al., 2021, composite) The submitted system (constrained) consists of several recurrent, convolutional, and dense layers. The neural architecture starts with a dense layer that is designed to remove sound harmonics from a raw spectral pattern. This is followed by a 1D convolutional layer that extracts audio frequency patterns (features). Then the features are fed into a stack of LSTMs that focuses on 'local' temporal constructs. The output of the stack of LSTMs is then additionally concatenated with the CNN features and is fed into one more LSTM module. Using the resulting representation, the final (dense) layer evaluates a categorical loss across 16 classes. The network was trained with Adam optimizer, the learning rate was set to be 5×10^{-4}. In addition, similar to Lipsia, the team implemented a data augmentation strategy: samples from validation set have been added to the training data.

Lipsia (Celano, 2021, Universität Leipzig) submitted a constrained system based on the ResNet-50 (He et al., 2016), a deep (50 layers) CNN-based neural architecture. The choice of the model is supported by a comparative analysis with more shallow architectures such as ResNet-34 and a 3-layer CNNs that all were shown to overfit to the training data. In addition, the authors proposed transforming MFCC features into corresponding 640x480 spectrograms since this data format is more suitable for CNNs. The output layer of the network is dense and evaluates the probabilities of 16 language classes.[2] Finally, the authors augmented the training data with 60% of the samples from the validation set because the training set did not present enough variety in terms of domains and speakers while the validation data included significantly more. Use of the validation data in this way seems to have greatly improved generalization ability of the model.

The model performed relatively well with no fine-tuning or transfer-learning applied after augmentation.[3]

NTR (Bedyakin and Mikhaylovskiy, 2021, NTR Labs composite), submitted an essentially constrained[4] system which uses a CNN with a self-attentive pooling layer. The architecture of the network was QuartzNet ASR following Kriman et al. (2020), with the decoder mechanism replaced with a linear classification mechanism. The authors also used a similar approach in another challenge on low-resource ASR, Dialog-2021 ASR[5]. They applied several augmentation techniques, namely shifting samples in range (-5ms; +5ms), MFCC perturbations (SpecAugment; Park et al., 2019), and adding background noise.

4 Results and Analysis

The main results in Table 2 show all systems greatly varying in performance, with the Lipsia system clearly coming out on top, boasting best accuracy and average F_1 score, and reaching the best F_1 score for nearly each language individually.[6]

All four systems' performance varies greatly on average, but nevertheless some interesting overall trends emerge. Figure 1 shows that while the Anlirika and Lipsia systems' performance on the different languages do not correlate with the baseline system (linear fit with Pearson's $R^2 = 0.00$ and $p > 0.8$ and $R^2 = 0.02$ and $p > 0.5$, respectively), the NTR system's struggle correlates at least somewhat with the same languages that the baseline system struggles with: a linear fit has $R^2 = 0.15$ with $p > 0.1$. More interestingly, in correlations amongst themselves, the Anlirika and Lipsia systems do clearly correlate ($R^2 = 0.57$ and $p < 0.001$), and the NTR system correlates again at least somewhat with the Anlirika system ($R^2 = 0.11$ and $p > 0.2$) and the Lipsia system ($R^2 = 0.19$ and $p > 0.05$).

Note that most systems submitted are powerful enough to fit the training data: our baseline achieves a macro-averaged F_1 score of .98 ($\pm$.01) on the training data, the Lipsia system similarly achieves .97 ($\pm$.03), the NTR system reaches a score of .99 ($\pm$.02). An outlier, the Anlirika system reaches only .75 ($\pm$.09). On held-out data from CMU Wilderness which matches the training data domain, the baseline achieves .96 F1. This suggests an inability to generalize across domains and/or speakers without additional data for adaptation.

Diving deeper into performance on different languages and families, Figure 2 shows confusion matrices for precision and recall, grouped by language family. We can see the superiority of the Lipsia

[2]The submitted system actually predicts one out of 18 classes as two other languages that weren't part of the eventual test set were included. The system predicted these two languages for 27 of 8000 test examples, i.e., $\approx 0.34\%$.

[3]The authors trained ResNet-50 from scratch.

[4]Although technically external noise data was used when augmenting the dataset, no language-specific resources were.

[5]`http://www.dialog-21.ru/en/evaluation/`

[6]Each of the "wins" indicated by boldface in Table 2 is statistically significant under a paired-permutation significance test (note that as we are not in a multiple-hypothesis testing setting, we do not apply Bonferroni or similar corrections). There are no significant differences between the baseline and the Anlirika system for kab, ind, por, rus, and eng; between the baseline and the Lipsia system for sun; between the baseline and the NTR system for ind, iba, and cnh; between Anlirika and Lipsia on rus; between Lipsia and NTR on rus; between Anlirika and NTR on ind and rus.

ISO	Anlirika		Baseline		Lipsia		NTR	
	Valid.	Test	Valid.	Test	Valid.	Test	Valid.	Test
Family: Afro-Asiatic	*.329*	.214	*.181*	.235	*.670*	**.453**	*.102*	.082
kab	*.329*	.214	*.181*	.235	*.670*	**.453**	*.102*	.082
Family: Austronesian	*.429*	.368	*.082*	.094	*.578*	**.498**	*.065*	.060
iba	*.692*	.696	*.029*	.018	*.980*	**.968**	*.020*	.031
ind	*.350*	.108	*.033*	.105	*.700*	**.338**	*.096*	.074
sun	*.406*	**.369**	*.160*	.149	*.090*	.140	*.086*	.082
jav	*.267*	.300	*.106*	.106	*.540*	**.547**	*.059*	.053
Family: Basque	*.565*	.405	*.100*	.090	*.850*	**.792**	*.077*	.016
eus	*.565*	.405	*.100*	.090	*.850*	**.792**	*.077*	.016
Family: Dravidian	*.351*	.246	*.202*	.138	*.807*	**.572**	*.074*	.053
tam	*.342*	.272	*.348*	.204	*.800*	**.609**	*.172*	.046
kan	*.188*	.168	*.000*	.042	*.820*	**.557**	*.004*	.015
tel	*.523*	.298	*.259*	.168	*.800*	**.550**	*.046*	.097
Family: Indo-European	*.439*	.225	*.130*	.144	*.722*	**.402**	*.114*	.047
hin	*.458*	.378	*.091*	.099	*.780*	**.635**	*.021*	.011
por	*.211*	.143	*.157*	.166	*.550*	**.358**	*.102*	.068
rus	*.630*	**.034**	*.014*	.014	*.900*	**.065**	*.050*	**.049**
eng	*.194*	.148	*.161*	.179	*.460*	**.414**	*.270*	.099
mar	*.701*	.423	*.229*	.263	*.920*	**.539**	*.126*	.010
Family: Niger-Congo	*.516*	.403	*.138*	.063	*.860*	**.763**	*.122*	.038
cnh	*.516*	.403	*.138*	.063	*.860*	**.763**	*.122*	.038
Family: Tai-Kadai	*.362*	.156	*.086*	.052	*.780*	**.401**	*.025*	.015
tha	*.362*	.156	*.086*	.052	*.780*	**.401**	*.025*	.015
F1, Macro Avg.	*.421*	.282	*.131*	.122	*.719*	**.508**	*.086*	.049
F1, Micro Avg.	*.436*	.298	*.145*	.137		**.532**		.063
Accuracy		29.9%		13.7%		**53.1%**		6.3%

Table 2: F_1 scores, their macro-averages per family, and overall accuracies of submitted predictions on validation and test data (validation results are self-reported by participants). The Lipsia system performed best across nearly all languages and consistently achieves the highest averages.

system and to a lesser degree the Anlirika system over the generally more noisy and unreliable baseline system and the NTR system which was likely overtrained: it classifies 23% of examples as tel, 20% as kab, and 16% as eng, with the remaining 41% spread across the remaining 13 languages (so $\approx 3.2\%$ per language).

Interestingly, the other three systems all struggle to tell apart sun and jav, the Anlirika and baseline systems classifying both mostly as sun and the Lipsia system classifying both mostly as jav. Note that the baseline system tends to label many languages' examples as sun (most notably mar, the test data for which contains only female speakers), eus (most notably also rus), and eng (most notably also iba), despite balanced training data. In a similar pattern, the Anlirika predicts tam for many languages, in particular ind, the other two Dravidian languages kan and tel, por, rus, eng, cnh, and tha.

Looking more closely at the clearly best-performing system, the Lipsia system, and its performance and confusions, we furthermore find that the biggest divergence from the diagonal after the sun/jav confusion is a tendency to label rus as por, and the second biggest divergence is that mar examples are also sometimes labeled as kan and tel; while the first one is within the same family, in the second case, these are neighbouring languages in

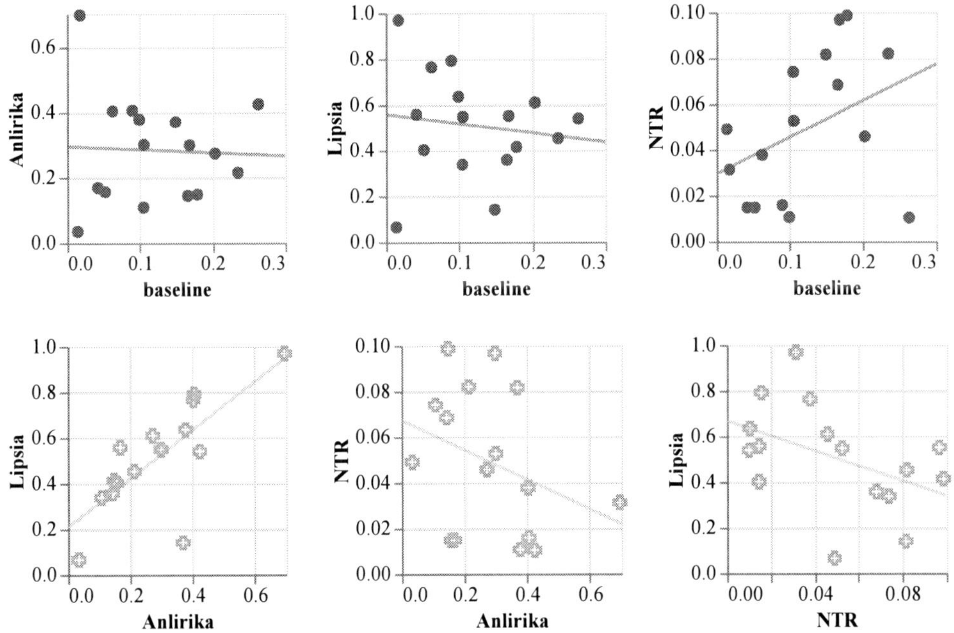

Figure 1: Correlating submitted systems' F_1 scores for our 16 languages on the test set. The lines are linear regressions as described in Section 4.

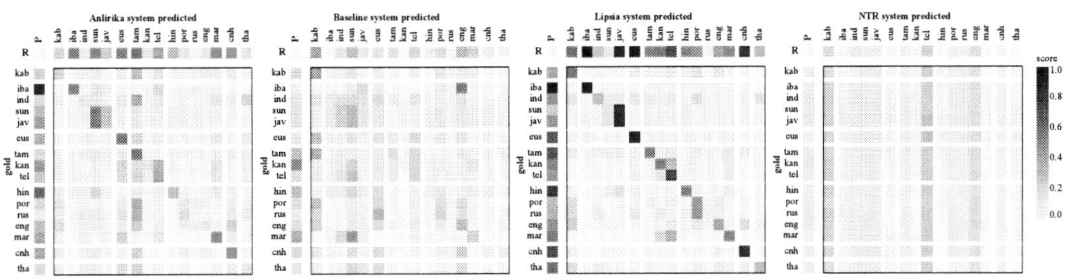

Figure 2: Visualization of Precision (P), Recall (R), and confusion matrices (scores are counts normalized by number of gold entries) for the Anlirika, baseline, Lipsia, and NTR system, grouped by language families.

contact and mar shares some typological properties with kan (and kan and tel belong to the same language family).

5 Conclusion

This paper describes the SIGTYP shared task on robust spoken language identification (SLID). This task investigated the ability of current SLID models to generalize across speakers and domains. The best system achieved a macro-averaged accuracy of 53% by training on validation data, indicating that even then the task is far from solved. Further exploration of few-shot domain and speaker adaptation is necessary for SLID systems to be applied outside typical well-matched data scenarios.

References

Badr M. Abdullah, Jacek Kudera, Tania Avgustinova, Bernd Möbius, and Dietrich Klakow. 2020. Rediscovering the Slavic continuum in representations emerging from neural models of spoken language identification. In *Proceedings of the 7th Workshop on NLP for Similar Languages, Varieties and Dialects*, pages 128–139, Barcelona, Spain (Online). International Committee on Computational Linguistics (ICCL).

Rosana Ardila, Megan Branson, Kelly Davis, Michael Kohler, Josh Meyer, Michael Henretty, Reuben Morais, Lindsay Saunders, Francis Tyers, and Gregor Weber. 2020. Common voice: A massively-multilingual speech corpus. In *Proceedings of the 12th Language Resources and Evaluation Conference*, pages 4218–4222, Marseille, France. European Language Resources Association.

Roman Bedyakin and Nikolay Mikhaylovskiy. 2021. Language ID Prediction from Speech Using Self-Attentive Pooling and 1D-Convolutions. In *Proceedings of the Third Workshop on Computational Research in Linguistic Typology*. North American Association for Computational Linguistics.

Alan W Black. 2019. CMU wilderness multilingual speech dataset. In *IEEE International Conference on Acoustics, Speech and Signal Processing (ICASSP)*, pages 5971–5975.

Giuseppe Celano. 2021. A ResNet-50-based Convolutional Neural Network Model for Language ID Identification from Speech Recordings. In *Proceedings of the Third Workshop on Computational Research in Linguistic Typology*. North American Association for Computational Linguistics.

Bernard Comrie. 1988. Linguistic typology. *Annual Review of Anthropology*, 17:145–159.

William Croft. 2002. *Typology and Universals*. Cambridge University Press.

Grégory Gelly, Jean-Luc Gauvain, Lori Lamel, Antoine Laurent, Viet Bac Le, and Abdel Messaoudi. 2016. Language recognition for dialects and closely related languages. In *Odyssey*, pages 124–131.

Javier Gonzalez-Dominguez, Ignacio Lopez-Moreno, Haşim Sak, Joaquin Gonzalez-Rodriguez, and Pedro J Moreno. 2014. Automatic language identification using long short-term memory recurrent neural networks. In *Fifteenth Annual Conference of the International Speech Communication Association*.

Fei He, Shan-Hui Cathy Chu, Oddur Kjartansson, Clara Rivera, Anna Katanova, Alexander Gutkin, Isin Demirsahin, Cibu Johny, Martin Jansche, Supheakmungkol Sarin, and Knot Pipatsrisawat. 2020. Open-source Multi-speaker Speech Corpora for Building Gujarati, Kannada, Malayalam, Marathi, Tamil and Telugu Speech Synthesis Systems. In *Proceedings of The 12th Language Resources and Evaluation Conference (LREC)*, pages 6494–6503, Marseille, France. European Language Resources Association (ELRA).

Kaiming He, Xiangyu Zhang, Shaoqing Ren, and Jian Sun. 2016. Deep residual learning for image recognition. In *Proceedings of the IEEE conference on computer vision and pattern recognition*, pages 770–778.

Pratik Joshi, Sebastin Santy, Amar Budhiraja, Kalika Bali, and Monojit Choudhury. 2020. The state and fate of linguistic diversity and inclusion in the nlp world. In *Proceedings of the 58th Annual Meeting of the Association for Computational Linguistics*, pages 6282–6293.

Sarah Samson Juan, Laurent Besacier, Benjamin Lecouteux, and Mohamed Dyab. 2015. Using resources from a closely-related language to develop asr for a very under-resourced language: A case study for iban. In *Proceedings of INTERSPEECH*, Dresden, Germany.

Sarah Samson Juan, Laurent Besacier, and Solange Rossato. 2014. Semi-supervised g2p bootstrapping and its application to asr for a very under-resourced language: Iban. In *Proceedings of Workshop for Spoken Language Technology for Under-resourced (SLTU)*.

Oddur Kjartansson, Supheakmungkol Sarin, Knot Pipatsrisawat, Martin Jansche, and Linne Ha. 2018. Crowd-Sourced Speech Corpora for Javanese, Sundanese, Sinhala, Nepali, and Bangladeshi Bengali. In *Proc. The 6th Intl. Workshop on Spoken Language Technologies for Under-Resourced Languages (SLTU)*, pages 52–55, Gurugram, India.

Samuel Kriman, Stanislav Beliaev, Boris Ginsburg, Jocelyn Huang, Oleksii Kuchaiev, Vitaly Lavrukhin, Ryan Leary, Jason Li, and Yang Zhang. 2020. Quartznet: Deep automatic speech recognition with 1d time-channel separable convolutions. In *ICASSP 2020-2020 IEEE International Conference on Acoustics, Speech and Signal Processing (ICASSP)*, pages 6124–6128. IEEE.

Lori F Lamel and Jean-Luc Gauvain. 1994. Language identification using phone-based acoustic likelihoods. In *Proceedings of ICASSP'94. IEEE International Conference on Acoustics, Speech and Signal Processing*, volume 1, pages I–293. IEEE.

Kong Aik Lee, Haizhou Li, Li Deng, Ville Hautamäki, Wei Rao, Xiong Xiao, Anthony Larcher, Hanwu Sun, Trung Nguyen, Guangsen Wang, et al. 2016. The 2015 nist language recognition evaluation: the shared view of i2r, fantastic4 and singams. In *Interspeech 2016*, volume 2016, pages 3211–3215.

Haizhou Li and Bin Ma. 2005. A phonotactic language model for spoken language identification. In *Proceedings of the 43rd Annual Meeting of the Association for Computational Linguistics (ACL'05)*, pages 515–522.

Ignacio Lopez-Moreno, Javier Gonzalez-Dominguez, Oldrich Plchot, David Martinez, Joaquin Gonzalez-Rodriguez, and Pedro Moreno. 2014. Automatic language identification using deep neural networks. In *2014 IEEE international conference on acoustics, speech and signal processing (ICASSP)*, pages 5337–5341. IEEE.

Daniel S Park, William Chan, Yu Zhang, Chung-Cheng Chiu, Barret Zoph, Ekin D Cubuk, and Quoc V Le. 2019. Specaugment: A simple data augmentation method for automatic speech recognition. *arXiv preprint arXiv:1904.08779*.

Seyed Omid Sadjadi, Timothee Kheyrkhah, Audrey Tong, Craig S Greenberg, Douglas A Reynolds, Elliot Singer, Lisa P Mason, and Jaime Hernandez-Cordero. 2018. The 2017 nist language recognition evaluation. In *Odyssey*, pages 82–89.

Andrei Shcherbakov, Liam Whittle, Ritesh Kumar, Siddharth Singh, Matthew Coleman, and Ekaterina Vylomova. 2021. Anlirika: an LSTM–CNN Flow Twister for Language ID Prediction. In *Proceedings of the Third Workshop on Computational Research in Linguistic Typology*. North American Association for Computational Linguistics.

Suwon Shon, Ahmed Ali, and James Glass. 2018. Convolutional neural network and language embeddings for end-to-end dialect recognition. In *Proc. Odyssey 2018 The Speaker and Language Recognition Workshop*, pages 98–104.

Shivam Shukla. 2020. Speech dataset in hindi language.

Benjamin V Tucker and Richard Wright. 2020. Introduction to the special issue on the phonetics of underdocumented languages. *The Journal of the Acoustical Society of America*, 147(4):2741–2744.

Language ID Prediction from Speech Using Self-Attentive Pooling

Roman Bedyakin[1], **Nikolay Mikhaylovskiy**[2, 3]
[1]AO HTSTS, Moscow, Russia, [2]NTR Labs, Moscow, Russia,
[3]Tomsk State University, Tomsk, Russia
{rbedyakin, nickm}@ntr.ai

Abstract

This memo describes NTR-TSU submission for SIGTYP 2021 Shared Task on predicting language IDs from speech.

Spoken Language Identification (LID) is an important step in a multilingual Automated Speech Recognition (ASR) system pipeline. For many low-resource and endangered languages, only single-speaker recordings may be available, demanding a need for domain and speaker-invariant language ID systems. In this memo, we show that a convolutional neural network with a Self-Attentive Pooling layer shows promising results for the language identification task.

1 Introduction

Spoken Language Identification (LID) is a process of classifying the language spoken in a speech recording and is an important step in a multilingual Automated Speech Recognition (ASR) system pipeline.

Differences between languages exist at all linguistic levels and vary from marked, easily identifiable distinctions (such as the use of entirely different words) to more subtle variations, which might have been lost or gained due to language contact. The latter end of the range is a challenge not only for automatic LID systems but also for linguistic sciences themselves.

In this memo, we show that a convolutional neural network with a Self-Attentive Pooling layer shows promising results in low-resource setting for the language identification task. The system described herein is identical to the one simultaneously submitted for Low Resource ASR challenge at Dialog2021 conference, language identification track, although the dataset is completely different.

1.1 Previous work

The first works on LID date back at least to mid-seventies, when Leonard and Doddington (1974) explored frequency of occurrences of certain reference sound units in different languages.

Previously developed LID approaches include:

- Purely acoustic LID that aims at capturing the essential differences between languages by modeling distributions in a compact representation of the raw speech signal directly.
- Phonotactics LID rely on the relative frequencies of sound units (phoneme/phone) and their sequences in speech.
- Prosodic LID use tone, intonation and prominence, typically represented as pitch contour.
- Word Level LID systems use fully-fledged large vocabulary continuous speech recognizers (LVCSR) to decode an incoming utterance into strings of words and then use Written Language Identification.

In the latest 10 years, intermediary-dimensional vector representations similar to i-vector (Dehak, et al. 2011a, 2011b, Kanagasundaram et al., 2011) and x-vector (Snyder et al., 2018) have been dominating the speech classification field, including LID. Additionally, starting from 2014 (Lopez-Moreno et

Proceedings of the Third Workshop on Computational Typology and Multilingual NLP, pages 130–135
June 10, 2021. ©2021 Association for Computational Linguistics

al., 2014), deep neural networks have been predominantly used for such tasks (see, for example, Bartz et al, 2017), Abdullah et al., 2020), Draghici et al, 2020), van der Merwe, 2020).

2 Model architecture

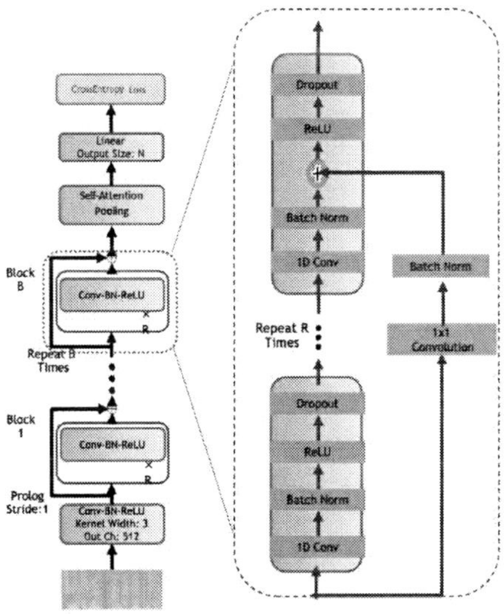

Figure 1: The model architecture

Similar to work of Koluguri et al., 2020, the model is based on 1D Time-Channel Separable convolutions, namely, the QuartzNet ASR architecture (Kriman et al., 2020) comprising of an encoder and decoder structures.

2.1 Encoder

The encoder used is QuartzNet BxR model shown in Figure 1, and has B blocks, each with R sub-blocks (Kriman et al., 2020). The first block is fed with MFSC coefficients vector of length 40. Each sub-block applies the following operations (Kriman et al., 2020):

- a 1D convolution,
- batch norm,
- ReLU, and
- dropout.

All sub-blocks in a block have the same number of output channels. These blocks are connected with residual connections (Kriman et al., 2020). We use QuartzNet 15*5, with 512 channels. All the convolutional layers have stride 1 and dilation 1 (Kriman et al., 2020).

2.2 Self-attentive pooling decoder

Similar to Cai et al., 2018, Chowdhury et al., 2018, we agree that not all frames contribute equally to the utterance level representation. Thus we use a self-attentive pooling (SAP) layer introduced by Cai et al., 2018 to pay more attention to the frames that are more important.

Namely, we first feed the frame level feature maps $\{x_1, x_2, \cdots, x_L\}$ into a fully-connected layer to get a hidden representation

$$h_t = tanh(Wx_t + b)$$

Then we measure the importance of each frame as the similarity of h_t with a learnable context vector μ and get a normalized importance weight w_t through a softmax function (Cai et al., 2018).

After that, the utterance level representation e can be generated as a weighted sum of the frame level feature maps based on the learned weights:

$$e = \sum_{t=1}^{T} w_t x_t$$

2.3 Loss Function

We have used cross-entropy loss function for this task.

3 Experiments

3.1 Datasets and tasks

For training models, speech data from the CMU Wilderness Dataset (Black, 2019) were used, which contain read speech from the Bible in 699 languages, but usually recorded from a single speaker. This training data were released in the form of derived MFCCs. The evaluation (validation, test) data come from different sources, in particular data from the Common Voice project, several OpenSLR corpora (SLR24 (Juan et al., 2014a, 2014b), SLR35, SLR36 (Kjartansson et al,. 2018), SLR64, SLR66, SLR79 (He et al., 2020), and the Paradisec collection.

There are 16 languages in the released train data, 4000 utterances per language. Table 1 summarizes the languages in the dataset. Validation and test data consist of 8000 utterances, 500 for each language.

Table 1: Summary of languages in the dataset

ISO 639-3 code	Language name	Genus	Family
kab	Kabyle	Berber	Afro-Asiatic
ind	Indonesian	Malayo-Sumbawan	Austronesian
sun	Sundanese	Malayo-Sumbawan	Austronesian
jav	Javanese	Javanese	Austronesian
eus	Euskara	Basque	Basque
tam	Tamil	Southern Dravidian	Dravidian
kan	Kannada	Southern Dravidian	Dravidian
tel	Telugu	South-Central Dravidian	Dravidian
hin	Hindi	Indic	Indo-European
por	Portuguese	Romance	Indo-European
rus	Russian	Slavic	Indo-European
eng	English	Germanic	Indo-European
mar	Marathi	Indic	Indo-European
tha	Thai	Kam-Tai	Tai-Kadai
iba	Iban	Malayo-Sumbawan	Austronesian
cnh	Chin, Hakha	Gur	Niger-Congo

3.2 Optimization and training process

We have used the attention vector size of 256. Models were trained until they reached a plateau on a validation set. Training was done using the Stochastic Gradient Descent optimizer with initial learning rate of 0.005 and cosine annealing decay to 1e-4.

4 Results and Discussion

We have experimented with SpecAugment augmentation introduced by Park et al., 2019 and run experiments both with and without augmentation.

The system described above allowed us to achieve the following results on the validation set (see Table 2). Somewhat surprisingly, detection of most languages was better without SpecAugment, Sundanese, Portuguese, Russian, and Iban being exceptions. Iban did not detect at all without augmentation. We can hypothesize that SpecAugment is more favorable for Indo-European and Austronesian languages detection than for other language families. This hypothesis requires further research.

Looking at the confusion matrix (Figure 2) we can see that most language samples determined as English, Kabyle or Telugu, independent of the language family. This means that there are more prominent speech features that hinder the language identification. Given the nature of the training set, that may be related to the gender of the readers.

Table 2: Results on validation dataset

		Without augmentation			With augmentation		
Language	**support**	**precision**	**recall**	**f1-score**	**precision**	**recall**	**f1-score**
kab	500	**0.0735**	**0.218**	**0.11**	0.0675	0.206	0.1017
ind	500	0.1102	**0.13**	**0.1193**	**0.125**	0.078	0.0961
sun	500	0.0747	0.082	0.0782	**0.0753**	**0.1**	**0.0859**
jav	500	**0.0692**	0.054	**0.0607**	0.0624	**0.056**	0.059
eus	500	**0.1925**	**0.072**	**0.1048**	0.1656	0.05	0.0768
tam	500	**0.3108**	**0.304**	**0.3074**	0.2244	0.14	0.1724
kan	500	**0.0339**	**0.004**	**0.0072**	0.0149	0.002	0.0035
tel	500	**0.0298**	0.112	**0.0471**	0.0284	**0.12**	0.0459
hin	500	**0.0933**	**0.014**	**0.0243**	0.0896	0.012	0.0212
por	500	0.0871	0.062	0.0724	**0.1061**	**0.098**	**0.1019**
rus	500	0.0482	0.032	0.0385	**0.0712**	**0.038**	**0.0495**
eng	500	**0.2065**	0.406	**0.2738**	0.1972	**0.428**	0.27
mar	500	0.3491	**0.118**	**0.1764**	**0.3654**	0.076	0.1258
tha	500	**0.2167**	**0.026**	**0.0464**	0.1014	0.014	0.0246
iba	500	0	0	0	**0.0638**	**0.012**	**0.0202**
cnh	500	**0.2039**	**0.104**	**0.1377**	0.1797	0.092	0.1217

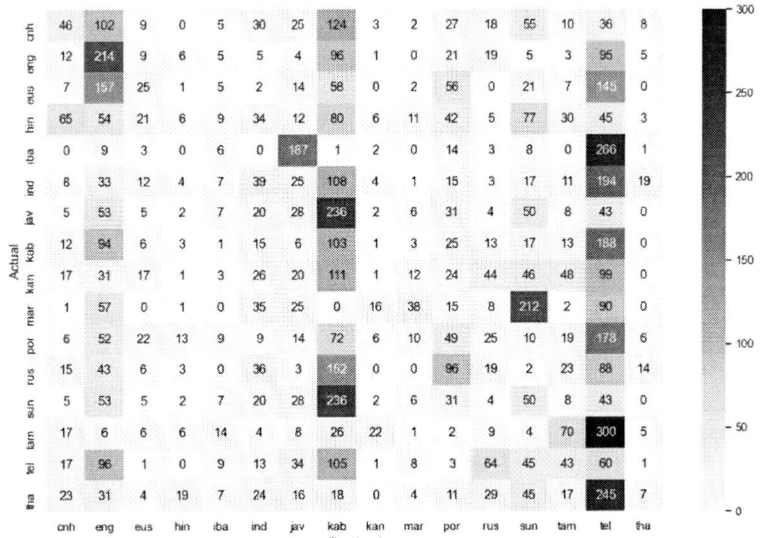

Figure 2: The confusion matrix for the validation set

Table 3: Test set results

	Without augmentation			**With augmentation**		
Lang	**precision**	**recall**	**f1-score**	**precision**	**recall**	**f1-score**
kab	**0.07**	0.194	**0.1029**	0.0668	**0.21**	0.1013
ind	0.1245	**0.176**	0.1458	**0.2113**	0.142	**0.1699**
sun	0.0767	0.088	0.0819	**0.0926**	**0.098**	**0.0952**
jav	**0.0844**	**0.068**	**0.0753**	0.0535	0.048	0.0506
eus	**0.1607**	**0.054**	**0.0808**	0.1194	0.032	0.0505
tam	0.3333	**0.306**	0.3191	**0.4234**	0.282	**0.3385**
kan	0.1642	**0.022**	**0.0388**	**0.1795**	0.014	0.026
tel	**0.0489**	0.162	**0.0751**	0.0446	**0.164**	0.0701
hin	0.2466	0.036	0.0628	**0.3231**	**0.042**	**0.0743**
por	0.1518	0.126	0.1377	**0.1765**	**0.174**	**0.1752**
rus	**0.1786**	**0.164**	**0.171**	0.1497	0.132	0.1403
eng	**0.1934**	0.408	**0.2624**	0.1679	**0.424**	0.2405
mar	0.1565	**0.036**	**0.0585**	**0.2024**	0.034	0.0582
tha	0.1587	**0.02**	**0.0355**	**0.186**	0.016	0.0295
iba	0.0057	0.002	0.003	**0.0072**	**0.002**	**0.0031**
cnh	**0.3556**	**0.16**	**0.2207**	0.2562	0.124	0.1671
Average	0.15685	0.1264	0.1170	0.1663	0.1211	0.1119

On the other hand, the test set results (see Table 3) have exhibited no statistically significant differences between augmented and not augmented training.

Acknowledgments

The authors are grateful to

- colleagues at NTR Labs Machine Learning Research group for the discussions and support;
- Anonymous reviewers who suggested multiple improvements to this memo and helped fix errors

References

Abdullah, B. M. *et al.* (2020) 'Cross-domain adaptation of spoken language identification for related languages: The curious case of Slavic languages', *arXiv*, (1). doi: 10.21437/interspeech.2020-2930.

Bartz, C. *et al.* (2017) 'Language identification using deep convolutional recurrent neural networks', *Lecture Notes in Computer Science (including subseries Lecture Notes in Artificial Intelligence and Lecture Notes in Bioinformatics)*, 10639 LNCS(1), pp. 880–889. doi: 10.1007/978-3-319-70136-3_93.

Bhattacharya, *et al.* (2017) 'Deep Speaker Embeddings for Short-Duration Speaker Verification', in *Interspeech 2017*. ISCA: ISCA, pp. 1517–1521. doi: 10.21437/Interspeech.2017-1575.

Black A. W., (2019) 'CMU Wilderness Multilingual Speech Dataset,' ICASSP 2019 - 2019 IEEE International Conference on Acoustics, Speech and Signal Processing (ICASSP), pp. 5971-5975, doi: 10.1109/ICASSP.2019.8683536.

Cai, W., et al. (2018) 'Exploring the encoding layer and loss function in end-to-end speaker and language recognition system', arXiv. doi: 10.21437/odyssey.2018-11.

Chowdhury, F. A. R. R. *et al.* (2018) 'Attention-Based Models for Text-Dependent Speaker Verification', in *ICASSP, IEEE International Conference on Acoustics, Speech and Signal Processing - Proceedings*, pp. 5359–5363. doi: 10.1109/ICASSP.2018.8461587.

Dehak, N. *et al.* (2011a) 'Language recognition via i-vectors and dimensionality reduction', in *Proceedings of the Annual Conference of the International Speech Communication Association, INTERSPEECH*, pp. 857–860.

Dehak, N. *et al.* (2011b) 'Front-End Factor Analysis For Speaker Verification', IEEE Transactions On Audio, Speech And Language Processing 1, pp. 1–11. Available at: http://groups.csail.mit.edu/sls//publications/2010/Dehak_IEEE_Transactions.pdf (Accessed: 28 March 2021).

Draghici, A. *et al.* (2020) 'A study on spoken language identification using deep neural networks', *ACM International Conference Proceeding Series*, (July), pp. 253–256. doi: 10.1145/3411109.3411123.

He, F. *et al.* (2020) 'Open-source multi-speaker speech corpora for building gujarati, kannada, malayalam, marathi, tamil and telugu speech synthesis systems', in *LREC 2020 - 12th International Conference on Language Resources and Evaluation, Conference Proceedings*, pp. 6494–6503. Available at: http://www.openslr.org/78/ (Accessed: 21 April 2021).

Juan S.S. et al. (2014a) 'Semi-Supervised G2p Bootstrapping And Its Application to ASR for a Very Under-Resourced Language : Iban' Grenoble, France. *SLTU-2014*:14–16.

Juan S.S. et al. (2014b) 'Using closely-related language to build an ASR for a very under-resourced language: Iban.' In *Oriental COCOSDA 2014 - 17th Conference of the Oriental Chapter of the International Coordinating Committee on Speech Databases and Speech I/O Systems and Assessment / CASLRE (Conference on Asian Spoken Language Research and Evaluation)*. Institute of Electrical and Electronics Engineers Inc.

Kanagasundaram, A. et al. (2011) 'i-Vector based speaker recognition on short utterances', in *Proceedings of the Annual Conference of the International Speech Communication Association, INTERSPEECH*, pp. 2341–2344. Available at: https://www.researchgate.net/publication/230643046_i-vector_Based_Speaker_Recognition_on_Short_Utterances (Accessed: 28 March 2021).

Kjartansson, O. *et al.* (2018) 'Crowd-Sourced Speech Corpora for Javanese, Sundanese, Sinhala, Nepali, and Bangladeshi Bengali', in. International Speech Communication Association, pp. 52–55. doi: 10.21437/sltu.2018-11.

Koluguri, N. R. *et al.* (2020) 'SpeakerNet: 1D Depth-wise Separable Convolutional Network for Text-Independent Speaker Recognition and Verification'. Available at: http://arxiv.org/abs/2010.12653 (Accessed: 20 March 2021).

Kriman, S. *et al.* (2020) 'Quartznet: Deep Automatic Speech Recognition with 1D Time-Channel Separable Convolutions', in *ICASSP, IEEE International Conference on Acoustics, Speech and Signal Processing - Proceedings*, pp. 6124–6128. doi: 10.1109/ICASSP40776.2020.9053889.

Latif, S. *et al.* (2020) 'Deep representation learning in speech processing: Challenges, recent advances, and future trends', *arXiv*, pp. 1–25.

Leonard R. and Doddington G., (1974) 'Automatic language identification.' Technical Report RADC-TR74-200 (Air Force Rome Air Development Center, Technical Report) August 1974

Lopez-Moreno, I. *et al.* (2014) 'Automatic language identification using deep neural networks', *IEEE International Conference on Acoustic, Speech and Signal Processing.*

van der Merwe, R. (2020) 'Triplet Entropy Loss: Improving The Generalisation of Short Speech Language Identification Systems'. Available at: http://arxiv.org/abs/2012.03775.

Navrátil, J. (2006) '*Automatic Language Identification, Multilingual Speech Processing*.' doi: 10.1016/b978-012088501-5/50011-1.

Park, D. S. *et al.* (2019) 'Specaugment: A simple data augmentation method for automatic speech recognition', *Proceedings of the Annual Conference of the International Speech Communication Association, INTERSPEECH*, 2019-Septe, pp. 2613–2617. doi: 10.21437/Interspeech.2019-2680.

Rao, K. and Nandi, D. (2015) Language Identification—A Brief Review. 10.1007/978-3-319-17725-0_2.

Sarthak, *et al.* (2019) 'Spoken language identification using convNets', *Lecture Notes in Computer Science (including subseries Lecture Notes in Artificial Intelligence and Lecture Notes in Bioinformatics)*, 11912 LNCS, pp. 252–265. doi: 10.1007/978-3-030-34255-5_17.

Snyder, D. *et al.* (2018) 'X-Vectors: Robust DNN Embeddings for Speaker Recognition', in *ICASSP, IEEE International Conference on Acoustics, Speech and Signal Processing - Proceedings*, pp. 5329–5333. doi: 10.1109/ICASSP.2018.8461375.

Wong, K. E. (2004) 'Automatic Spoken Language Identification Utilizing Acoustic and Phonetic Speech Information', *PhD Thesis*, (Queensland University of Technology).

A ResNet-50-based Convolutional Neural Network Model for Language ID Identification from Speech Recordings

Giuseppe G. A. Celano
Leipzig University
Faculty of Mathematics and Computer Science
Institute of Computer Science
celano@informatik.uni-leipzig.de

Abstract

This paper describes the model built for the SIGTYP 2021 Shared Task aimed at identifying 18 typologically different languages from speech recordings. Mel-frequency cepstral coefficients derived from audio files are transformed into spectrograms, which are then fed into a ResNet-50-based CNN architecture. The final model achieved validation and test accuracies of 0.73 and 0.53, respectively.

1 Introduction

In the SIGTYP 2021 Shared Task, participants are asked to predict language IDs from speech recordings. The novelty of this Shared Task consists in (i) the variety of the languages involved, which comprises very different language genera/families (see Table 1), and (ii) the use of speech form.

Indeed, many linguistics-related Shared Tasks seem to focus on a restricted number of related languages (often Indo-European ones) and model their spellings.[1] In particular, this latter feature poses a number of theoretical and practical challenges, especially when some language comparison is involved, as in typological studies.

Writing systems, as is known, can highly diverge in what they represent, even when they are segmental scripts (not to mention that a language can be encoded in different writing systems, like, for example, Kabyle). If we consider the languages in the Shared Task dataset, it would be very hard to find a meaningful way to compare, for example, the Javanese writing system with the Portuguese one: the former could be written in the *scriptio continua* of its traditional script,[2] while the latter's alphabetical script distinguishes space-delimited tokens (mostly corresponding to morphosyntactic words). Interestingly enough, it is no less challenging to compare word-based scripts, in that there is no single definition of graphemic (let alone morphosyntactic) word across languages, and even within the same writing system, inconsistencies are not uncommon.

The use of language recordings instead of written documents should therefore ensure a more direct and consistent encoding of languages. Recordings also allow us to capture intonation structure, which is usually absent (or represented in a minimal form) in writing systems, despite its crucial role in conveying information (see Lambrecht, 1996 and, more in general, information structure studies).

On the downside, speech recordings are sensitive to idiolect variances, which a statistical model should however be able to properly address by not overfitting the training data. This is even more relevant for the SIGTYP 2021 Shared Task, in that its goal is to train a model being able to generalize to recordings of not only different people, but also very different genres/content.

In the following sections, I present the model I built to tackle the multiclass classification task at hand. In Section 2, the training and validation sets are described. Section 3 details the training phase of a number of models, including the ResNet-50-based CNN one, which I chose to participate in the SIGTYP 2021 Shared Task. Section 4 summarizes the results of the ResNet-50-based CNN model, while Section 5 contains some concluding remarks.

2 The training and validation sets

The training and validation sets are released by the organizers of the Shared Task as `npy` files containing mel-frequency cepstral coefficients (MFCCs) computed from audio files. The training set consists of 72,000 readings of the New Testament (each of them usually corresponding to a verse), while the validation set consists of 8,000 instances from different sources.

18 languages are included in the training set (4,000 instances per language), while only 16 lan-

[1] Interestingly, though, Gorman et al. (2020) concerns mapping of graphemes onto phonemes.

[2] Nowadays, however, Javanese is more commonly written in a Latin script.

Proceedings of the Third Workshop on Computational Typology and Multilingual NLP, pages 136–144
June 10, 2021.

Language	Genus	Family	ID
Basque	Basque	Basque	eus
Eastern Bru	Katuic	Austro-Asiatic	bru
Hakha Chin	Gur	Niger-Congo	cnh
English	Germanic	Indo-European	eng
Hindi	Indic	Indo-European	hin
Iban	Malayo-Sumbawan	Austronesian	iba
Indonesian	Malayo-Sumbawan	Austronesian	ind
Javanese	Javanese	Austronesian	jav
Kabyle	Berber	Afro-Asiatic	kab
Kannada	Southern Dravidian	Dravidian	kan
Marathi	Indic	Indo-European	mar
Portuguese	Romance	Indo-European	por
Vlax Romani	Romani	Indo-European	rmy
Russian	Slavic	Indo-European	rus
Sundanese	Malayo-Sumbawan	Austronesian	sun
Tamil	Southern Dravidian	Dravidian	tam
Telegu	South-Central	Dravidian	tel
Thai	Kam-Tai	Tai-Kadai	tha

Table 1: Languages in the training dataset.

guages are in the validation set (500 instances per language, with the languages Eastern Bru and Vlax Romani missing). Each instance is encoded as a 2-dimensional tensor, whose shape is $(39, x)$, with $x \in \{x : x \in \mathbb{Z} \land 300 < x < 2729\}$.

MFCCs are often used as features in ML. Basically, they allow leverage of sound frequencies, which can offer a richer representation than that of a pure sound waveform (see Xu et al., 2004 for more details and their computation).

3 Method

3.1 A baseline model

A baseline can be calculated by feeding a model directly with MFFCs. The training and validation data contain tensors whose second dimension length varies. A solution for that can be slicing/padding them as to get shape $(39, 501)$, since about 80% of the training instances have a shape of $(39, x)$, with $x \in \{x : x \in \mathbb{Z} \land 300 < x < 502\}$.

A model is trained with three RNN layers and two densely connected layers, the last of which outputs the final probabilities for each label (see Appendix A). The RMSProp optimizer with learning rate 0.00001 is chosen. The first dimension of each input tensor can be interpreted as representing time steps or a sequence. Each time step (except the first one) receives the output of the previous time step:

$$h_t = tanh(Wx_t + Uh_{t-1} + b), \quad (1)$$

$$y_t = tanh(Vh_t + c). \quad (2)$$

At each time step, the relevant input vector x_t is multiplied by its weights and then added to the product of the (hidden) vector of the previous time step and its weights (b and c are the bias vectors, $tanh$ the activation function, and y_t the output vector).

The RNN model performs poorly (see Figure 1), since it cannot generalize at all. This is due not only to the model architecture, but also to the data mismatch between the sets, the validation data containing very different kinds of speech recordings. I therefore added part of the validation data (60%) to the training set and trained a new model with the same RNN architecture and hyperparameters. Figure 2 shows that this model returns very similar results: it also overfits the training data, the validation accuracy invariably remaining around 0.1.

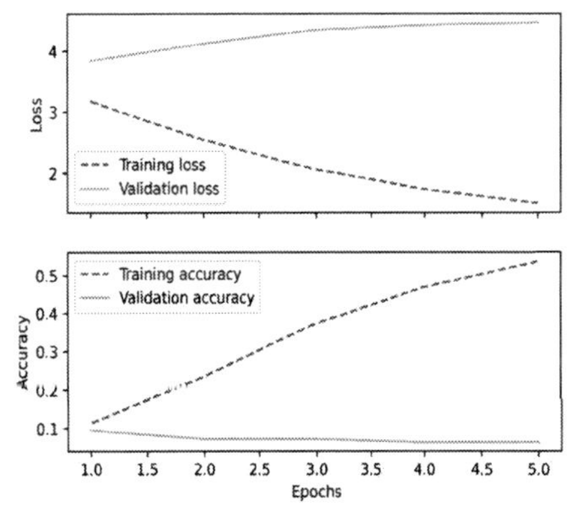

Figure 1: Performance of the baseline model.

3.2 A CNN approach

MFFCs can be used to create spectrograms, which allow transfer of a sound waveform into the image domain. Spectrograms return a visual representation of the unfolding of a sound wave through time, and have proved to provide promising results in a variety of ML tasks (see, for example, Chourasia et al., 2021 and Reddy et al., 2021).

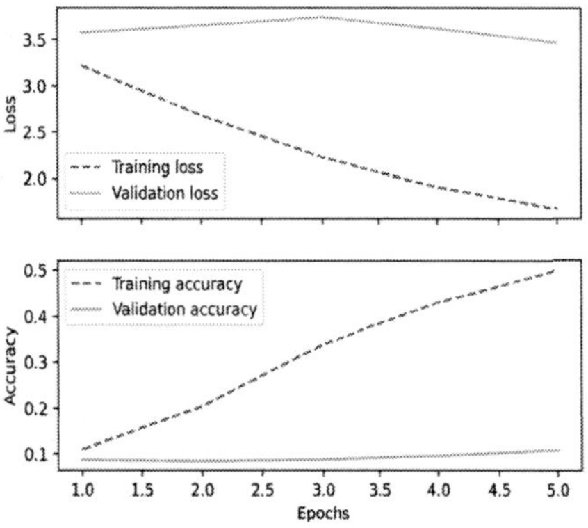

Figure 2: Performance of the baseline model with training set augmented with some validation data.

Using the default arguments of the function `specshow` (among which are `sr = 22050`, i.e., sample rate, and `hop_length = 512`) within the Python package `librosa`, the MFFCs are converted into images of shape $(640, 480)$ (Figure 3 shows an example of a spectrogram).

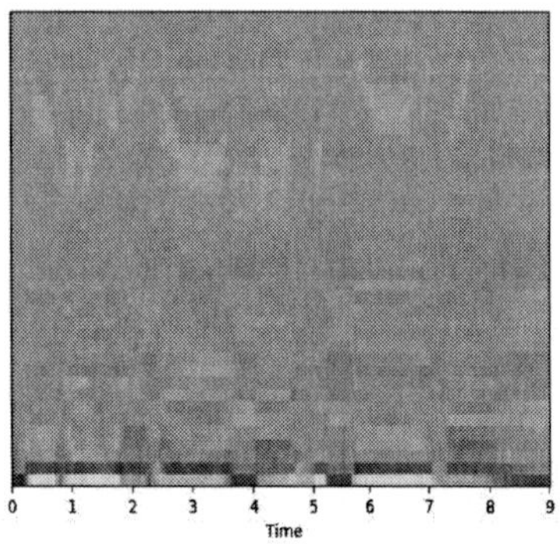

Figure 3: Spectrogram of a Hakha Chin instance.

The conversion allows one to take advantage of CNN architectures. In order to deal with the high variance of the model, 60% of the validation set is made part of the training set by stratified sampling: 300 instances of each language (i.e., 16×300) are randomly selected and added to the training set.

Two CNN architectures have been compared using the same dataset described above: a 3-layer CNN[3] and ResNet-50 (He et al. 2016). Despite its moderately deep architecture (see Figure B), the 3-layer CNN model (with RMSProp optimizer and learning rate 0.001) quickly overfits the training data (Figure 4) and therefore, like the RNN model, proves to be inadequate for the task at hand.

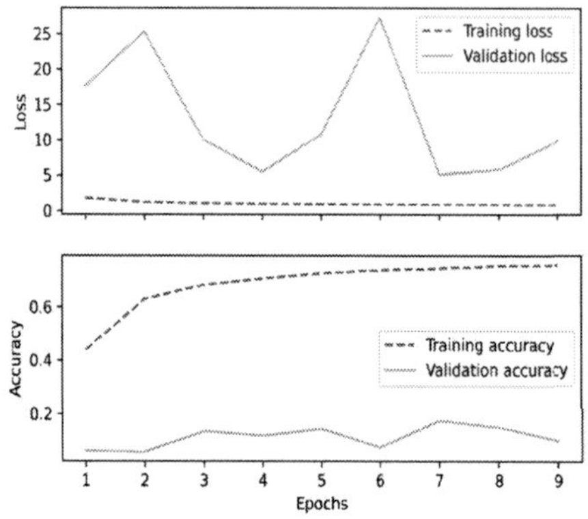

Figure 4: Performance of the 3-layer CNN model.

ResNet-50 is an extremely deep CNN architecture, which tries to overcome the degradation problem using residual learning. An input x is added to an output, so that a function $H(x)$ is redefined as

$$H(x) = F(x) + x, \tag{3}$$

which is hypothesized to make learning easier (He et al., 2016, p. 2). In Figure 5, one residual unit of ResNet-50 is shown: the layer `conv2_block1_out` is added to the layer `conv2_block2_3_bn` within the layer `conv2_block2_add`, as the same shape of the two layers shows $(120, 160, 256)$.

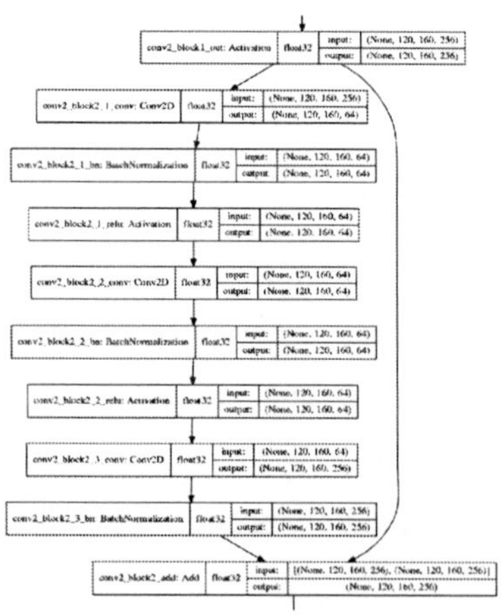

Figure 5: Detail of the ResNet-50 model.

There exist many ResNet architectures, such as ResNet-34, ResNet-50, and ResNet-101, each of

[3] 3 refers only to the CNN layers.

Language	Precision	Recall	F1
Eastern Bru	0.00	0.00	0.00
Hakha Chin	0.86	0.85	0.86
English	0.68	0.34	0.46
Basque	0.77	0.94	0.85
Hindi	0.92	0.68	0.78
Iban	0.95	1.00	0.98
Indonesian	0.78	0.64	0.70
Javanese	0.41	0.80	0.54
Kabyle	0.57	0.81	0.67
Kannada	0.92	0.73	0.82
Marathi	0.85	0.99	0.92
Portuguese	0.56	0.54	0.55
Vlax Romani	0.00	0.00	0.00
Russian	0.94	0.85	0.90
Sundanese	0.15	0.06	0.09
Tamil	0.84	0.77	0.80
Telegu	0.72	0.91	0.80
Thai	0.86	0.71	0.78

Table 2: Precision, recall, and F1 scores calculated on the validation set (ResNet-50-based model).

which is called after the number of the CNN layers and fully connected layers it contains. ResNet-50 has 50 of them, and according to the results reported by Xu et al. (2004), it performed better than ResNet-34, but worse than ResNet-101 and ResNet-134, in an ImageNet classification task (in reference to top-one and top-five error rates).

The ResNet-50 architecture has been employed to fit the training data of the SIGTYP 2021 Shared Task, without, however, transfer learning, in that the original weights were computed on completely different kind of data, and therefore are unlikely to be any useful. Of course, experimenting with different ResNet and non-ResNet architectures, as well as with different sets of hyperparameters, would be useful; the sizes of the architectures and the amount of training time needed to do that, however, made me focus only on ResNet-50, which turned out to return good results without requiring much optimization.

In order to accommodate the data of the SIGTYP 2021 Shared Task, the top layer was substituted with one allowing for the shape (480, 640, 3), while the output layer was replaced by a densely connected layer outputting an 18-dimensional vector, i.e., a probability score for each of the 18 languages. The Adam optimizer with learning rates of 0.0001 (first 7 epochs) and 0.00001 (8th epoch) was chosen.

4 Results and Discussion

The ResNet-50-based model provides good training and validation accuracy scores (0.98 and 0.73, respectively). Importantly, both accuracy scores grow during training, and both loss scores get smaller and smaller. In Figure 6, the algorithm seems to have converged. However, the final accuracy score (0.53) calculated on the test set released by the organizers seems to suggest that some overfitting has occurred.

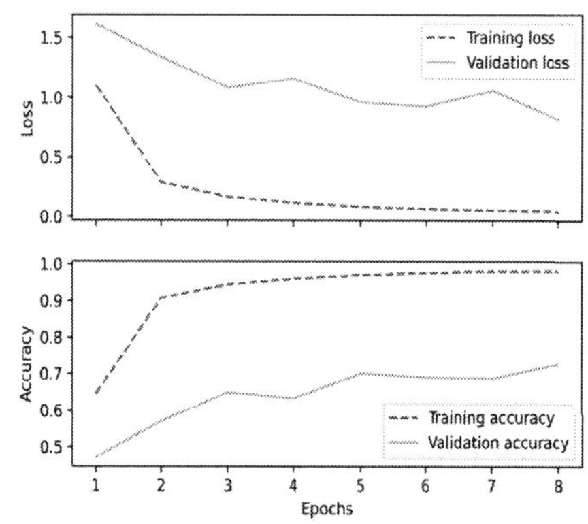

Figure 6: Performance of the ResNet-50-based CNN model.

The confusion matrices (Appendix C and D), the heatmaps (Appendix E and F), as well as the tables containing precision, recall, and F1 scores (Table 2 and 3), show that the model performs well, with a few exceptions. Sundanese is very often misclassified as Javanese. Appendix D reveals a more complex picture: English, Portuguese, Russian, and Thai are often also misclassified as Kabyle. Similarly, the model often associates Telegu with Kannada and Marathi. On the contrary, it can identify Iban very well. These results require further future investigation to ascertain whether these misclassifications can be ascribed to similarities between the languages.

Notably, the rows for Eastern Bru and Vlax Romani are not available in the heatmaps (Appendix E and F) because the languages are absent in both the validation and test sets.

Tweaking the hyperparameters and especially experimenting with deeper ResNet architectures could probably lead to an improvement of the results.

5 Conclusions

In the present paper, a ResNet-50-based CNN model has been presented, which was used to fit the data of the SIGTYP 2021 Shared Task. Attempts

Language	Precision	Recall	F1
Eastern Bru	0.00	0.00	0.00
Hakha Chin	0.72	0.81	0.76
English	0.48	0.37	0.41
Basque	0.69	0.93	0.79
Hindi	0.80	0.53	0.63
Iban	0.97	0.97	0.97
Indonesian	0.46	0.27	0.34
Javanese	0.41	0.83	0.55
Kabyle	0.36	0.06	0.45
Kannada	0.55	0.57	0.56
Marathi	0.57	0.51	0.54
Portuguese	0.31	0.43	0.36
Vlax Romani	0.00	0.00	0.00
Russian	0.33	0.04	0.06
Sundanese	0.21	0.10	0.14
Tamil	0.71	0.53	0.61
Telegu	0.44	0.73	0.55
Thai	0.64	0.29	0.40

Table 3: Precision, recall, and F1 scores calculated on the test set (ResNet-50-based model).

to tackle the task with relatively simple RNN and CNN architectures were unsuccessful. ResNet-50, however, proved to offer a robust architecture to train linguistic data for language ID prediction. The task at hand was challenging because the training data differ considerably from the validation data, and therefore any model needs strong ability to generalize. The ResNet-50-based CNN model proposed in this article shows good validation and test accuracies (0.73 and 0.53, respectively). Notably, Sudanese is very often misclassified as Javanese.

Acknowledgements

This work has been supported by the German Research Foundation (DFG project number 408121292).

References

Mayank Chourasia, Shriya Haral, Srushti Bhatkar, and Smita Kulkarni. 2021. Emotion recognition from speech signal using deep learning. In *Intelligent Data Communication Technologies and Internet of Things: Proceedings of ICICI 2020*, pages 471–481. Springer Singapore.

Kyle Gorman, Lucas F.E. Ashby, Aaron Goyzueta, Arya McCarthy, Shijie Wu, and Daniel You. 2020. The SIGMORPHON 2020 shared task on multilingual grapheme-to-phoneme conversion. In *Proceedings of the 17th SIGMORPHON Workshop on Computational Research in Phonetics, Phonology, and Morphology*, pages 40–50, Online. Association for Computational Linguistics.

Kaiming He, Xiangyu Zhang, Shaoqing Ren, and Jian Sun. 2016. Deep residual learning for image recognition. In *Proceedings of the IEEE Conference on Computer Vision and Pattern Recognition*, pages 770–778.

Knud Lambrecht. 1996. *Information Structure and Sentence Form: Topic, Focus, and the Mental Representations of Discourse Referents*. Cambridge University Press.

M. Kiran Reddy, Pyry Helkkula, Y. Madhu Keerthana, Kasimir Kaitue, Mikko Minkkinen, Heli Tolppanen, Tuomo Nieminen, and Paavo Alku. 2021. The automatic detection of heart failure using speech signals. *Computer Speech & Language*, 69:1–11.

Min Xu, Ling-Yu Duan, Jianfei Cai, Liang-Tien Chia, Changsheng Xu, and Qi Tian. 2004. Hmm-based audio keyword generation. In *Pacific-Rim Conference on Multimedia*, pages 566–574. Springer.

A Architecture for the baseline model.

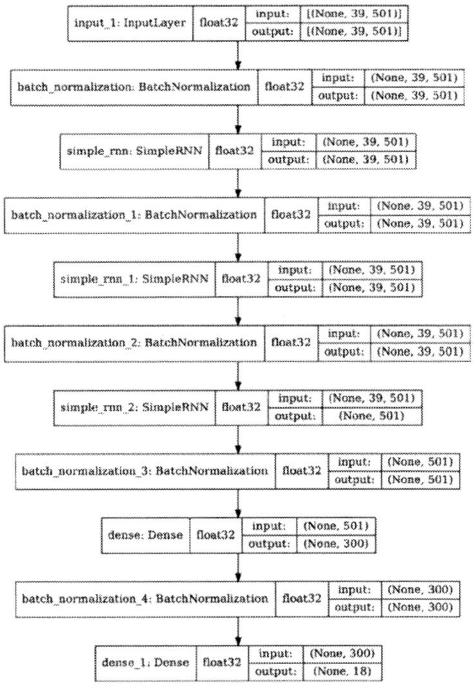

B Architecture for the 3-layer CNN model.

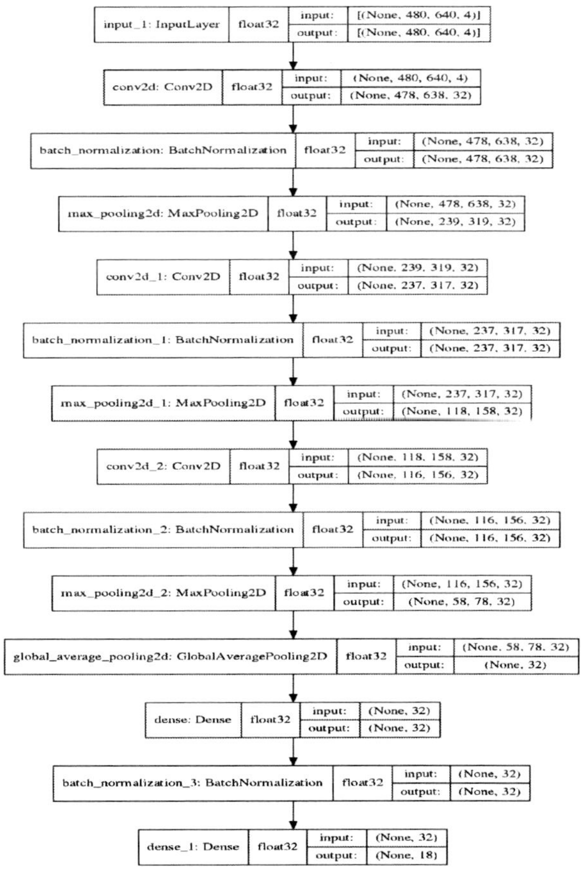

C Confusion matrix for the validation data (ResNet-50-based model).

	bru	cnh	eng	eus	hin	iba	ind	jav	kab	kan	mar	por	rmy	rus	sun	tam	tel	tha	class error rate
bru	0	0	0	0	0	0	0	0	0	0	0	0	0	0	0	0	0	0	
cnh	0	170	4	2	0	2	3	7	4	0	0	0	0	0	8	0	0	0	0.15
eng	0	17	69	6	6	2	7	11	40	0	3	20	0	3	0	2	9	5	0.66
eus	0	0	0	189	0	0	0	0	7	1	0	1	0	0	0	0	2	0	0.06
hin	1	0	2	6	135	2	1	10	6	1	7	5	6	4	7	2	5	0	0.33
iba	0	0	0	0	0	200	0	0	0	0	0	0	0	0	0	0	0	0	0.00
ind	0	0	2	3	0	3	127	3	19	0	1	16	0	0	2	9	4	11	0.36
jav	0	0	1	0	0	0	2	160	1	0	0	0	0	0	36	0	0	0	0.20
kab	0	0	5	1	2	0	4	0	163	3	1	7	1	0	2	3	8	0	0.18
kan	0	0	0	6	0	0	2	1	2	147	3	0	0	0	0	3	36	0	0.27
mar	0	0	0	0	0	0	0	0	0	0	199	0	0	0	0	0	1	0	0.01
por	0	3	11	18	1	1	5	8	19	1	3	107	0	3	8	5	5	2	0.47
rmy	0	0	0	0	0	0	0	0	0	0	0	0	0	0	0	0	0	0	
rus	0	0	1	0	0	0	4	0	2	0	0	18	0	171	0	1	0	3	0.14
sun	0	0	1	0	0	0	1	185	1	0	0	0	0	0	12	0	0	0	0.94
tam	0	1	1	5	3	0	1	0	9	2	7	9	0	0	3	154	2	3	0.23
tel	0	0	2	5	0	0	1	0	2	3	4	0	0	0	1	0	182	0	0.09
tha	1	6	3	6	0	0	5	3	11	1	6	8	0	0	3	4	0	143	0.28

D Confusion matrix for the test data (ResNet-50-based model).

	bru	cnh	eng	eus	hin	iba	ind	jav	kab	kan	mar	por	rmy	rus	sun	tam	tel	tha	class error rate
bru	0	0	0	0	0	0	0	0	0	0	0	0	0	0	0	0	0	0	
cnh	1	404	19	0	4	0	1	11	20	3	1	10	0	2	16	1	5	2	0.19
eng	1	72	183	8	3	2	9	9	105	4	9	45	0	8	9	5	20	8	0.63
eus	0	0	1	463	0	3	2	0	10	1	9	4	0	0	0	1	5	1	0.07
hin	4	2	9	14	264	6	2	65	12	6	39	17	16	2	31	2	9	0	0.47
iba	0	0	0	2	2	483	0	3	0	4	4	2	0	0	0	0	0	0	0.03
ind	1	8	2	47	4	2	134	32	51	7	4	63	0	2	26	40	21	56	0.73
jav	0	0	0	0	10	0	8	416	1	0	0	6	1	0	52	0	6	0	0.17
kab	0	3	44	17	13	0	11	11	300	7	2	51	0	3	7	10	19	2	0.40
kan	0	0	0	9	0	0	1	0	2	283	40	1	0	3	0	6	154	1	0.43
mar	0	0	0	1	0	0	0	1	4	88	257	0	0	0	0	0	149	0	0.49
por	0	13	47	18	2	0	17	16	95	2	7	215	1	14	6	21	22	4	0.57
rmy	0	0	0	0	0	0	0	0	0	0	0	0	0	0	0	0	0	0	
rus	0	3	23	48	17	2	27	0	84	36	0	225	0	18	0	4	11	2	0.96
sun	0	0	0	0	10	0	8	416	1	0	0	6	1	0	52	0	6	0	0.90
tam	0	20	4	9	3	0	21	20	46	15	27	19	1	1	21	267	20	6	0.47
tel	0	4	5	20	0	0	6	2	2	59	35	0	0	1	0	3	363	0	0.27
tha	0	30	47	13	0	0	47	18	93	1	19	37	0	1	22	17	9	146	0.71

E Heatmap with validation set error rates (ResNet-50-based model).

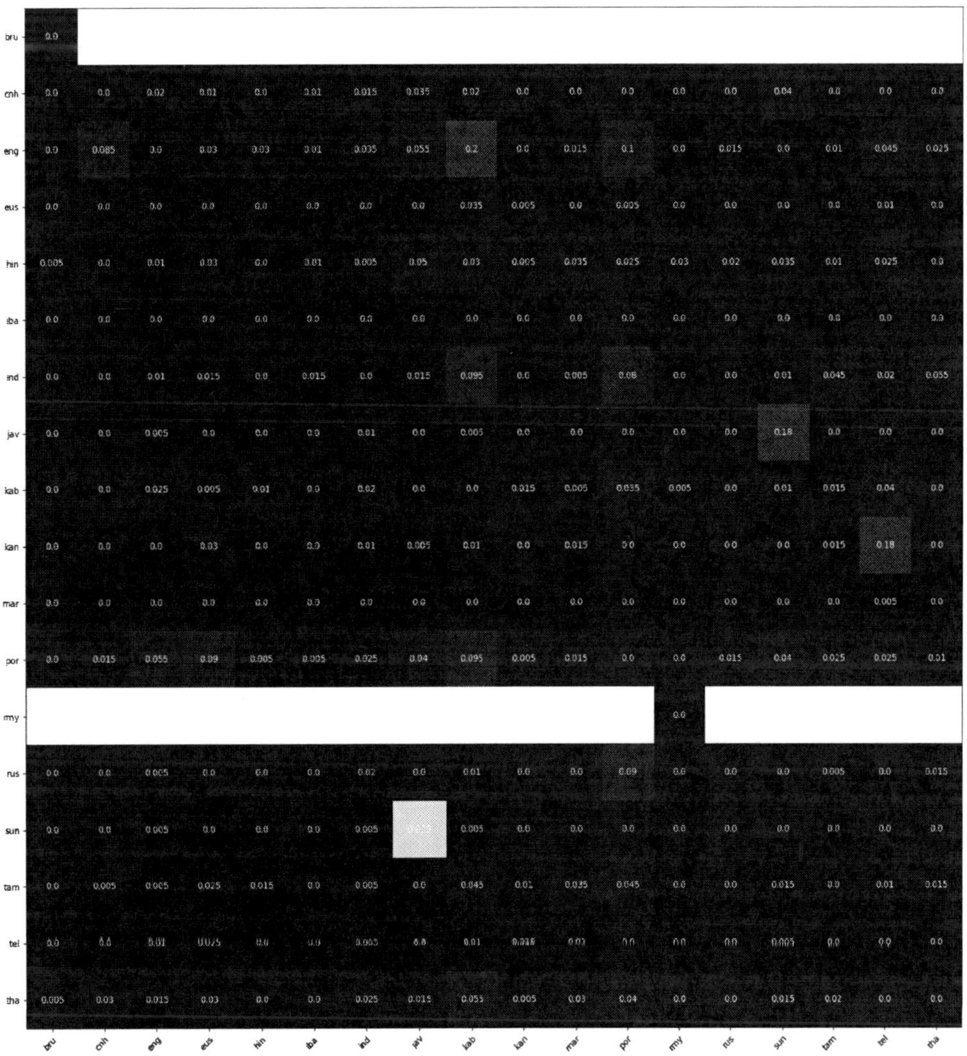

F Heatmap with test set error rates (ResNet-50-based model).

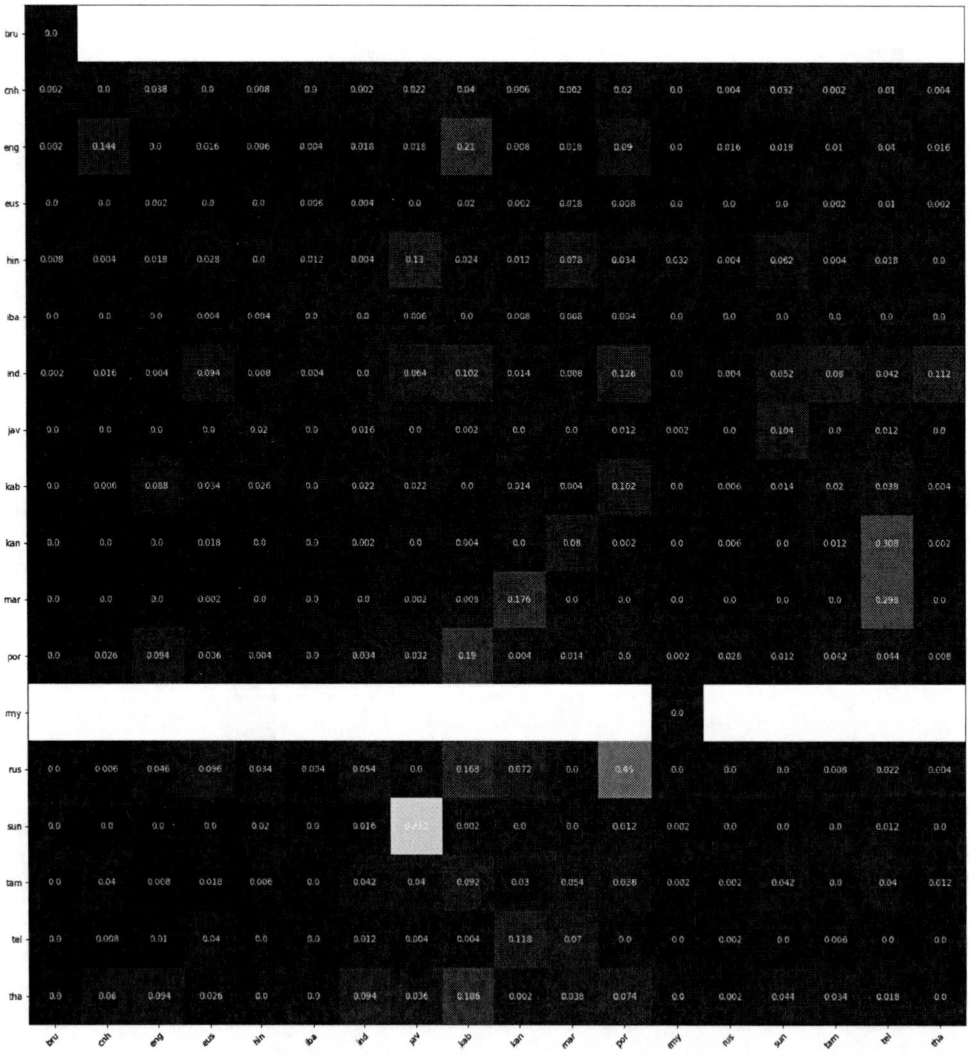

Anlirika: an LSTM–CNN Flow Twister for Spoken Language Identification

Andrei Shcherbakov[♮] **Liam Whittle**[◁] **Ritesh Kumar**[•]
Siddharth Singh[•] **Matthew Coleman**[◁] **Ekaterina Vylomova**[♮]
[♮]University of Melbourne [◁]Monash University [•]Bhim Rao Ambedkar University

ultrasparc@yandex.ru

Abstract

The paper presents Anlirika's submission to SIGTYP 2021 Shared Task on Robust Spoken Language Identification. The task aims at building a robust system that generalizes well across different domains and speakers. The training data is limited to a single domain only with predominantly single speaker per language while the validation and test data samples are derived from diverse dataset and multiple speakers. We experiment with a neural system comprising a combination of dense, convolutional, and recurrent layers that are designed to perform better generalization and obtain speaker-invariant representations. We demonstrate that the task in its constrained form (without making use of external data or augmentation the train set with samples from the validation set) is still challenging. Our best system trained on the data augmented with validation samples achieves 29.9% accuracy on the test set.

1 Introduction

Among approximately 7,000 world languages, over 43% are oral only and do not exhibit any writing system. Still, even in less exotic cases language processing systems may have to solely rely on vocal representations. Spoken language identification (SLI) is essential sub-task in many approaches to multilingual automated speech recognition and machine translation. In addition, it also has practical applications as a standalone task. Automated assignment of a call center operator to a client is one of possible use case scenarios.

The paper provides a description of "Anlirika" system[1] that was submitted to SIGTYP 2021 Shared Task on *Robust* SLI (Salesky et al., 2021). In terms of the task, systems are trained to predict a language class (id) from an audio signal. Importantly, the task aims at development of robust systems that can generalize well to new domains and speakers. Many languages are under-resourced, and the situation when the language data exist only for a very limited number of speakers or domains is common. For instance, the largest multilingual SLI dataset, namely CMU Wilderness (Black, 2019), has been derived from the Bible in ≈ 700 languages and lacks speaker diversity. Therefore, it is essential for a system to be speaker-invariant and robust.

2 Related Work

Most work on SLI focused on Indo-European languages such as English, German, Russian, French, Hindi. It is also common to transform raw audio signal into the log-Mel spectra or MFCC features. Recent approaches such as Bartz et al. (2017), Revay and Teschke (2019), and Shukla et al. (2019) make use of various convolution-based neural architectures. For instance, Bartz et al. (2017) proposed a hybrid model that used convolutional layers to extract spatial features and recurrent units (bidirectional LSTMs) tp capture temporal characteristics. Revay and Teschke (2019) explored the ResNet-50 (He et al., 2016) architecture dynamically adapting learning rate.

3 Dataset

The dataset comprises 16 typologically diverse languages from Afro-Asiatic, Austronesian, Basque, Dravidian, Indo-European, Niger-Congo, and Tai-Kadai families. The training data is derived from the CMU Wilderness dataset (Black, 2019) which represents a single domain (speech utterances from the Bible) and has predominantly a single speaker per language. The validation and test sets were collected from multiple corpora such as Common Voice (Ardila et al., 2019) and present a variety of recording conditions with multiple speakers per language. The length of each speech utterance ranged

[1]The code is available at https://github.com/andreas-softwareengineer-pro/speech-language-classifier

Proceedings of the Third Workshop on Computational Typology and Multilingual NLP, pages 145–148
June 10, 2021.

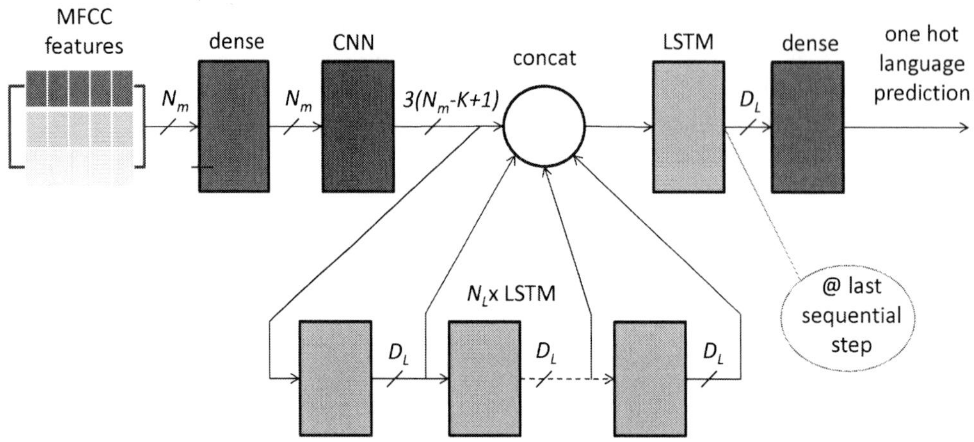

Figure 1: Architecture used in language classifier

between 3 and 7 seconds. The training data contained 4,000 utterances per language, while validation and test sets comprised 500 samples each. Importantly, the utterances were provided in the form of Mel-Frequency Cepstral Coefficients (MFCC) features rather then raw audio signal.

4 Architecture

As illustrated on Figure 1, we used a multi-layer neural network solution with two dense layers, one CNN and 1–7 LSTM layers. The design of neural layer stack is motivated by the following general vision of how a sample should be processed:

- We suggest that a raw spectral pattern first needs to be multiplied by a square matrix in order to remove sound harmonics. That is why we are using a dense layer as the front one;

- Then we try to recognize features related to the spectral line shape. Therefore, we use a one-dimensional CNN (convolving by input feature vector index [frequency]);

- Then we recognize "local" temporal constructs with a stack of LSTMs;

- We use yet another LSTM to reduce temporal patterns into a single-vector representation (only the final time step output goes to the next layer);

- Finally, we classify it into one of 16 languages with a dense layer.

The layer stack we used is summarized in Table 1.

4.1 Batching mechanism

We employed a batched learning process with a fixed number of processed samples per batch (64) and with variable number of time steps. Such a mechanism works as follows. An initial batch is filled with randomly chosen samples. The number of temporal steps in the batch is determined by the shortest sample currently present in a given batch. Once a batch is fed forward through the neural network layers:

1. The samples which ends happen to be aligned with the end of the batch, are done now (within a given epoch). We replace them with next randomly chosen training samples when forming the next batch. If a sequential layer contains hidden states (which is true for the LSTMs in our model), zero hidden states are supplied to the respective threads of batch. Final prediction values for such threads are used to calculate the loss;

2. The samples which do not fit within the batch length, are passed to the next batch for further processing, having their already-processed prefixes removed. Start hidden states for the respective threads are initialized with the values of final hidden states computed in the preceding batch, as shown with blue arrows in Figure 2.

This process repeats until all the samples are pro-

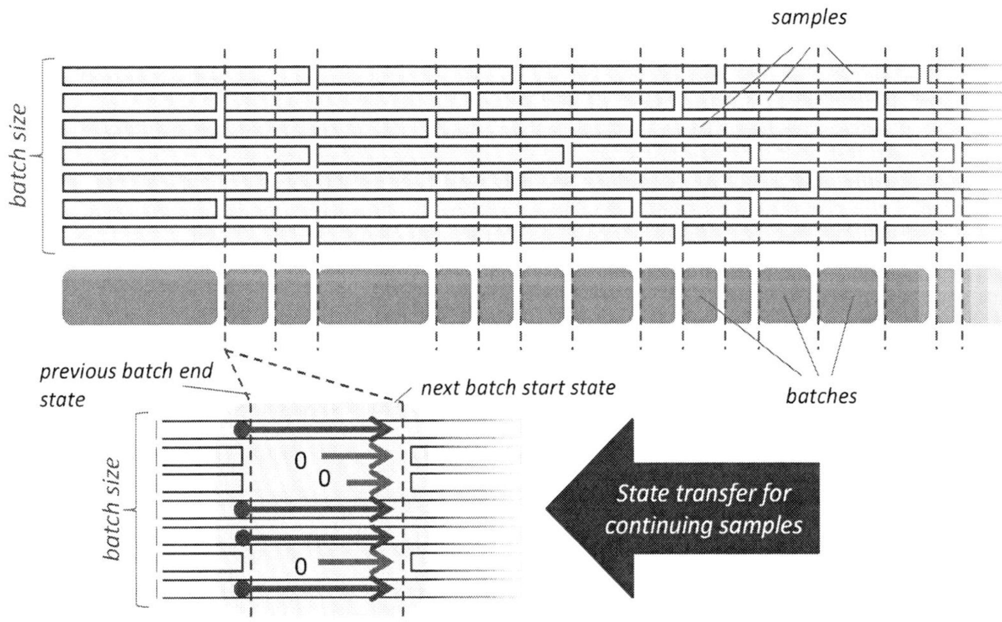

Figure 2: Batch shaping

Layer Type	Output Size	Output Type	Hyperparamers
dense	N_m	per-timestep	$N_m = 39$
1D CNN	$D_{CNN} = 3(N_m - K + 1)$	per-timestep	K=4 – kernel size
$N_L\times$ LSTM	D_L ea.	per-timestep	-
concat	$D_{CNN} + N_L D_L$	per-timestep	-
LSTM	D_L	per-sample	-
dense	Num. languages=16	per-sample	-

Table 1: Layer stack summary

cessed, i.e. a training epoch is done. Some trailing batches may be underpopulated with threads, in which cases output values of unused threads are ignored. Figure 2 summarises the description above.

A drawback of such a batching technique is constraining of temporal depth when the backpropagation through time takes place in LSTM layers. A batch is typically much shorter in time steps than a sample. Therefore, a single backpropagation operation (that cannot run across batches) may modify less weights than it would be expected without batching. We regarded this effect as minor, however, its influence to the overall learning capability is yet to be investigated.

5 Experiments

We varied N_L, the number of extra sequential LSTM layers (which outputs were concatenated to the output of the CNN layer). We tried the following options: {0,2,4,6}. A number of units in each LSTM layer was chosen from {200,300}. We used equal numbers of units across all the LSTM layers present in the model.

Using the original train set. A learning dynamic we observed in our experiment was generally slow. In most trials the model failed to learn with the learning rate value greater than $4 \cdot 10^{-4}$. With lower learning rates, it trained at an extremely slow pace gaining about 0.1% train set accuracy per epoch. At the time of this report writing, we achieved an overall accuracy value of about 12% at validation set. It is curious to note that accuracy figures for train and validation sets did not correlate as expected, the fact that may indicate significant difference in domains. Typically, a predicted distribution of languages was limited to 2-3 classes, the list of which was volatile. We also noticed that the model converged much faster at small subsets of training sets (50-500 samples).

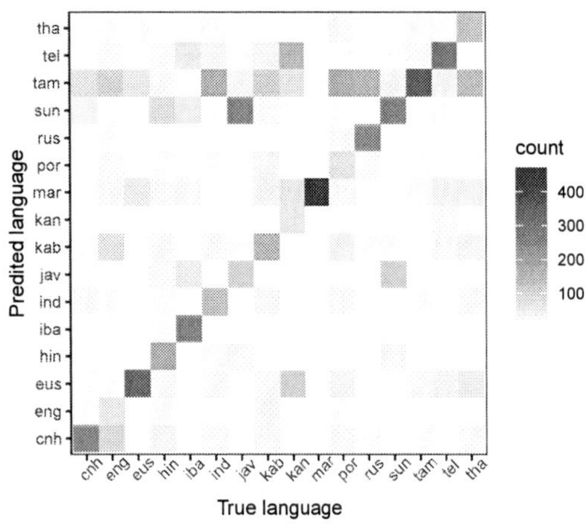

Figure 3: Confusion matrix for mixed set holdout validation ($N_L = 2, D_L = 200$)

Augmenting training data with validation set samples. A quite different picture was observed when we combined training and validations sets and randomly split them again into training and validation portions. A much superior accuracy of 74% on validation set was achieved. The confusion matrix is shown on Figure 3. Such a relatively high prediction accuracy is not surprising, as a validation holdout is likely to share speaker identities with the respective training subset, the fact that leads to a significant loosening of required generalization ability. However, a drastic improvement in convergence dynamics remains a noticeable and unexpected effect.

Tuning of hyperparameters. A choice of$N_L = 2$ was found to be producing the highest accuracy. Increasing D_L from 200 to 300 didn't lead to any significant difference in performance.

Shared task submission. The final submitted version was trained on an augmented set. The performance figures are shown in Table 2.

Set	Acc.	F1, Micro Avg	F1, Macro Avg
Test	29.9%	29.8%	28.2%
Valid.	43.6%	43.6%	42.1%

Table 2: Aggregated performance metrics for the final model version

6 Conclusion & future work

To address the task of language classification in speech samples, we implemented and explored a neural network model. The model's architecture was inspired by an idea of phoneme sequence recognition. Our experiments are yet in progress, still it is clear that the generalization across domains appears to be the main challenge.

Following a maxim of keeping model as light as possible, we are going to explore architecture modifications that directly enforce some kind of phonetic generalization, for instance, by insertion of "bottlenecks" (layers with low output size).

References

Rosana Ardila, Megan Branson, Kelly Davis, Michael Henretty, Michael Kohler, Josh Meyer, Reuben Morais, Lindsay Saunders, Francis M Tyers, and Gregor Weber. 2019. Common voice: A massively-multilingual speech corpus. *arXiv preprint arXiv:1912.06670*.

Christian Bartz, Tom Herold, Haojin Yang, and Christoph Meinel. 2017. Language identification using deep convolutional recurrent neural networks. In *International conference on neural information processing*, pages 880–889. Springer.

Alan W Black. 2019. Cmu wilderness multilingual speech dataset. In *ICASSP 2019-2019 IEEE International Conference on Acoustics, Speech and Signal Processing (ICASSP)*, pages 5971–5975. IEEE.

Kaiming He, Xiangyu Zhang, Shaoqing Ren, and Jian Sun. 2016. Deep residual learning for image recognition. In *Proceedings of the IEEE conference on computer vision and pattern recognition*, pages 770–778.

Shauna Revay and Matthew Teschke. 2019. Multiclass language identification using deep learning on spectral images of audio signals. *arXiv preprint arXiv:1905.04348*.

Elizabeth Salesky, Badr M Abdullah, Sabrina J Mielke, Elena Klyachko, Oleg Serikov, Edoardo Maria Ponti, Ritesh Kumar, Ryan Cotterell, and Ekaterina Vylomova. 2021. SIGTYP 2021 shared task: Robust spoken language identification. In *Proceedings of the Third Workshop on Computational Research in Linguistic Typology*, pages 136–142.

Shikhar Shukla, Govind Mittal, et al. 2019. Spoken language identification using convnets. In *European Conference on Ambient Intelligence*, pages 252–265. Springer.

Author Index

Association for Computational Linguistics
209 N. Eighth Street
Stroudsburg, Pennsylvania 18360

CURRAN ASSOCIATES INC.
proceedings
.com

ISBN 978-1-7138-3028-3
9 781713 830283